# RECIPES FROM THE
# SPANISH KITCHEN
## NICHOLAS BUTCHER

GRUB STREET • LONDON

IN MEMORY OF MY PARENTS, GEOFFREY AND AUDREY BUTCHER

This new edition published 2012
by Grub Street,4 Rainham Close, London SW11 6SS
post@grubstreet.co.uk
www.grubstreet.co.uk

First published in 1990 as *The Spanish Kitchen* by Macmillan

Jacket design: Sarah Driver

The publisher gratefully acknowledges the permission granted to reproduce the copyright material in this book. Every effort has been made to trace copyright holders and to obtain their permission for the use of copyright material. The publisher apologises for any errors or omissions and would be grateful to be notified of any corrections that should be incorporated in future reprints or editions of this book.

A CIP catalogue for this book is available from the British Library

ISBN 978-1- 908117-24-3

Printed and bound by MPG Ltd, Bodmin, Cornwall
on FSC (Forest Stewardship Council) paper

# Contents

# Foreword
## TO THE NEW EDITION

When I first started exploring Spain and acquiring the information which would eventually form the basis of this book, getting around the country was often a frustratingly slow process. Roads in some places were improving, but only some, and the country and its possibilities seemed to stretch out in front of you for ever. Now, of course, you can speed comfortably from one corner of the peninsula to the other. The effect of these efficient motorways, and high-speed trains and planes has been to make Spain, in effect, shrink.

I have to admit that the pleasure has perhaps shrunk a little too. While being aware of the romantic trap of nostalgia, I am convinced that much is lost when hurtling along the country's modern roads with their gentle curves and easy overtaking. When driving around Spain now, a quarter of a century later, my gratitude at reduced journey times is tempered by a sadness that somehow I am no longer able to appreciate my surroundings in quite the same way as before. In addition, my route from A to B no longer takes me through quiet small towns and villages, too numerous to remember. They have been sidetracked by the rush to save time.

Yet if you take the trouble you can still find solitude in this great country and find yourself on roads where you have to go so slowly that you can hear the birds singing over the noise of the engine. Here you do have time to pause and listen, and to gape in gratitude and wonder at the sights Spain has to offer.

So much has changed, but who would expect less as the twentieth century became the twenty-first? Spain's food has changed; the face of Spain too, and it seems foolish to resist, even if perhaps one should not rush to total surrender. It is reassuring that its people still have an inexhaustable willingness to enjoy themselves at a frenetic pace, yet can offset this by an admirable ability to switch off, to never take anything too seriously for too long, to say to the uptight foreigner, 'Tranquilo, hombre', take it easy, nothing is worth getting in such a state about. I think this geniality communicates itself to Spain's food and wine, which in their turn provide a civilised framework for cordial enjoyment and relaxation.

It is not a perfect country. One can only wince at naïve attempts to romanticise Mediterranean attitudes to alcohol consumption when one now sees children barely into their teens incapacitated by drink on a regular basis. Natural regional pride can morph into a prickly, inward-looking local nationalism when encouraged to do so by self-serving politicians. Spanish television can astonish at its fatuousness and its ability to make you feel grubby just for watching it, and by no means all Spanish families sit down together in front of that television with a healthy balanced meal based on the so-called Mediterranean diet.

On the up-side, interest thrives in both traditional and avant-garde food. This means it is no longer all but impossible to try foods and wines from beyond your region, and, in good part thanks to the internet, there is now a wonderful freedom to explore the country's cooking, to seek out and share knowledge. People no longer think you are eccentric to make your own bread, or to drink a red wine from somewhere other than La Rioja or Ribera del Duero.

How to condense it all into one volume? One can only be guided by one's preferences and prejudices, and I hope the reader will forgive mine (I have an obvious bias to the food of Andalucía where I live) and any favourites I have omitted. The book is much the same as when first published, but with mistakes corrected (I hope) some things added, others removed.

Finally, a word of very belated thanks to all those who helped bring this book to fruition. To all at Macmillan, who first published the book, especially Adam Sisman, Hazel Orme, Katrina Whone and Katie Owen, for their confidence in me, patience and hard work on my behalf. I am also hugely grateful to Anne Dolamore for having enough faith in the book to want to republish it.

And as always a big thank-you to José Alaminos, Pepe, who's been the best companion on my travels around his wonderful country that anyone could wish for.

Nicholas Butcher

# Introduction

Trying to define Spanish food poses a problem. It is that 'Spanish food' as a coherent concept simply does not exist. True, certain dishes have been adopted on a national scale and appear on menus throughout the country; but with regard to the rest of the food the Spanish eat, you may as well compare the cooking of Cataluña with that of Andalucía as that of Normandy with that of Provence, or that of Piemonte with that of Calabria.

Spanish food, in other words, is better thought of in regional terms. It is far more helpful and accurate to talk of Basque food or Galician food or Murcian food, although these headings are still vague. This regional individuality is reflected in, or is a reflection of, the individuality of Spain's different peoples, its Gallegos, its Basques, its Catalans, its Andaluces, and so on. Each region insists, with varying degrees of conviction and historical justification, on its autonomy. Nevertheless, despite the apparent slide this would suggest towards a federal state, I believe there is a strong thread uniting all Spaniards, a seam in the various strata of the Iberian character, that is mirrored in their food. There is something tantalisingly indefinable and yet unmistakable about all Spain's regional food. One can detect influences from elsewhere, similarities too, but never is one in any doubt when eating genuine Spanish cuisine – this could not be France or Italy or anywhere else. Spain stamps its personality, and what a personality it is, ineradicably.

It is now much easier to find Spanish food beyond its borders – the popularity of tapas bars has seen to that – but comparatively few holiday-makers return home with any knowledge of the cuisine of the country they have just visited. Nor do they go with any intention of finding out. For too many people Spain is just somewhere to drink cheap wine in the sun all day and complain about their sunburn in the disco at night. In the face of such indifference it is not surprising that the Spanish shrug their shoulders and make little attempt to promote their cooking. Instead, tourists are happily palmed off with what they expect, an 'international' cuisine of dishes that will be exactly the same wherever they go. A few token 'typically Spanish' dishes will be available – appalling paellas or mass-produced supermarket tortillas – but it is a dispiriting experience for anyone who might wish to know how the Spanish themselves eat. 'There is a fanfare to the very name of Spain,' wrote Jan Morris, but not, alas, to its food.

But things are improving. There are now any number of guides available in print or on the internet to help more adventurous visitors discover Spanish food, and even without them a fairly reliable way of finding out how the Spanish eat is to follow the crowds. If you're out driving at lunchtime, look for lorries and commercial vehicles outside roadside restaurants. The food will be basic but good value. On Sundays, discover where Spanish families are eating. Wandering around a Spanish town, pluck up courage and enter that not-too-prepossessing bar which is packed to the gunwales. Or just ask; people will be more than willing to help.

Even better is to acquire a little Spanish before you go. It is not only a basic courtesy to a charming people but it will also help you get what you want rather than what people *think* you want. You may even make friends with some Spaniards, and your novelty value will make you hugely popular at first, ensuring riotous trips around favourite tapas bar. Once a little interest has been shown, no one is more anxious than a Spaniard to show off the best his or her country has to offer.

Because eating *en la calle* (in the street) is so popular in Spain, and there is so much competition, the general standard of the food to be had is high. Indeed, there are said to be more bars, taverns and so on in Spain than in the rest of Europe put together. That may be hard to believe, but a walk round any Spanish town will reveal scores of them, many little bigger than a handkerchief. One such was described by H. V. Morton in his book *A Stranger in Spain* (1955) as 'like the hide-out of a robber gang, in whose dark interior, filled with wine barrels and bottles, [one] may dimly see garlic and every manner of sausage hanging from the ceiling and wooden benches and trestle-tables scrubbed white. Sometimes an assassin walks to the door and gives the apprehensive stranger a charming smile. It is not unusual that the rougher the exterior the finer are the manners to be met inside.'

Eating is perhaps the most important activity in a Spaniard's day. Breakfast is taken at about ten o'clock, when the local cafés will be full of people munching on French-style sandwiches, *bocadillos*, filled with anything from cured ham or cheese to salted anchovies. Toast is popular with oil or flavoured lard, while the Catalans adore their *pa amb tomàquet* – bread rubbed with a cut tomato and seasoned with salt and oil. This is at its best prepared with real country bread (*pa de pàges*) with a firm crumb, quite thickly sliced. Normal bread just goes soggy and makes you wonder why they bother. Another traditional breakfast would consist of the famous fritters called *churros*, made from a simple flour-and-water paste which is piped into terrifying cauldrons of boiling oil. The skilled fryers manipulate the tubes of paste with two giant chopsticks into huge Catherine wheel shapes, let them go brown and crisp and then drain them, often rather perfunctorily. The wheel is snipped into manageable lengths with scissors and served piled on a plate or on a sheet of paper with milky coffee or thick dark chocolate the consistency of custard.

This breakfast may take place as early as four or five o'clock in the morning – before you go to bed. The traveller in Spain can rest assured that there is no more comforting pick-me-up (and insurance against hangover) after a long night's carousing at the local *feria* than a good helping of *churros con chocolate* – and it is certainly more digestible at this time than first thing in the morning.

One of the more civilised aspects of life in Spain is the period set aside for lunch. Having finished the first shift at about one-thirty, the average Spaniard can devote at least a couple of hours to eating lunch before going back to work in the late afternoon. Lunch is called simply 'the meal', *la comida*, and is the highlight of the day. It is the time for conversation and tapas, that untranslatable word which means a little plate of something, hardly more than a mouthful, to eat with ice-cold lager, sherry or wine (sensibly, Spaniards rarely drink on an empty stomach, and will keep eating at a steady pace as the drink flows). Often they will talk about food too, not with pretension but as naturally as we talk about the weather. Eventually, if appetite is intact, you go home for lunch, a siesta if there is time, and then back to work. You will not eat so much in the evening, but will meet up with friends again, eat a few tapas, have a few glasses of wine . . .

Some bars pride themselves on having a wide range of tapas, others offer just a few. Some include the tapa in the price of a drink (a very cheap way of eating, this) but most of them charge nowadays. Many bars also have a selection of cured hams, cheeses and sausages, and many do full-scale platefuls too. If a particular tapa takes your fancy you can ask for a bigger helping – *una media ración* for half a portion, *una ración* for a full-size one.

It would be difficult to describe the food in such places or in Spanish homes as refined or delicate, though there are exceptions –*jamón serrano* (see page 35) being an obvious example. Spanish cookery does not give much thought for the hesitant stomach or weak constitution inclined to indigestion. Nor, as a quick glance through the recipes contained herein will confirm, is it ideal for those who are concerned about their weight. It is down-to-earth stuff, much of it designed, like traditional English food, to warm one from within during a hard winter or to refuel a worker during a long day in the fields. While very much a fan of this sort of food, I am not trying to romanticise 'peasant' cooking, which can be every bit as bad or as dull as the most pretentious *nouvelle cuisine*. It depends, like any sort of cookery, on the cook and what he or she has to work with.

Spanish cooking still turns something of a blind eye to the health police who want to forbid us numerous foods we've been eating for centuries. Nor is it cooked to impress, with unnecessary show or decoration; based on a tradition of family cooking, it can be judged solely on the criterion of whether it tastes good. These dishes have been cooked in much the same way, for generations, and many of the most popular Spanish eating places are those that continue the tradition.

The new, modern Spain, now solidly democratic and enthusiastic about European union, bears little resemblance to Spain before the Civil War, beloved of such chroniclers as Laurie Lee and Kate O'Brien. The landscape may still provoke awe, many towns and villages may still maintain an almost medieval atmosphere, but glance through a window nowadays and you will catch sight of the average Spanish family TV tuned to the latest must-see reality TV show, while in the street the children will be chewing their 'do-nuts' to see them over to the next meal.

In her book *Spain* Jan Morris caught the atmosphere of change, and lamented the diminution of the Spanishness of the country: 'It may be foolish to be proud and insular, but at least it makes for

style.' But one feels, despite it all, that Spain's style will never be completely extinguished, that the traveller new to Spain will still have to learn to wait and to realise that time there travels at a slower tempo, that modern hurry and rush, while very present in many people's lives, are alien to the Spanish character. And perhaps having discovered a little of Spain he or she will agree with that indomitable traveller George Borrow: 'With all that pertains to Spain, vastness and sublimity are associated.'

A volume such as this can only scratch at the surface of Spain's cookery. Its purpose is to try to provide some insight into what the Spanish eat, how and why. Wherever possible I have kept as close to the original spirit of the dishes as I can, for books on foreign cookery should surely aim to give their readers an accurate account of what these dishes are like in their homeland, even though, as Elizabeth David points out in *French Provincial Cooking*, 'A country's national food appears completely authentic only *in* that country.' Although inevitable, it is not cause for despair, except for the exceptionally pedantic. With a little resource and ingenuity nearly all the recipes in this book are within the reach of a reasonably competent and experienced cook who knows how to shop. Alternatives may have to be found for some of the more unusual ingredients (I make suggestions where appropriate) and a modicum of common sense is needed – please don't mix a can of baked beans with some beef sausages and chopped-and-shaped 'ham-style' chunks and think you are serving a *fabada asturiana*.

All recipes are for four people unless stated otherwise, four British people that is. The Spanish seem to have gargantuan appetites – Bernard Wall, author of *Spain of the Spaniards* (1938), likened them to boa-constrictors – and many is the time I've been defeated by the size of the meals served to me in Spanish homes and restaurants, even though I am by no means a meagre eater. Such huge meals are perhaps a reaction to the times when so many Spaniards went hungry and when, conversely, to eat frugally at all times was considered by the poor to be only fit and proper.

Both metric and imperial measurements are given, but should by no means be followed slavishly. Individual adjustments are up to the cook.

# A Journey Through the Regions of Spain

## ANDALUCÍA AND MURCIA

There is still romance to be found in a journey through Spain. Nowhere else surprises the traveller quite so relentlessly with so many sudden, sweeping panoramas, so many quiet little towns built on to the side of a precipice or sheer gorge, or overlooked by some outcrop of rock with its ruined castle or religious statue. Above all, there is so often in Spain that lonely sense of being in the middle of nowhere. Travelling through miles and miles of nothing, each new town is an adventure, a magnet in the emptiness and with an air of unassuming drama in its setting.

One never seems to be far from mountains in Spain. Along the south coast they follow you all the way, changing hue with the light or peering mysteriously through the clouds, but always there, thrusting abruptly up from the sea or where the sea once was, a majestic and uncompromising barrier between the tourist and the real Spain. Crossing these mountains, winding your way up to Granada for example, you can only gape, not just at the views but at the feats of engineering that made it possible for you to be there in the first place. Often you can see traces of the old roads. Narrow, tortuous and

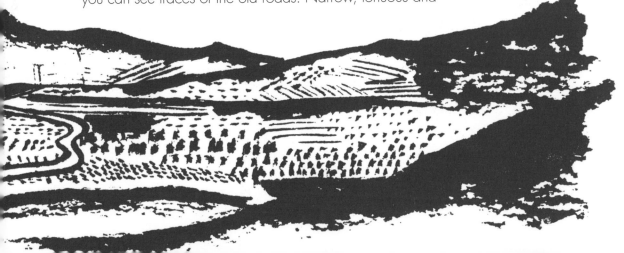

incredibly slow, these more than anything help to explain Spain's well-defined regionality. It used to take five hours to get from Málaga to Almería, both in Andalucía, and even longer to reach Murcia, the next region to the east. Small wonder that there are marked differences in their cuisines, so marked that the people of one province will often be completely ignorant of the cooking of their neighbours.

Where the sea has retreated from the sierras of eastern Andalucía, great plains have been left which are heavily cultivated. Almuñecar, for example, looks as if it's about to be drowned beneath the green forest of chirimoyo trees, their scented leaves a good indication of the heavenly flavour of the custardy pulp of the fruit. Further on, one can barely see for the plantations of sugar cane, and in the Campo de Dalías, the plain beneath the Sierra de Gádor, all one can see for mile after mile in all directions are the *invernaderos*, a sea of white plastic beneath which vegetables are grown at electrifying speed.

Beyond the city of Almería the road takes you northwards into a stark, barren, desert landscape where the scarred yellow mountains seem to writhe in the arid heat. Nothing appears to grow in these scrub lands except tough-skinned grapes, but crossing into Murcia you start to see fields of stunted thistles that turn out to be artichokes, and the white bloom of cotton. Murcia city is at the centre of a great *huerta* – fertile land dedicated to the cultivation of fruit and vegetables. The city has great charm, and beautiful buildings. One is reminded of Brighton, for Murcia has the same sense of slightly faded grandeur, of calm and friendly elegance.

The market here is a fine Spanish-Modernist building near the river Segura. Its upper floor is devoted almost entirely to local vegetables, including hairy-bearded bunches of young garlic shoots and huge garlands of dried red peppers. The garlic might go into a tortilla or into scrambled egg with prawns or chopped ham; or the shoots can be combined with the dried pepper, salt-cod and black olives for a salad called *mojete*. Downstairs are fish and meat. Much of the fish is preserved – there are great black planks of cured tuna, *mojama*, huge dried boards of salt-cod, dried bonito, and grey mullet roe, pressed and cured and needing the occasional dust and polish with a scrubbing brush to keep it looking in the pink of health, as one stall holder unashamedly demonstrated. The local sausages sold there include great squidgy *sobrasada*, delicious on hot toast, small round morcillas, the blood sausage that usually comes in a loop and goes into soups and stews all over Spain, and thick black *butifarras*, the Catalan blood sausage quite a way from home. Now we can smell vinegar and spices, and find several stalls putting out their basin piled high with olives of all colours and sizes, and pickled vegetables and capers. Even pickled caper plants are on sale.

Food markets inevitably make you pay closer attention to the wares in the neighbourhood pastry shops. In Murcia you'll probably want to try *pasteles de carne* – round, flat pies of very crisp pastry filled with chopped meat and hard-boiled egg, topped with a clever swirl of tissue-thin pastry looking like mashed potato – or *cordiales*, little marzipan sweets made with pine-nuts instead of almonds. Another curiosity to look out for is *paparajotes*, lemon leaves dipped in batter and fried. You eat the batter, but not the leaves themselves.

# VALENCIA

Heading north-east out of Murcia you enter an area recently devastated when the Segura burst its banks after heavy rain, submerging everything in mud. It is a dreadful sight, the fruit trees barely holding their branches above the surface and the great palms of Orihuela looking pathetic in their muddy puddles and ponds. There are many more palms in Elche (or Elx), where they make up for an otherwise rather dull town. This is the biggest plantation in Europe, and the chances are that the palm frond you wave on Palm Sunday came from here. They are bleached by wrapping them in black plastic, and look like dark thorns against the skyline.

Unless you want to go to Benidorm (actually a weirdly interesting experience) it is best to leave the coast at Alicante. For up in the scruffy, unkempt-looking hills to the north, all pleats and folds, is Jijona, home of Spain's *turrón* industry. From September to December they work flat out producing Spain's favourite Christmas sweetmeat, a mixture of almonds, sugar and eggs. The factory may close for the rest of the year, but to stay open some are now producing turrón ice cream and trying to sell turrón overseas. A visit round a turrón factory is a must, if only for the smell of roasting almonds.

A second place of pilgrimage is farther up. The road twists and climbs way above the *huerta*, into greener mountains and Alcoy. As you leave Alcoy look for a stone horse trough. It belongs to the *Venta del Pilar*, one of those precious Spanish restaurants (no longer with us, sadly: Ed) that actually go out of their way to serve regional specialities, dishes that are usually long forgotten or ignored by the restaurant trade. Indeed, there is something not quite right, something uncomfortable, about preserving local traditional dishes in this way, as if they were museum pieces. But if the alternative is that they are forgotten then I suppose we should be grateful, though I will never be happy eating such country food off expensive china with two or three waiters forever at my elbow with their linen cloths and bow ties.

Here we were brought *bajoques farcides*, large peeled red peppers stuffed with rice, and a little dish of *pericana*, something almost impossible to reproduce here but consisting of dried red peppers very briefly fried without prior soaking, then crumbled and mixed with tiny pieces of salt-cod, garlic and oil: delicious and surprisingly delicate. This was followed by *conejo espatarrat*, an extremely rich dish of rabbit and potatoes gratinated under a thick layer of garlic mayonnaise, and some fillets of fresh tuna fried with garlic shoots. Also on the menu were *borreta* (see page 113), the local version of *cocido* called *olleta*, and two regional rice dishes, *paella de sabater* and *arroz con costra*.

If some of these names sound a little strange to an ear accustomed to Castilian Spanish, this is because they come from the local Valencian version of Catalan. Now we are in what is cumbersomely known as the Valencian Community, the signposts tend to be in both Castilian and Valencian, and are frequently disfigured if not, with the Valencian word obliterating the Castilian.

Valencia itself is the commercial centre of a giant agricultural area, whose principal product appears to be oranges. I never thought I would tire of seeing those neatly rounded trees brightly decked with fruit like orange light bulbs, but as one trudges through the flat *huerta*, a stream of lorries crawling in both directions, the attraction begins to pall.

Entering the city is something of a nightmare, a sprawling confused mess of concrete and cars. Despite one's first impressions, however, Valencia does have some beautiful architecture, for like most of Spain's urban conglomerations it preserves something of its past at the centre. It has a fine cathedral, and you can climb the Miguelete bell tower to get a view over Valencia, a considerably tougher assignment than the similar trip up the Giralda in Seville. But the market is the place to go. Here you can naturally buy all you need for a paella, starting with the stall that sells the special pans on the steps outside. There are baskets of snails of various sizes and prices, all very well-behaved (in Granada I watched them climb all over the stall holders' walls and ceilings). There are sacks of *garrafones*, the large white butter beans that form part of the authentic Valencian paella. The vegetables here seem if anything even crisper and greener than those of Murcia, and we find great red volcanoes of paprika and beautiful mounds of gritty *rovellons*, flame-coloured fungi flecked with mossy green. There is horse meat too, if you want it, enormous plumber's lengths of white sausage, tripe hanging up like a washing line of peculiar nappies; and in the fish section an endless variety of prawns, monstrous monkfish and hake, cuttlefish (their roe sold separately), a much larger version of Málaga's *chanquetes* resembling our own whitebait in size, and, of course, eels, slithering slimily around their boxes. They are one of Valencia's greatest specialities in dishes such as *all i pebre*. Then there are boxes of dried octopus, salted tuna (called *tonyina*) and much more. These Spanish markets, as well as being an education, are a delight to the senses.

Apart from the hundreds of rice dishes, and the fish dishes of the coast, the region has a few other interesting things: the *caragolada* for example, made with little snails called *avellanencs* and spicy with chilli, a stew of goat or lamb called *tumbet* or *tombet*, the various versions of gazpacho and *flaons*, the little pastries stuffed with curd cheese and flavoured with cinnamon which come from Morella, a romantic fortress of a town in the northernmost part of the region.

## CATALUÑA

While still officially very much part of Spain, Cataluña can make that hard to believe at times, as every sign you see, every notice, every conversation you hear, seem to be in that clipped, chunky language with its slightly awkward words (for a Castilian speaker) ending in t and c. The fiercely insular pride of many Catalans is extremely irritating to non-Catalans, but sweeping down into Barcelona along its great long avenues one soon falls under the spell of Cataluña and its difference from the rest of Spain. This confident, cosmopolitan, forward-looking metropolis may be second to Madrid in size, but in every other department it is the peninsula's first city. Here we seem to be in an accelerated Spain, the Spain of the future.

One gets the taste of Barcelona walking down the Ramblas, the series of avenues that run together into one down to the port, with a *paseo*, or promenade, down the middle which is sensibly much wider than the traffic lanes. Here are stalls selling flowers or pets (in the widest sense – some of the stalls are almost mini-zoos) and tables where you can have your fortune told. As you pass the Liceo opera house, you may feel the rumble of the metro coming up from the Barceloneta. Down there, around the harbour, it can scarcely be described as attractive, but it's a good place to eat fish or *zarzuela*, Barcelona's fish stew. You can also try a tapa of a *bomba*, a fried cannonball shape of meat and mashed potato served with an explosive sauce. It seems these fishermen like their food hot – some *patatas bravas* I tried were almost lethal.

Along the Ramblas, too, is one of Barcelona's principal markets, that of Sant Josep, more popularly known as La Bokería. In autumn there is a mind-boggling display of fungi, most prodigiously the *rovellón* or *bolet* (*Lactarius deliciosus*) but of all colours, shapes and sizes, including a most peculiar one called *pie de rata* (rat's foot) which is white with numerous shaggy brown fronds, looking like a sea anemone or a species of coral.

Here, it seems, you can buy anything. Black truffles at £150 a kilo, tiny wood strawberries, *madroños*, the fruit of the strawberry tree and symbol of Madrid (and which will supposedly make you drunk if you eat more than a few), green hairy squashes called *chayotas*, all manner of tropical fruit and nut, and trendy balsamic vinegar. If it's the season for game, you can buy wild rabbits and hares, delicious in those original Catalan combinations with snails or prawns or chestnuts, or maybe even in a dark chocolate sauce; there are partridge for stewing with stuffed cabbage leaves; and pheasants and even thrushes. The latter are called for in *niu*, perhaps the strangest, most cacophonous dish in Spain. This calls for *peixopalo* (stockfish), the innards from a salt-cod, thrushes (or pigeons), squid or cuttlefish, pork sausages, potatoes and hard-boiled egg.

Then there are some fine yellow chickens, boxes of coxcombs for all those weird garnishes to be found in *Le Répertoire de la Cuisine*, stalls where you can buy nothing but salt-cod, already soaking in its salty bath water. And the fish market, a snow-scape of ice and wet floors, where there is surely enough fish to feed all Barcelona for a week. There is *dorada*, that splendid member of the bream family with a gold bridge across its nose, plenty of hake, as ever, and monkfish, here forced by unnatural gymnastics to display themselves with their tail curled over their heads and clamped into their own gaping jaws. They will be delicious in a burnt garlic sauce. And one lady has a box of freshwater crayfish, *cangrejos*, belligerent little creatures in scarlet, some of them climbing over the ice in a chilly bid for freedom. Can there be any fish markets more exciting than those of Spain?

Catalan food is perhaps the most interesting in Spain but eating it in Barcelona is not easy, as the restaurants that specialise in it are extremely popular, making reservations almost essential. The Catalans go for combinations which appear barbaric to other Spaniards: you can try pigs' trotters with aubergines, snails or chicken with prawns, duck with dried figs, goose with pears, as well as a host of less outlandish dishes. Pudding after a Catalan meal is often *crema catalana*, custard topped with scorched sugar and very similar to our own burnt cream; or *mel i mató*, an inspired combination of fresh curd cheese and honey. Look out too for *cocas* or *coques*, a sort of Catalan pizza really, but rectangular with rounded corners, like a billiard table. They can be sweet or savoury, crispy or chewy. I particularly recommend the *coca de llardons*, with pork scratchings on top.

## ARAGÓN

A vast plain divides Aragón, once desert and previously sea. Marooned in the middle is Zaragoza, with its famous baroque basilica, home to the much-revered *Nuestra Señora del Pilar*. It's to be found alongside Spain's greatest river, the Ebro, which, in autumn sunshine, with the burnished leaves of the trees along its banks, and stroking oarsmen, reminds you almost of the Thames at Putney.

Aragón's food is little known and tends towards the plain and simple. There are good dishes of baby goat or lamb, sometimes accompanied by a powerful allioli; game such as venison or wild boar; famous hams from Teruel in the chilly mountains of the south; a sort of *cocido* called *recao*, thick with beans and rice; a dish well known to readers of cookery books called *espárragos montañeses* which are not mountain asparagus but stewed lambs' tails; and the two dishes perhaps most famous in the rest of Spain, *bacalao al ajo arriero* and *magras con tomate*. The first takes its name from the muleteers, the *arrieros* who once travelled Spain with their merchandise, preparing meals on the way with whatever dry stores they had with them and whatever they could scrounge (or pilfer) from the surrounding countryside. The accepted version of *bacalao al ajo arriero* generally contains dried red pepper, tomatoes, onions and, of course, garlic. *Magras con tomate* are thin slices of ham in tomato sauce, which is excellent if both the ham and the sauce are of the highest quality – a salty, watery disaster if nor. For pudding you should try the lovely firm peaches poached in red wine or *cuajada con miel*, junket with honey.

## NAVARRA AND THE BASQUE COUNTRY

The great plain of Aragón continues into Navarre, desolate and with its few flat-topped hills huddled together against the raw wind that sweeps across them in winter. Gradually the road rises and the foothills of the Pyrenees, powdered with snow like icing sugar on a cake, appear before you. Suddenly, there is Pamplona, a vibrant city at the crossing of historic pathways.

Pamplona is renowned abroad, thanks to Ernest Hemingway, for its *San Fermines*, a week-long festival in July when bulls go charging through the streets every morning after (and often over) the sprinting crowd of daredevils who run before them. Even out of season, however, you can detect the racy blood that flows in Pamplona veins. You also see the first signs of the Basques, with their flat caps and impenetrable language of x's and z's and k's.

You can walk up to the old walls and behold a bleak scene, humbling because of its weight of history. There before you are the ramparts of the Pyrenees and, beyond, the Roncesvalle pass into France. You feel that you might just catch sight of Charlemagne retreating into the distance, hear the forlorn call of Roland on his horn echoing through those gloomy valleys, or spy a caravan of distant pilgrims on their way to Santiago. The sunny personality of the *pamploneses* seems a bit of a miracle considering the dour country they inhabit.

A meal I once had here was a minor miracle too, for the people of the Basque country are very serious about their food and conscientious in its preparation. At the Shanti we were served by two efficient but pleasantly unprofessional ladies struggling to keep their feet on the polished stone floor. They brought us a meal which, though it was to defeat us for the rest of the day, was unusual in that it was impossible to fault. First we tried the local red peppers, *pimientos de piquillo*, roasted and peeled and dressed with oil and a little garlic. They were meaty, yet with a lovely yielding texture I haven't found in other sorts of pimiento, and with a natural, very light piquancy. With them came a little dish of egg scrambled with fungi, *revuelto de setas*, perfectly seasoned and creamy. These were followed by a *cazuela* of rice and large clams 'an *arroz caldoso*' that most difficult of rice dishes to get just right, but perfectly tender and juicy; and *cordero al txilindrón*, a Navarre classic of lamb in a simple sauce based on dried red peppers. Somehow we managed to share a dish of *natillas* for pudding. This is Spain's version of a true custard, scented with a little cinnamon and lemon and topped with two blobs of poached meringue. We paid little more for this than many a less memorable meal.

Other Navarre dishes to look out for include a giant country dish called *calderete*, a stew of lamb, rabbit and snail flavoured with ham and chorizo; the local beans, especially the red ones, perhaps cooked with borage or quails; *cochifrito*, a popular shepherd's dish of stewed lamb; and trout (see page 227 for *trucha a la navarra*) and *ajo arrieros* as in Aragón, perhaps with freshwater crayfish added.

In the Basque country itself, Euskadi, you are in one of the *best* places in all Spain for eating tapas, or *pintxos* as they are called locally, with sharp local *txakolí* wine to accompany them, served in a wide tumbler called a *txikito* or a *pote*. There is nowhere better than the País Vasco for a *chuletón*, a whacking section of beef rib worthy of Desperate Dan that you will remember for the rest of your days, while in traditional Basque restaurants you will find good fish and shellfish preparations, the most famous being baked spider-crab in a rich tomato sauce (*txangurro a la donostiarra*); sticky gelatinous *kokotxas*, the prized pieces of meat from under a hake or cod's mouth with garlic and parsley sauce; *chipirones en su tinta*, squid in their own very black ink, and various hake and salt-cod recipes well known throughout Spain.

Interestingly, especially around San Sebastián, you will also find a whole swarm of multi-Michelin-starred chefs whose restaurants are at the vanguard of modern Spanish cooking. I have been a reluctant convert to their ideas to an extent, but convert I am. Some of the dishes dreamt up by these people, Juan Mari Arzak, for example, are astonishing – and quite astonishingly expensive to boot.

## LA RIOJA

South of Pamplona is La Rioja, the little region whose name must now be known to every lover of good wine. It is a splendid area of sweeping hills and dales, the reddish earth given over almost exclusively to vines. We are back in the valley of the Ebro, and straddling it is the capital, Logroño, appearing suddenly from the surrounding fields, as abruptly as do Pamplona or Vitoria in the Basque country. Logroño is somehow a flavourless city, though by no means ugly, but it does have at its heart a charming wooded square and a range of excellent tapas bars in Calle del Laurel.

Here I am yet again reminded of, and delighted by, Spain's regionality, most obviously seen in the pastry shops. So often something available in one area, or even in one particular town, can be seen nowhere else. In Vitoria, for example, a peaceful little city, I came across *alcachofas*, sponge and densely whipped cream cleverly wrapped in chocolate leaves to look like artichokes. Here in Logroño you find *fardelejos de arnedo*, a spring-roll-shaped fritter filled with a spongy almond cream; and here also they make coffee-flavoured toffees that are famous throughout Spain.

Logroño has a good market, too. In La Rioja, it seems, they grow things on a giant scale – great unwieldy clumps of saw-toothed cardoons, the splayed celery-like crowns of borage, huge heads of cauliflower and endive; these may well go into the rich *menestras*, or thick vegetable soups, for which the area is well known. In the *matanza* season, the time in late autumn when the family pig is slaughtered and sausages are made to put by for the year, you will see sausage skins for sale as well as sacks of the especially aromatic paprika that goes into chorizo. We are also at the start of the territory famous for its roasts, and everywhere are young lambs and goats, and in separate piles, neatly and cleanly displayed, are their little feet and heads, as well as pigs' ears and cows' noses and feet, and blocks of congealed blood looking like liver. The Spanish waste nothing and have no qualms about it, as Norman Lewis, in *Voices of the Old Sea* (1984), discovered in his Catalan fishing village:

'Meat, hardly to be seen in Farol for years, began to reappear. Somewhere in secret a steer was slaughtered, and although the best of it, for roasting and stewing purposes, would have been delivered to the Muga mansion by discreet men at the dead of night, not even the numerous members of the Muga family and their many hangers-on could eat a whole beast in a matter of days when refrigerators were not to be had, so large amounts of perfectly acceptable offal found its way into the butcher's shop.

*When the news got round of this first windfall of tripe, liver, lights, brain, of knuckles, tail and hooves, of glandular sacs, arterial conduits and membraneous messes, there was a stampede to the shop, and Carmela soon returned with a grim smile of triumph and a prize in its bloody package. I was ordered from the kitchenette while the cooking got under way. "Don't look, sir, whatever you do. Just leave it to me. Appearances don't count. It's all in the mind.*

*The meal, reflecting ingenuity and resource based on a great culinary tradition, was a memorable one. ("Pardon me, but don't stare at your food like that, sir. Everything is good. If there's something you don't fancy the look of, just pass it over to me.") As usual Carmela shovelled the remains into a bag, hid it away in the party frock she had worn for so many years, and was off.*

## CASTILLA Y LEÓN

Crossing into Castilla from Cantabria, an English traveller can feel quite at home. As you wind your way through the mountains there are all the familiar colours of an English autumn, sparkling in the sunshine. This is a lush green land with plenty of cows. The country rolls gently down to Burgos, but there are snow-capped mountains in the distance, glowering like icy fangs, and one is reminded that Castilla is a land of terrible extremes of climate. A mighty plain, extending to the horizon and beyond, is what now opens up before you. There is barely a tree to be seen in the undulating vastness, and the people who inhabit this *alta meseta* (high plateau) have to endure a crushing, unrelenting sun in summer and a pitiless, bone-chilling cold in winter when the seas of wheat are frozen with snow.

Nearing Segovia, the terrain suddenly changes as we encounter a river and pine forests. Then, turning a corner, there is the city before you, a romantic sight as it surveys the plain from its long hilltop, the cathedral silhouetted against a filmy background in the early evening light, with the chocolate box *Alcázar* to the right and the magnificent Roman aqueduct to the left. The cathedral echoes that of Burgos in its breathtaking size, but is immeasurably more restrained, with its pale, honey-coloured stone, and light, elegant interior.

Madrid is Spain's capital for no other reason than that it happens to be more or less in the centre of the country. Apart from its climate, which is nearly insupportable, it is fairly tolerable as big cities go, somehow more amiable than other capitals. This is, I'm sure, partly because people actually live in its centre, so that as they leave their homes for an evening *paseo* there is a definite, almost provincial, sense that it is a neighbourhood rather than an urban conglomeration of office blocks. But despite the feast of art on offer at the Prado, and the regional cooking in the restaurants, it is a relief to head south for Toledo.

The famous outline of Toledo has been described by Jan Morris in *Spain*:

*She is built on a rocky mound in a bend of the Tagus, and is thus surrounded on three sides by a deep gorge, with shingle and grey rock running down to the water's edge. The river runs fast here, with a clutter of old stone mills and two excellent bridges; a castle stands sentinel across the stream; harsh grey hills are all about: the setting of Toledo is all abrasion – nothing soft, nothing amusing, nothing hospitable. This is the Spanish character at its most intractable. If a city can be said to look like a person, then Toledo looks just like one of those El Greco characters who were in fact conceived here – towering, handsome, humourless, sad, a little bloodless.*

That the city has been preserved as a national monument means that it attracts tourists in summer like wasps to a jam pot, swarming from one standard sight to the next as if they were so many blossoms to be depollinated. But it is easy enough to get away from them: as evening falls take a long walk round the city and discover why Toledo is the archetypal Spanish place. It has all the requisite narrow, tall-sided streets, many little more than alleys, and as you wander the dimly lit cobbled lanes, the tattered exteriors of sombre, silent houses frowning over you, you feel much of the time as if you're in a remote and long-abandoned Spanish village.

To the south lie the plains of La Mancha, the monotonous, mind-numbing steppe-like expanse of the *alta meseta*. Here they produce Spain's greatest cheese, Manchego, from ewe's milk, and which, at its best and when properly cured and aged, rivals Parmesan, which it resembles. Try buying a whole one and keeping it submerged in olive oil for a year. Or if you can't bear to wait that long, take a short cut: slice a piece of Manchego into thin wedges, but without trimming off the rind. Arrange in a dish and pour over enough good oil to cover. Leave the cheese to soak for up to a week (it is not necessary to put it in the fridge) before dipping into it when the mood takes you. You should not, of course, waste the oil. Have it trickled over good toast for breakfast.

Back up north in Burgos you may decide to head west along the pilgrim's way instead of south to Segovia. Whichever you decide you should first stop at the Hostal Landa Palace, to be found on the Madrid road as you leave the city. It is a splendid old inn, lovingly and beautifully cared for, and they have an old-style baker's oven which they use to cook their, and Castilla y Leon's, speciality, baby lamb.

With the embers from the oven they cook chorizo in an interesting way: the sausages are wrapped in brown paper dampened with white wine, placed in a large ladle and covered with the hot embers. The ladle rests on a thick wooden tablet which sits at the side of your table while the chorizo cooks. Then the waiter deftly cuts open the charred paper and out slips the sausage, bright, glistening and juicy.

The road to Santiago crosses plains which must have seemed endless to the pilgrims of long ago. There is little sign of life apart from the occasional bored and lonely shepherd, his flock and his dog. The land stretches around them as far as the eye can see in all directions and the emptiness, the sheer weight of open space under the Castilian sky is hypnotic.

Occasionally the landscape varies a little near the rivers that cut through the *meseta*, and the small villages or even cities built around them. They seem lively enough, Palencia, Valladolid and so on, but are soon left behind and once more you find yourself alone on that straight, straight road, with nothing to distract the eye but the occasional hay barn, round and clay-plastered.

'Nothing is edible in the Castilian countryside,' said the painter Darío de Regoyos. 'On the contrary, it's the countryside that consumes the man.' And though it is mistaken to talk of the cooking of Castilla as if it were one homogeneous area, its culinary tradition can seem limited. Apart from its roasts (and these were formerly the prerogative of the rich landowners and could still hardly be called everyday food), the typical dishes tend to be basic high-calory concoctions of pulses and the cheapest bits of pork, the ears, trotters, tail and so on, or else stews of game such as pigeon or partridge. There is also magnificent bread, described by James Michener in *Iberia* (1968):

> *Of the bread I can say only that I ate it as if it were cake. Served in crusty small loaves, it seems to be made of honey, cream, rock salt and coarse grain which has lost none of its goodness through milling. Once I was in the area with a friend who at each meal ate three loaves, by himself. When I commented on this, he asked, 'Why eat meat when this is here?'*

The pilgrim must have felt a surge of excitement on approaching León in the north-west corner of the region, for mountains finally come into view, the mountains that run parallel to the north coast and separate Castilla y León from Asturias and Cantabria. One feels for those who arrived in winter, as the cold here seems to cut through even the thickest clothing with a cruel, knife-like quality and sends you scurrying to the nearest bar for a fiery aguardiente. The country people who set up their stalls of fruit and vegetables in the Plaza Mayor deserve a medal for endurance as they stamp their feet and rub their hands and build little fires from broken orange boxes around which they huddle in the raw air. You can buy gigantic onions here, huge curly heads of endive or take your pick from the sacks of dried beans or little green lentils, but the intense cold makes it difficult to stop and linger.

'There is nothing remarkable in León, which is an old gloomy town, with the exception of its cathedral . . .' So said George Borrow in 1842 in *The Bible in Spain*, but what an exception it is! There is no more ethereally beautiful sight in all Spain, for it is a wonderland of stained glass. There seems to be no corner of the cathedral where the glass is not visible and, straining one's neck and open-mouthed in astonishment, one feels as if one were admiring the display of some celestial jeweller. It is a wonderful refreshment after the gloom and doom of those dark monsters in Burgos and Seville.

Heading south, with Portugal just a little way away over the horizon, a good place to stop is Tordesillas, to be found beside the Duero, another of Spain's great rivers. Overlooking the river is the Convent of Santa Clara, where there is a closed order of a dozen or so Poor Clare nuns who make lovely little cakes and biscuits. You ring a bell (only once, warns the guide, or the nun will go to another door) beside a revolving wooden hatch, and a faint, gentle voice asks what you want. The hatch revolves and you are sent samples from which to choose, a difficult task, for all are exquisitely light and delicate.

Everyone who visits Salamanca further south seems to fall in love with it. It should ideally be seen in sunshine, which makes the warm yellow sandstone, of which most of this grand old city is composed, glow like gold. Salamanca is the home of what was once one of the world's most prestigious universities and is crammed with beautiful architecture. It still bustles with students, the bars are lively, noisy and cheap, but one cannot help but lament its fall from glory.

From its northern approach you would never guess that Salamanca was famous for its *chacinería*, but arriving in the market, close by the magnificent Plaza Mayor, one finds the stalls bulging with cured hams, loins and sausages of every kind, including the local speciality, *farinato*, a smooth-textured, bready sausage resembling chorizo in flavour. There is even a lending library here for the students, set up like any other stall, an unusual sight in a land notorious for its lack of readers.

There is plenty of game too, with row upon row of hare and wild rabbit and plump pigeon. The hare could be used in a favourite dish in Salamanca called *lebrada de pregonaos*, marinated hare in a sauce of red wine, pounded almonds, pine-nuts and the animal's blood. It is a traditional dish for the celebrations following the publishing of the banns of an engaged couple.

This abundance of game and pork products is explained by the countryside south of the city, which is green and rolling and dotted with what one comes to think of as the emblem of Extremadura, the ilex or holm oak. Its acorns are eaten by the black Iberian pig before it is turned into Spain's great ham, *jamón ibérico*.

## EXTREMADURA

Extremadura is divided from Castilla by the Sierra de Béjar, not a very tall range of mountains, to be sure, but some of the most beautiful in Spain. The road descends to the gentle curves of the region's uplands, boulder-strewn and divided into little fields by low dry-stone walls. Then the terrain becomes almost like moorland, empty but for pigs, cows and bulls.

From the wilderness that is so much of Extremadura came that mighty troop of conquerors of the New World, the *conquistadores*, and there are many traces of them in the provincial capital Cáceres, bushy-topped with the nests of its distinguished visitor, the stork.

Cáceres hardly has the air of a regional capital, more that of some small country town. Despite the students at the local university, the atmosphere is almost one of hush, like after hours in a museum. Indeed, Cáceres *is* almost a museum, or at least the old part is, and to wander around those ancient cobbled streets at night, shiny with light drizzle and dimly lit by the odd lamp stuck on a wall, is an eerie experience. Any moment you expect to see some grizzled conquistador lurch heavy with drink from a doorway and stagger to his horse waiting patiently in the shadows.

The name Extremadura is a composite of words meaning 'extreme' and 'hard', and may have prompted some commentators to suggest that because life in Extremadura was hard, and because the *conquistadores* were a formidably hard breed of men, the one was somehow the inevitable product of the other. But Extremadura would surely have been no more demanding a region to live in than Castilla with its awful scorched plains or Andalucía with its harsh sierras.

Certainly, the desire to escape one's miserable *pueblo* and to seek fortune abroad is not exclusive to Extremadura. Galicia used to be famous for exporting its people to the Americas, and many of Barcelona's citizens are emigrant Andalusians who came there in search of work or fortune, much as young people in Britain head for London. It was probably just chance that Cortes and Pizarro were from Extremadura.

The local food reflects the pastoral nature of the area. Apart from the excellent hams and charcuterie, there is a 'shepherd's' gazpacho, a stew rather than a soup of rabbit and snails eaten with flat unleavened bread; *frite*, mature lamb fried with paprika; *migas* of fried bread, eaten with thick hot chocolate; various stews of lamb called *caldereta* or *cochifrito*; the usual imaginative dishes using offal such as liver and lights and blood (I once had a tremendous dish of young goat's kidneys in Plasencia); and delicious tench and carp fresh from the rivers. They can be put into a *pisto de peces*, a dish of cleaned fish layered with onions, tomatoes and peppers, with garlic and herbs added for savour. For pudding, look out for *repápalos*, little fried balls of egg and breadcrumbs served soaked in milk with sugar and cinnamon. There are stupendous cheeses, too, called *tortas*, either *del Casar* or *de La Serena*. You don't cut this in wedges; instead you remove its lid, and underneath is a glorious, smelly, fondue-textured cheese, which once tried soon becomes addictive.

## THE NORTH-WEST – GALICIA AND ASTURIAS

Entering Galicia after the great central mass of Castilla is not only like stepping into another world but also like travelling back in time. For rural Galicia often barely seems to have arrived in the twenty-first century.

It has immediate charm and, as anyone who has read anything about Spain will know, it bears uncanny resemblances to much with which the British are familiar. The hills and thickly forested mountains are perhaps grander and more severe, the architecture of the villages is definitely peculiar to the region, but winding down a country lane it is often possible to believe that perhaps you have been transported to a lonely corner of lushest England. The people here speak Spanish (if they have to) with a pronounced and difficult Portuguese accent, since they have their own language, a hybrid of Spanish and Portuguese, which is very widely spoken.

Their food, meanwhile, is robust, warming and served in awe-inspiring quantity. A request for a portion of *empanada*, for instance, can result in a great platter brought to your table piled high with slices of pie. This is only your starter, for you may then be brought a great earthenware *cazuela* packed with delicious hake in a rich sauce full of squid and clams, potatoes, prawns and vegetables. Octopus is a Galician passion, and in fact all their locally caught seafood is justifiably famous. The region's beef is better than most in Spain, and they cure beef hams to make good *cecina*. The forelegs of pigs go to make *lacón*, ham, which goes into one of the area's classic dishes, *lacón con grelos*, a boil-up with potatoes, chorizo and turnip greens. A typical sweet would be *filloas*, very thin pancakes cooked on an iron griddle, often filled with pastry cream or similar. Wine will be brought in a white jug and is drunk from shallow, wide-mouthed cups, not glasses. Cheese, more often than not, will come in the shape, gently rounded like a breast, of *tetilla*, its name meaning precisely what its shape indicates. There is a chaster, flat version and a smoked and cured one called *San Simón*.

An excellent place to eat Galician food is Santiago, the last stage of a long pilgrimage dedicated to St James. At the market you can buy all the scallops you can eat, as well as various species of crabs and clams. There are the usual nasty-looking bits and pieces in the anatomy section, and they sell a powerful rye bread, sticky and chewy and looking like an enormous chocolate cake. Then you see great round baskets containing *pimientos de Padrón*, tiny green peppers from the coastal town down the road. They will be fried and eaten whole, seeds and all. This can be nerve-wracking: famously there are always one or two which pack a severe kick of chilli and leave you gasping if you drew the short straw.

The trays of scarlet-coloured meat on sale at the butchers' are for making *zorza*, a delicious preparation of little pieces of pork marinated in paprika and garlic, then fried, the original idea being to fry the mixture for stuffing chorizos. The same mixture can be found in neighbouring Asturias, where it is known as *picadillo* and is especially good when mixed with the local peas, called *arbejos*.

The Galician coast, wild and windswept, is a pleasant change after the over-exploitation of other parts of Spain, and as you make your leisurely way along the road that takes you round the *rías* (the inlets and bays belonging to the river estuaries) you catch tantalising glimpses of the Atlantic, its waves breaking on one empty beach after another.

The road leads eventually to the end of the world, for so the cape of Finisterre was long thought to be. Near the lighthouse on the headland a path takes you down to a view of the Atlantic. What a thing to believe, that the great mass of ocean spread out before you under a threatening sky was the very edge of everything. It is a bleak, lonely, dangerous place (this part of the coast is called *La Costa de la Muerte*, the coast of death), and it is easy there to give credence to the old legend.

Asturias is subtly different from Galicia. It is still green and fertile but the land is considerably more open. The weather is similar to Britain's and many country people protect their shoes, as they splash through the mud and puddles, with *zuecos*, wooden clogs. The houses in the countryside, white with red-tiled roofs, are not unlike Swiss chalets, while the *hórreos* (granaries) are bigger than in Galicia and supported on stone toadstool-like feet.

Asturias produces three things famous in all Spain: milk, beans and cider. The local milk puts a white moustache round the mouths of children all over the country, and makes very good rice pudding, as I discovered at a restaurant called La Máquina in Lugones, a nondescript satellite of Oviedo, itself not the most attractive place in the region.

The restaurant does its best not to be noticed: no sign indicates its trade save an ageing, anonymous menu out of sight round the side. You know it must be the one because of the little model train outside its front, but apart from that it appears to be a private house, dead to the world. A meal here is *fabada asturiana* followed by *arroz con leche*. There are a few other token offerings on the menu but it would be folly to ask for anything else. The *fabada* is unsurpassable, the great fat beans melting in the mouth, the smoky home-made sausages, the *compango*, luscious and tender. The rice pudding, thick and creamy and tasting of real farm milk, is a treat.

The local still cider can be sampled in any number of *chigres* or *sidrerías*. Here you can watch as the barman, with varying degrees of success, pours the cider from a bottle held up above his head to a large glass in his other hand at about knee level. The potent smell of a *chigre* and the basic nature of their floors, bears witness to the fact that the barman's aim isn't always spot on – and that the acidity of the spilt cider ruins conventional floor coverings. The tumbler is only filled to the depth of a couple of fingers (a measure called a *culín* or *culete*) and you must drink the cider immediately, while it is still aerated and with a thin head on it. If it goes flat it is thrown away – on the floor.

The Asturians are also good at sweet-making. A charming cake shop and delicatessen in Oviedo called Camilo de Bias sells a bewildering variety of good pastries (try the little *duquesitas* of pastry and egg yolk); the Tejeiro family in Grado produce rich and sticky *tocinillos*, a highly concentrated form of crème caramel where only the yolks are used, having been mixed with thick sugar syrup; and up in Salas you find something that should merit three stars in the green Michelin guide – *carajitos del profesor*, heavenly home-made macaroons made with hazelnuts instead of almonds. Imitations are made elsewhere, but only in Salas do you find genuine *carajitos* still made by descendants of the original *profesor*.

Not surprisingly, the Asturians also make a great deal of cheese, the most famous being the mouth-tingling, creamy blue *cabrales*, wrapped in maple leaves and matured in damp caves. Known as *picón* in neighbouring Cantabria, it is of uneven quality. More to my taste is a much firmer blue cheese, *gamoneu*. There are several others, such as *queso de Casín* and the quaintly named *afuega'l pitu* or 'throat-choker', and you can try them in a cheese restaurant called Babilonia in Oviedo. The blue ones are best with a glass of the local sweet muscat wine, *tostadillo*.

# The Spanish Larder

## OLIVES, OLIVE OIL
*(aceitunas, aceite de oliva)*

Olive trees are grown in vast numbers in Spain, the orchards stretching as far as the eye can see, the trees carefully spaced out with an almost military regularity and the soil between them spotlessly clear of grasses and weeds. From the air the landscape resembles nothing so much as a giant sheet of pegboard.

To walk among these twisted, knotty trees with their spiky leaves is to remind oneself of ancient history, for olive trees are rooted deep, not just in the earth but in the Mediterranean subconscious — they were a familiar sight 5000 years ago in the countryside of the Levant. It was the Greeks who introduced them to the rest of Europe, the secret of the olive having been revealed to them, according to legend, by Aristaeus, son of Apollo and Cyrene. It was to become the symbol of prosperity, victory and peace, so it is ironic that it was invading Roman legions who introduced the taste for olive oil to Spain, where previously lard had been used. Those later invaders, the Moors, developed the technology of olive cultivation and its culinary and medicinal uses. They also gave Spain its words for oil and for olive, aceite and aceituna, and for oil press or mill, almazara.

Hispanic oil became in Roman times the finest and most expensive in the Mediterranean, with large quantities being exported all over the Roman empire from the olive mills of Andalucía. Today Spain is the world's greatest producer. In the province of Jaén, for example, the olive plantations of Seas de Segura are said to be the most extensive in the world, with more than two million trees. As you drive through towns in olive-oil-producing areas the rather foetid smell (the locals have grown up with it and don't notice) is that of *alpechín*, the nasty toxic by-product of the milling process.

The best eating olives are said to be those from the trees that are visible from the top of the Giralda tower (not many in modern Seville) but there are several varieties. Black olives are simply the fruit left to ripen completely on the tree, green olives are in effect the unripe ones. Whereas olives for normal quality oil are beaten down from the trees with long poles on to sheets spread around their trunks, olives for eating and for the best oil must be picked to avoid bruising. They are inedible at this stage, and their natural bitterness must be drawn out and softened. While in Spain you may care to buy some and do this yourself back home.

Make a split to the stone in each olive with a sharp knife, discarding any bruised ones. Olive juice stains, so wear an apron and gloves. Place the olives in a large jar or bowl, cover them with water and add a good quantity of salt, enough to make the water taste salty. Next day drain them and repeat the process. Continue like this for several days, until when you taste an olive there is no acrid sensation on swallowing and the olive tastes good enough to eat. Now, to your final brine, add lightly crushed whole cloves of garlic, strips of lemon peel if you like, and sprigs of fresh thyme, oregano or any other fresh herbs you have to hand. Leave the olives in this *aliño* for a few days and they will be ready. They will get saltier the longer they are left, and are at their most delicious when newly made. This is just one of a host of ways of preparing olives, and is time-consuming, so if you are in Spain visit the local market or look in shops – there are bound to be bowls of these olives on display and you can buy them loose.

Good Spanish olive oil is now widely available in the UK, which is fortunate because unless you buy it in cans in Spain, airline security restrictions mean you can't take bottles home on the plane (unless you pack the bottle in your suitcase, which is asking for trouble). Even in Spain olive oil is not cheap: after all, it requires four or five kilos of olives to produce one litre of oil. Yet, for small growers, life is difficult – the local mills will only pay a pittance for olives and often the grower will opt to have his payment in oil.

Cheaper oil is to be had from sunflower seeds, but is tasteless and really only suitable for deep frying, for which it is very good, or for making a neutral-flavoured mayonnaise. It is popular because of its cheapness. Lard is still commonly used outside oil-producing areas in the north and is a key ingredient in many of the rich little sweetmeats popular at Christmas.

It should be noted that the oil used in the recipes in this book refers to olive oil unless stated otherwise. You can use extra virgin if you want, but don't expect to notice a huge difference in cooked dishes, as the heat neutralises much of the taste of what is in effect the raw juice of the fruit. Extra virgin does go a bit further, however, because it thins on heating. It is of course the best for giving a final dressing to any number of things such as grilled vegetables or the best anchovy fillets. In salads, however, the taste can get a bit lost when competing with vinegar, so don't use your most prized extra virgin there.

In Spanish shops you will see other varieties of olive oil on sale: *virgen* is the next best in quality, and can be very good. Plain *aceite de oliva* is olive oil that has been completely refined but with some *virgen* added afterwards to make it taste of something. *Aceite de orujo de oliva* is extracted from the residues left over from making the other sorts and is not very good, but cheap.

Finally, extra-virgin olive oil does not keep indefinitely. It depends rather on the variety of olive used, but on average you should try to use up your oil within about a year of its pressing.

## BREAD

### (pan)

Many chroniclers of Spain have sung the praises of its bread. The traditional loaf is of a very stout crumb and chewy crust, dryish and long lasting. This loaf has been widely superseded, partly perhaps to cater for foreign tastes, by a French-style loaf with a crackling crust and softer, damper crumb and which is now the bread generally used for *bocadillos* or *emparedados*, the large Spanish sandwich, though it is not nearly as good toasted as the traditional loaf. Spanish housewives have also been persuaded that they like pre-sliced, plastic-wrapped bread which, though different in style from the British kind, is equally lacking in body or taste.

Bread made from all-wheat flour was at one time reserved for the tables of the wealthy. The common folk had to make do with bread made from barley, spelt, maslin (a mixed grain), or emmer wheat, a species still to be found in Asturias. The arrival of maize from America meant the birth of corn bread, often called *borona* or *boroña*, which would be wrapped in leaves and left among the embers of the fire overnight. These breads nearly died out, partly because they were considered too indigestible but mainly because maize became more important as a cattle feed. However, interest in them is reviving. A flat Basque corn bread called *talo* also survives, and is made at local fiestas to be eaten with chorizo sausage.

Since it was so important, bread grew to have an almost religious significance – in many places it is traditional to kiss a piece of bread should it fall on the ground, as it was in Gerald Brenan's village in

the Alpujarras, as he relates in *South from Granada* (1957):

> *Before cutting a new loaf it was proper to make the sign of the cross over it with a knife. If a loaf or rosca fell to the ground the person who picked it up would kiss it and say, 'Es pan de Dios' (It's God's bread). Children were never allowed to strike it or treat it roughly or to crumble it on the table, and it was considered shocking to offer even stale crusts to a dog. When once I jabbed my knife into a loaf I was reproved and told that I was 'stabbing the face of Christ'. Bread was, in fact, sacred, and this, according to Dr Americo Castro, is not, as one would suppose, a derivation from the cult of the Sacrament but a notion borrowed from the Arabs.*

Stale bread is rarely wasted in Spain. It is used to thicken soups and stews, for making sweetmeats and dumplings, and to make breadcrumbs for *migas* or for coating foods for frying.

## TOMATOES
### (tomates)

One would suppose these to be as traditional a part of Spanish and Mediterranean cooking as olive oil and garlic, but they are actually a comparative newcomer, having been brought to Europe from America by the Spanish *conquistadores*. As with most new foods, tomatoes took time to become popular, and Norman Lewis describes in his wonderful book *Voices of the Old Sea* how this mistrust had lingered on in the remote village where he lived in Catalonia and where he was told that 'the decadence of modern times . . . [could be blamed on] . . . the cinema which displayed the godlessness and luxury of the rich to the poor, and the widespread consumption of tomatoes – recently introduced into local agri-

birthrate.'

*marmande* type, achieved a once-justified fame for
nately, even in Spain the growers have fallen prey
tomatoes one sees in Spanish food markets are
der plastic mean they don't have a chance to ma-
possible to get decent tomatoes, but you always
ng raw, the bulbous, segmented *raf* tomato, of
e. It is only in season from December to March.
it, and it tastes better when green anyway. An-
Organic growers, farmers markets or tomato-

t.
to
a d
ture
seen
the *m*
Don't
other o
growing

Toma
mixture
dishes. Th
one weighi
tomatoes ar

most commonly as part of the *sofrito*, the
which forms the base of so many Spanish
rge *marmande* ones, so '1 tomato' means
in use a little tomato concentrate. Tinned

It is gener
potato peeler.
there are a gre
most of your t
skinned tomato
wards the end.

are usually firm enough to peel with a
nute and the skins will slip off easily. If
m as well, but that can mean you lose
lternative to chopping: halve the un-
e of the grater. Mind your fingers to-

## ONIONS
### *(cebollas)*

I have used large Spanish onions for the recipes in this book. They weigh about 225g/8oz each. They
are a good all-purpose onion, not too powerful for salads but with enough flavour for cooking. A good
tip when using onion for salads is to rinse and soak the chunks in several changes of cold water before
using. This sweetens it, useful if the onion is very sharp.

Spring onions are known as *cebolletas* or *cebollas tiernas;* button onions as *cebollitas;* chives (very
little used) as *cebollino.*

# GARLIC
## (ajo)

Where would the Spanish be without garlic? The Spanish are renowned for their love of this ancient bulb, and use it wherever they can, sometimes indiscriminately. Indeed, if you're at all fussy about garlic this book is not for you. Spanish cookery without garlic would be unthinkable, so don't imagine that if you leave the garlic out when you make one of these dishes that you are 'adapting'. You are not, you are destroying. Reduce the stated amount of garlic if you must but don't leave it out altogether.

# TOCINO

This means pork fat but is used loosely to describe a variety of preserved fats and bacon-type products. More precisely: *tocino fresco* is fresh, unrendered pork fat with skin attached, maybe with a few veins of meat running through it; *tocino salado* is salted pork fat or belly (in which case it may be called *tocino entreverado*), salted in coarse salt, not brine; *tocino rancio* is one of the above left to age sufficiently to turn yellowish and acquire a rancid taste. Small quantities of it are added to some dishes for flavouring purposes, though it is not eaten; *tocino de jamón* is the delicious fat of a cured ham. Lard is *manteca*, while *beicon*, naturally enough, is British-style streaky bacon, also called *panceta*. Unsmoked bacon, Italian *panceta* and salt-pork are acceptable alternatives to *tocino salado* which is used in a number of Spanish dishes.

# BONES
## (huesos)

Beef or pork bones are used for flavouring broths. They may be fresh marrow bones (*cañas*), salted (*huesos salados*) or rancid (*huesos añejos*).

# BROTH or STOCK
## (caldo)

Few Spanish housewives brew up a stockpot specially. Instead, leftover broth from boiled meals (*ollas* or *pucheros*) will be used, or else a stock cube. Several recipes in this book include broth; I suggest you either follow the Spanish way (stock cubes are not as bad as they're made out to be if used in moderation), use your own if you're in the habit of making it, or simply use water. Occasionally a good stock is essential and this has been noted in the recipes concerned.

## GREEN AND RED PEPPERS

*(pimientos verdes, pimientos rojos,* the latter being the ripened version of the former)

These come in all shapes and sizes in Spain, from tiny ones the length of a thumb, tapered and gnarled cone-shaped ones and the more familiar 'bell' peppers. These very large ones are best peeled for use in salads. If they are not of too irregular a shape this can be done with a potato peeler. Otherwise you can roast them first, which also improves the flavour, by putting them in a hot oven, under the grill or on a griddle until they are charred black. Put them in a bowl, cover them with a plate and leave them until you need them – the steam they give off loosens the burnt skin and makes it much easier to peel off. Even confirmed pepper-haters will now find them palatable.

Long dried red peppers, called *pimientos choriceros*, are used all over the country but particularly in northern parts. Their pulp is now sold in jars and is a useful alternative standby.

## NUTS

*(frutos secos)*

Hazelnuts (*avellanas*), pine-nuts (*piñones*), walnuts (*nueces*). chestnuts (*castañas*) and almonds (*almendras*).

Almonds are grown extensively all over southern, eastern and north-eastern Spain, often clinging to the most precipitous of hillsides and making a wonderful sight when they blossom in spring. Apart from their obvious uses in sweet cookery they find their way into many savoury dishes, being pounded to a paste which will thicken and flavour the sauce. They are usually fried or toasted first. It is nice to see almonds on sale loose in Spain in great boxes in the grocers' instead of being confined to expensive little plastic packets. You should buy them shelled but still in their dusty brown skins. To remove these simply blanch the almonds in boiling water for a minute. The nut then slips out easily, glistening and creamy-coloured, like ivory.

You know when winter is coming in Spain when the chestnut roasters set up their braziers on street corners. Chestnuts once formed an important part of the winter diet in northern areas before the advent of the potato but their consumption has also declined because of a disastrous chestnut blight which has devastated the trees. Dried chestnuts are used in some recipes and are called *pilongas*.

Hazelnut and walnuts are other northern Spanish crops now a less important part of the diet than they once were. Hazelnuts are frequently pounded up like almonds to thicken and flavour sauces, while walnuts are more commonly eaten as a pudding, though they do appear in some savoury dishes.

Pine-nuts are expensive little nuts with a delightful, delicately creamy taste which can be augmented considerably by frying them. They are either pounded for sauces and soups or added whole to dishes. When in Spain look out for sugared pine-nuts, a lovely titbit for nibbling after meals.

# VINEGAR
## *(vinagre)*

Apart from its obvious use in salads, vinegar is principally used in making *escabeches*, the pickling mixture which preserves fish and game, and in gazpachos. The days when vinegar in a British cookbook meant malt vinegar are long gone, thank heavens, and you should naturally use a good wine vinegar.

Sherry vinegar (*vinagre de Jerez*) was rather the vogue in French *nouvelle cuisine* in the seventies, something which would have surprised many housewives in the sherry-producing areas of south-west Spain who have long used it for their gazpachos and salads. It is more expensive than ordinary vinegar, but its concentrated flavour means that you need to use less. It is also called *vinagre de yema*, 'of the yolk', i.e. the best part, because it is made from a pure, unfermented grape juice obtained without pressing the *orujo*, the refuse of skins, seeds and stalks. It is then aged in oak barrels for a minimum of two years, often considerably longer.

# SPICES
## *(especias)*

The Moors gave the Spanish a taste for the spices they brought with them, a taste that originally could be enjoyed only by the wealthy. Barcelona's status as a Mediterranean trading port later ensured that the richer classes could satisfy their craving for these exotic flavourings, and many a meal in medieval and renaissance Spain would have been overpoweringly flavoured by today's standards. The legacy such meals left Spanish cookery was the widespread use of spices in both savoury and sweet dishes. Most common are:

| | |
|---|---|
| cinnamon (*canela*) | nutmeg (*nuez moscada*) |
| aniseed (*matalahúva*) | black pepper (*pimienta*) |
| sesame seed (*ajonjolí*) | cloves (*clavos de especia*) |
| cumin (*comino*) | saffron (*azafrán*) |

Ginger, mace, cardamom and galingale (another sort of ginger) were also popular, but the taste for these has not survived and they are very rarely used.

The most influential spice to result from the discovery of America was *pimentón*, the red pepper made by grinding up dried red capsicums and better known in Britain by its Hungarian name of paprika. It may come from *ñoras*, which appear in several recipes in this book. They are stubby, rounded and dented dried peppers of a very dark scarlet colour (also called *pimientos de bola*) which are essential for the cooking of many dishes from Murcia and Alicante. They are a particular speciality of

Guardamar, where they dry their peppers on the sand-dunes. Murcian *pimentón* is widely used in Spain and is made by milling *ñoras*. In fact they have very little flesh, but it is of an extremely concentrated colour and flavour. To use *ñoras*, pull out the stalk and shake out as many seeds as possible. Soak the pepper in cold water for an hour or so, by which time it should have softened. Cut the *ñora* in half and scrape the flesh from the skin with a teaspoon.

An especially delicious Spanish paprika is called *pimentón de la Vera* from Extremadura, where red peppers of various sorts are dried and smoked before milling. It comes in three varieties, sweet (*dulce*), hot (*picante*) and *agridulce* (somewhere between the two). I love this spice and find myself using it more and more in my cooking, as it seems to have the useful effect of adding to the general savouriness of a dish, intensifying the flavours whilst subtly blending in. If possible, always try to use Spanish *pimentón* when making recipes in this book.

Vanilla (*vainilla*) was another important American spice, originally from Mexico. It is used in some Spanish puddings and in *carquinyolis*, a dried biscuit which is used pounded up in some Catalan savoury dishes.

## A NOTE ON SAFFRON

This precious spice, which lends its golden colour and inimitable taste to so many Spanish dishes, comes from the purple-flowered saffron crocus, *Crocus sativus*, first grown in Spain by the Moors and still cultivated in vast fields in La Mancha. It consists of the dried stigmas of the crocus, just three of them to each flower. Since seventy-five thousand such flowers are needed to produce 450 grams (1lb) of saffron it's no wonder that it has always been the most expensive spice in the world, in medieval times even more costly than gold. Fortunately one needs very little to flavour a dish – I generally direct 'a good pinch' in the recipe in this book. Try to use genuine La Mancha saffron if possible.

Though cheaper than elsewhere, saffron is still expensive in Spain (3000 euros a kilo at the time of writing) and many people cannot afford to use it on an everyday basis. Saffron often appears in Spanish cooking as much for its colour as for it taste – there's many a Spanish soup or stew that would look distinctly unappetising without that special warm yellow that glows so appealingly on the plate. When this is the case many Spanish cooks use *colorante*, cheap saffron colouring that comes in little envelopes of bright orange powder. *Colorante* is an extremely virulent dye called tartrazine. Scare stories now abound about it but the extremely small quantities needed to colour a dish shouldn't do you any harm at all.

Unfortunately, many Spanish restaurants substitute *colorante* for saffron where they really shouldn't – in paella for example. I tend to use both, the one for flavour, the other to boost the colour if necessary.

# HERBS

## (hierbas)

Spanish cooks are on the whole quite restrained when using herbs.

## PARSLEY (perejil)

This is the most important herb in the Spanish kitchen. It is used on a massive scale, something which may seem odd to those accustomed to seeing it as a discarded garnish at the side of a plate. In Spain it is usually given away free by greengrocers and butchers, and is the flat-leaved variety, not to be confused with coriander which it resembles. There are those who insist that it is superior in flavour to the British curled-leaf type, but I'm sure in a blind tasting nobody could spot the difference. I do recommend that you grow it yourself, however, whichever form you prefer, and pick it just before you need it: its flavour is immeasurably fresher and more concentrated. If you buy it, keep it fresh and crisp in the following way: rinse it under the tap, shake off the excess water and put it in a clean coffee jar or similar. Screw on the lid and keep it in the fridge. The stalks are full of flavour and can be used for flavouring stocks. Do not use dried parsley unless you like the taste of grass clippings.

## BAY LEAVES (hojas de laurel)

These are indispensable for many Spanish dishes, especially those requiring long cooking. A small leaf or half a large one is usually sufficient. Fresh leaves are considerably more aromatic. Bay leaves are often to be seen hanging up in Spanish markets still on the branch.

## THYME (tomillo)

Quite widely used in slowly cooked dishes. It grows wild in great profusion in the Spanish country-side.

## ROSEMARY (romero)

George Borrow reported that rosemary was thought to be 'good against witches and mischances on the road'. It is found wild in abundance in Spain, though not used a great deal in cookery. However, rosemary twigs added to the fire will produce a fragrant smoke that will flavour paellas or barbecued meats.

## BASIL (albahaca)

Extraordinarily, considering its status in Italy, basil is hardly used at all except for keeping flies out of the kitchen or for chucking in bunches at bullfighters. Nobody seems to know why – my friends were rapturous over a jar of pesto brought from Italy. So perhaps, as in Britain, a basil cult may yet start in Spain. (It is indeed more popular now, though hardly a cult – Ed.)

## FENNEL *(hinojo)*
Another herb that is easy enough to find when walking around Spain. Used occasionally in thick soups (*potajes*), with chestnuts and in a few fish dishes.

## OREGANO *(orégano)*
Used a great deal, especially for marinades. A tisane of oregano sweetened with honey was given to me as a bedtime drink when I was suffering from a nasty cold, and very comforting it was too.

## MINT *(hierbabuena)*
Found occasionally in cooking, in some broad bean and chicken dishes for example, and for mint tea (pennyroyal or *menta poleo* is used for this). A charming custom when the *cruces de mayo* (May Crosses) are constructed and displayed in the streets on 3 May, the feast of the Finding of the Cross, is to strew the ground round about with abundant sprigs of *mastranzo* or apple mint. The action of the feet of the passers-by fills the air with a most pleasing scent. You may also find a sprig of mint in the hot broth taken as a hangover cure at *feria* time.

# CURED HAM AND CHARCUTERIE
## *(jamón curado, los embutidos)*

These are the unsung glories of Spanish eating. Before coming to live in Spain I had no idea of the variety and quality of the preserved pork products to be found there. I soon discovered that the Spanish have a justifiable pride in them and a taste for them that leads to some extraordinary statistics. For example, nearly a whole *jamón serrano* is consumed per Spanish man, woman and child per year. These hams which weigh around 4-5kg/8-12lb are to be found hanging in shops and bars throughout Spain, sometimes with little conical cups attached to the bottom to catch the fatty drips. Spanish barmen slice it most expertly, using a special apparatus for holding it steady and a long, thin-bladed knife for carving.

Generally speaking, the best ham comes from the pig-farming areas of Extremadura, parts of Castilla Y León and western Andalucía, such as Montánchez, Guijuelo and Jabugo, where the favoured pig for hams is the native *Ibérico*, distinguished by its black trotters and black or red hide. Its flesh, fattier than that of other breeds and thus more succulent and flavoursome, has become increasingly popular over the last few years for eating as pork, and the meat marbled with this fat produces wonderfully tender ham. The most prized ham of all, *jamón de bellota*, comes from pigs allowed to roam free amongst the local groves of cork trees and holm-oaks; these pigs are gluttons for the acorns that their keepers beat down for them, and which imbue their meat with such a special flavour.

There is quite a difference between these black-footed hams (*jamón pata negra, jamón ibérico*) and ordinary serrano ham. The latter is the much more widely eaten for it comes from mass-produced white pigs that are farmed rather like battery hens. These pigs became popular because of the quality of their meat which is much leaner than that of their black-footed cousins. Their ham, though it can be good, lacks the finesse of a *pata negra*.

Like *prosciutto di Parma* these hams are not cooked or smoked (cooked ham is known everywhere as *jamón de York*). They are first left in coarse salt (about a day and a half per kilo) then washed and hung up to dry. When they start to 'sweat' they are removed to cool cellars where they are hung up to mature. Mass-produced ones mature for just a few weeks, *pata negra* for eighteen months or more. The coolness is vital, which is why mountainous areas such as the Sierra Morena and the Alpujarras are so favoured, and why hams are sent to be cured there from warmer parts of Spain.

Despite being expensive, Spanish ham is an enormously popular tapa. It goes perfectly with a chilled bone-dry sherry or a glass of *cava*, and many people order a plateful to share between friends. It is generally cut in thin (but not wafer-thin) slices by hand, though some people prefer their ordinary serrano ham cut in *tacos*, small cubes, as it is leaner. The fat can be heavenly, especially on a *pata negra*, and should not be discarded out of guilty thoughts about cholesterol or waistlines.

Cured ham is also used in cookery, where a little goes a long way. Buy it in thick slices and dice it as you need it. If buying thin slices for tapas at home, eat them as soon as possible or have them vacuum-packed: the best of the flavour starts to evaporate as soon as the ham is sliced. Parma ham is the only acceptable alternative to serrano ham in Spanish cookery; don't, whatever you do, put *pata negra* in the cooking pot.

The word *embutidos* covers the whole enormous range of Spain's superb *charcuterie*, also often

called *chacina*. Each region produces its own, and it is always worth buying the local sausages wherever you go as the general standard is extremely high. Remember that the word *ibérico* on the label will indicate that it's made from that particular breed of pig and will probably be more expensive.

The principal types are:

## CAÑA DE LOMO

This can rival *pata negra* for flavour and delicacy. It consists of the whole boned loin of the pig first rubbed with spices and oil, then encased in a skin and left to cure for several months.

## MORCÓN

At its best this can be exquisite. It is a fat, round, unevenly shaped sausage encased in the large intestine of the pig (its *morcón*) and is generally made from the shoulder and the off cuts from the loin, seasoned with paprika and other spices, and cured.

*El botillo* from the region of El Bierzo in León is a powerful-tasting smoked boiling sausage made using the *morcón* for the casing and eaten with potatoes and cabbage. *El chosco de Tineo* from neighbouring Asturias is made along similar lines.

## SALCHICHÓN

A firm, compact, fine-textured sausage which is effectively Spain's salami. Often studded with peppercorns. Perhaps the best comes from Vic in Cataluña.

## SOBRASADA

Mallorca's famous soft-textured sausage, more like a pâté or spread than a conventional sausage. It is also produced in some parts of Cataluña and Valencia, and consists of finely shredded pork mixed with fat and various spices.

## BUTIFARRA

Cataluña's sausage, of which there are several types, principally *blanca* and *negra*, the latter being a blood sausage. Some need cooking, like our own fresh sausages, others have already been boiled.

## LONGANIZA

A generic term for a long thin sausage, the character of which varies from region to region. *Fuet* and *xolís*, for example, are two popular Catalan versions. It may require cooking, as in the case of *chistorra* from the Basque country.

## CHORIZO

If, heaven forfend, I should ever be banished from Spain never to return, one taste of a chorizo could whisk me back there. For me, these coarse-textured sausages flavoured with paprika and garlic summon up the essence of Spanish cookery – it was my first taste of a chorizo that made me realise there was more to Spanish food than meets the eye. I was hooked, and I hope you will be too, whether eating them simply on their own, perhaps *al infierno* – toasted over blazing alcohol in an earthenware chafing dish – or with good fresh eggs and fried potatoes, or as part of the many soups and stews to which they lend their inimitable flavour.

A chorizo is usually stubby, about four inches long or less, and with a pronounced red colour. When cooked it will ooze bright scarlet juice (or else squirt it over you when you pierce it with a fork – you have been warned).

There are many other members of the chorizo family which do not require cooking. *Chorizo de Pamplona,* for example, delicious in a crusty roll, is more like a large close-textured salami; and whole pork loins may be given the chorizo treatment and called *chorizo de lomo.*

## MORCILLA

This is a cousin of our own black pudding, being a soft-textured, spiced blood sausage, and is widely eaten as a tapa or alongside chorizo in soups and stews. Morcilla varies enormously from region to region and in quality, perhaps the best being the smoked version of Asturias, the one containing rice from Burgos and a Basque version with onion and leek from the town of Beasain. Failing Spanish morcilla the only alternative is to use a top-quality black pudding. If you can't get hold of either, leave it out of the recipe altogether or make something else.

## CECINA

This is a ham made usually with beef (though versions exist made of sheep, goat, donkey or horse) which is popular in some parts of northern Spain, particularly León. It is made in much the same way as a serrano ham and will generally be smoked. Though well worth trying, it is not comparable, at least in my experience, to a good *jamón serrano.*

One should perhaps draw a veil over the mass-produced Spanish pork sandwich fillings with names borrowed from overseas which have become popular because of their cheapness. The principal offenders are *mortadela, chopped* (pronounced *chopé*) and *lunch:* they are all vile-tasting 'luncheon meats' to be avoided.

# EQUIPMENT

You could probably make all the dishes in this book without buying any special equipment, though a paella for more than three or four people might cause problems (see my comments on paella pans in the rice chapter). However, the following equipment is that most frequently used in this book.

1. Earthenware *cazuelas* or casseroles of various sizes. These are unglazed on the outside and not only look charming but cook evenly and hold the heat well. In Spain they cost next to nothing. They must be seasoned before using for the first time or they will crack: half-fill the *cazuela* with water and a good splash of vinegar. Bring it gently to the boil and let it boil until the liquid has evaporated. One drawback with earthenware is that it may start to pong a bit after a lot of use, and nowadays I tend to cook in normal pans, keeping the *cazuelas* for attractive serving dishes.

2. A large pestle and mortar. Indispensable in the Spanish kitchen, though the hand-held liquidiser has come as a godsend for making things like gazpacho. I would recommend using a pestle and mortar where stated in a recipe, for the texture will be better than that produced by the whirring blades of a liquidiser. It is also more satisfying and fun, a reminder of how it's been done in Spain for centuries.

3. A set of frying pans. I use a small one (13cm/5in base) for frying things like almonds and garlic, a medium-sized one (18cm/7in base) for frying fish, and a large one (25cm/10in base) for *sofritos*. This also serves as a paella pan for small numbers. For frying potatoes I use a large, deep iron pan (23cm/9in base, about 10cm/4in deep).

# Tapas/
## Pintxos

Nobody knows how the Spanish habit of eating tapas originated, and theories abound. The word itself means cover or lid, and a common theory is that tapas started life as slices of bread or sausage which the innkeeper would place over a customer's glass of wine or sherry. Some people reckon that this was to keep off flies, but a plausible explanation is that the Spaniards' love of conversation, combined with their taste for slowly sipped drinks such as sherry, produced a need for something solid to nibble at to temper the effects of the wine on a hungry stomach. H. V. Morton would have put it down to the Spaniards' breakfast ('deplorable') and, indeed, the time between breakfast and lunch in Spain often requires a little something to see you through. I wonder if it is too fanciful to see a connection between *tapar*, meaning not only 'to cover' but also 'to stop up' or 'to plug', and the need to stop up the appetite before lunch.

The custom, whatever its origins, is a comparatively new one, not having become established until the middle of the nineteenth century. Now it is an integral part of Spanish eating, and you can eat your way round Spain very cheaply, and with great variety, simply by living off tapas.

Entering a Spanish bar at lunchtime, particularly one that specializes in a wide variety of tapas, can be an intimidating experience, not least because of the immense din of conversation that is the inevitable result when more than two Spaniards congregate in a confined area. You have to shout to catch the busy barman's attention and give your order; he will shout back what they have in the way of tapas – the plates of tempting food you can just see along the length of the bar beyond the mass of animated bodies. If you are lucky and of good hearing you might understand about one third of what the barman is shouting, but you can hardly expect him to repeat himself with so many clamouring for his attention, so it's a good idea either to point at something and hope for the best, or stop the barman in mid-flow when you recognise something and say 'one of those'. If you order something that needs to be cooked – a plate of fried anchovies, for example, makes an excellent tapa for a group of four or five – he will shout your order to the kitchen from where he's standing. Somehow they manage to hear him above the racket.

You don't pay yet, of course. If in agreeable company you soon want more drinks and more tapas. More shouts. Miraculously, the barman will keep track of it all, or else ask you what you had when you come to pay (more shouting required). You will try and remember to the best of your ability and shout back. You would think this a situation ripe for exploitation by the dishonest, but this has always been the way the Spaniard has paid for his food and drinks and he wouldn't dream of leaving without settling up honestly. I can heartily recommend eating in such places for it is an excellent way of immersing oneself in the atmosphere of Spain.

Tapas, though in theory only meant to keep hunger at bay, can be quite substantial. When first taken on tapas expeditions my Spanish was poor and I would happily eat my fill of the things that were ordered for everyone to share. All too often I discovered to my dismay that I had missed hearing that in the meantime it had been decided to go to a restaurant for a 'proper' meal. On other occasions I would forgo too many tapas, thinking myself wise in preparing for the meal that would surely follow. I would learn too late that no such meal was planned, that the meal was the tapas.

A tapa can be anything, from a frugal slice of sausage or cheese to small bowls of tripe and chickpeas, from a little saucer of olives or prawns to a rich helping of broad beans cooked with serrano ham. The recipes that follow are some of the commonest tapas, or else they are dishes best suited to eating in small quantities, dishes to whet the appetite rather than sate it. However, many recipes from other chapters can be served as tapas – that is the joy of eating them, for you can sample many different things before you are full. Indeed, one of the best ways of having a Spanish meal at home for several people is just to put several plates of various Spanish foods round the table; provide good bread, plenty of wine, let people help themselves, and you have the makings of a memorable occasion.

# GILDAS

These are an ideal *pintxo* with your first drink. They are simply two or three pickled green chillies (the very mild Basque kind) skewered on a toothpick with an anchovy fillet and a green olive. They were named after the character played by Rita Hayworth in the film of the same name. Why? The film was very popular at the time they were invented and the mixture of tastes, so the legend goes, was a combination of the naughty, the charming and the spicy, just like Gilda. Incidentally, the name should be pronounced 'Hilda', as in Spain.

Similar things, called *banderillas*, are an assortment of pickles on sticks. They share a name with the barbed sticks used in bullfighting.

# Ajo colorado
## (also known as *ajobacalao*)

Literally, red garlic. This is a favourite dish in parts of Andalucía for Holy Week and is a typical example of the near-miracle the Spanish cook can conjure up from next to nothing, in this case bread, oil, garlic and a little piece of dried fish. Serve it with good toasted bread – the quantities given here will serve a good-size party, say twelve – but I like to eat it over several days, for the flavour matures with keeping (but don't eat it cold straight from the fridge if you can help it). It is rich and very, very moreish: without doubt one of the great Spanish dishes.

piece of salt-cod, about 120g/4oz, soaked (see page 44)
5 cloves garlic, peeled
2 heaped teaspoons paprika
280g/10oz white breadcrumbs
500ml/18fl oz oil
juice of 1 lemon
salt (optional)

Drain the salt-cod and cover it with fresh water. Bring it to the boil in a small pan and simmer it for 5 minutes. Remove the cod, reserving the cooking liquor. Skin and bone the cod, then crumble it into small pieces. Pound the garlic to a pulp in a mortar, then place it in a large mixing bowl. Rinse out the mortar with some of the cooking liquor and stir it into the garlic, along with the paprika. Add about half the breadcrumbs and the rest of the liquor, mixing it well with the pestle. Start gradually adding the oil, pounding and mixing well between additions. Add the crumbled cod and pound well. You may need to add extra water at this stage if it seems too thick. Add the lemon juice also, mixing all the while

– the smooth texture of *ajo colorado* depends largely on ceaseless pounding and mixing. Finally, check for salt – it may need a little.

# Soldaditos de Pavía

These 'little soldiers', saffron-coloured fingers of fried salt-cod, were created by the people of Madrid in honour of a regiment of hussars under General Pavía. They were stationed in Madrid in the nineteenth century and their gaily coloured yellow dress-coats endeared them to the local people; or at least that is one story. Manuel Martínez Llopis, in *La cocina típica de Madrid* (1981) provides a connection between the little soldiers and the coup that ended Spain's first republic:

> The name recalls the famous deed perpetrated by General Pavía in the early morning of 3 January 1874, when Castellar was defeated in the national assembly and offered his resignation and that of all his ministers. On hearing the news, Pavía called out his troops from their barracks and surrounded the Palace of Congress, inviting the members to leave the building. As they resisted, he sent the troops into the chamber and the members had to abandon their seats, thus dissolving the parliament.

As Pavía was from Cádiz and the hussars established by him wore a little red jacket beneath their blue dolmans, his name was appropriated for the delicious pieces of fried *bacalao*, a comparison being drawn with the strips of pepper that they used to be wrapped in. The use of this decoration gradually died out but the name was retained.

225g/8oz piece of salt-cod, cut from the thickest part in the middle
juice of ½ lemon
2 tablespoons oil
½ teaspoon paprika
black pepper
1 quantity Frying Batter (page 45) with the addition of a ground pinch of saffron
oil for deep-frying

Take out as many bones as possible from the cod without breaking it up, and remove the skin. Cut the fish into fingers 5-8cm/2-3in long and rather less than 1.25cm/½in wide. Remove any more bones that appear. Soak the fingers in cold water for about 4 hours, changing the water a couple of times. Don't soak them too long or they will be insipid; nibble a piece if you're unsure and drain them once they've lost their excessive saltiness. Dry them carefully on kitchen paper.

Now they must be marinated: pour the lemon and oil over them and sprinkle with the paprika and a touch of black pepper. Mix and leave for 3 or 4 hours – longer won't hurt. Drain, and turn them in the frying batter. Deep-fry in hot oil until crisp and golden brown.

# Gambas con gabardinas

There are some tapas so irresistible that one finds oneself helplessly devouring vast quantities of them, in the end abandoning any idea of a conventional meal. These 'prawns in mackintoshes' are one such tapa. They are simply fried in batter, which puffs up into a light, crispy, golden shell enclosing the succulent prawns within. Added crunch is provided by leaving the tails and last joints of the prawns intact.

If at all possible, try to get raw prawns in the shell for this recipe. Frozen prawns can be used, but the ready-peeled kind tend to be insipid.

1 quantity Frying Batter (see below)
450g/1lb prawns in their shells
sunflower oil for frying
salt

While the batter is resting shell the prawns, leaving the last joint and tail intact. (Use the debris to flavour the broth for a fish soup.) Heat a good amount of oil in a frying pan until very hot but not smoking. Holding the prawns by the tail, trail them through the batter, coating them thoroughly. Fry a few at a time until well browned, then drain on kitchen paper. When all are done sprinkle them lightly with salt and eat promptly. (It is of course a cook's perk to test the odd one, while they're frying, for crispness, consistency, seasoning or for any other reason he or she can dream up if challenged.)

# Frying Batter

This uses not eggs but beer, although no trace of its flavour remains in the finished product, which produces a wonderfully light and crisp coating. Even better, it is completely foolproof. (It is quite in order to leave out the colouring if you don't fancy it, but it is commonly used in Spain and does improve the colour.) It is also a very good-natured batter, puffing up to order many hours after it's made.

120g/4oz plain flour
½ teaspoon salt
1 teaspoon baking powder

1-2 tablespoons oil

about 150ml/5fl oz light beer

saffron colouring (optional)

Mix the flour with the salt and baking powder, then add the oil and beer, beating well until smooth (you shouldn't need an electric beater). Add more beer and oil if it seems very thick and pasty: the end result should be the consistency of double cream. Add a pinch of colouring (or a sprinkle if you don't want to stain your fingers) to give a lemony colour. Leave it to rest for 20 minutes.

If you find you have some left over, make *tortillas del campo*: simply add finely chopped onion and garlic to the batter and drop spoonfuls into hot oil.

# Tortillitas de camarones

Walking around the fish markets in Sanlúcar de Barrameda on the Cádiz coast, or nearby Jerez, you will see vendors of *camarones*, tiny shrimp so fresh they are still leaping like fleas from the tubs and buckets. These go unpeeled into a batter which is fried into thin, lacy, crispy fritters called tortillas or *tortillitas*. Nowhere makes them better than in Casa Balbino in Sanlúcar, the drawback being their popularity. At peak times experience of rugby scrums can come in useful when trying to order them at the bar.

Reproducing *tortillitas* at home is a challenge, especially if you can't get hold of really small shrimp. The best solution seems to me to cut slightly larger shrimp into chunks. You can either leave them unpeeled, or use the heads and shells to make a broth that then becomes the liquid for the batter. The flavour of the shells is vital.

150g/5oz small shrimp or prawns in the shell

200ml/7fl oz water or prawn-shell broth

50g/1½oz chickpea flour

50g/1½oz plain flour

60g/2oz onion, finely chopped

1 tablespoon chopped parsley

salt

oil for frying

If using prawns, first make a broth with the shells and heads: cover them with water, bring to the boil, skim and simmer for 10 minutes. Drain and leave to cool. Meanwhile, cut the prawns into smallish chunks.

Put the cold water or broth into a wide bowl. Add the two sorts of flour and mix in well with a whisk, then stir in the shrimps or prawn pieces, the onion, parsley and a couple of pinches of salt. You are aiming for a fairly thin consistency and quite a high proportion of shrimp to batter.

In a wide frying pan heat a good depth of oil until very hot. Using a very large tablespoon or kitchen spoon, ladle the batter into the hot oil, as you do so trying to push the batter out as thin as possible. Don't worry about the *tortillita* being of an irregular shape. You will probably only have room for a couple at a time. Fry until crisp and well browned on both sides, then drain on kitchen paper. Do not let them get cold. You will probably find you will end up eating them as you go.

# Gambas al pil-pil

These come to the table in little earthenware dishes (*cazuelas*) bubbling and sizzling, hence the onomatopoeic name. Raw prawns are cooked briskly with paprika, a little chilli and plenty of garlic and oil. With decent prawns and good oil this can be a splendid tapa, with lots of bread to mop up the lovely juices. With poor ingredients it is a disaster.

550g/1¼lb raw prawns
8 cloves garlic
2 teaspoons paprika
a small dried red chilli
oil
salt

Peel the prawns and divide them between four individual earthenware *cazuelas* or one larger one, or use any ovenproof dish. To each dish add two of the garlic cloves, roughly chopped, half a teaspoon of paprika, two or three little pieces of chilli and enough oil just to cover the prawns. Season with salt and leave the prawns to marinate for 3-4 hours.

Place the dishes over a high heat or in a very hot oven. Let the prawns bubble in the oil for 2-3 minutes and then carry them sizzling to the table. Let them cool a little before eating.

If you leave out the paprika you will have a dish of garlic prawns, or *gambas al ajillo.*

# Bacalao al pil-pil

Though sharing the same name as the previous recipe, and also originating in the Basque country, this rich dish of salt-cod is made in a rather different way. The juices and natural gelatine of the cod emulsify with the garlicky, chilli-spiked olive oil to form what is in effect a warm mayonnaise without the egg. Some unprincipled chefs cheat and add flour. Serve with lots of bread, as the sauce will be more than popular. Small new potatoes are also very good with it.

4 pieces (about 150g/5oz each) salt-cod, soaked (see page 44)
and patted dry with kitchen paper
250ml/8fl oz olive oil
4 large cloves garlic, sliced thinly
1 large dried chilli, cut in rough pieces or thin rings, seeds removed

Choose a frying pan, saucepan or *cazuela* large enough to hold the fish in a single layer without too much crowding. Heat the oil over a moderate heat and fry the garlic and chilli until the garlic is brown. Remove the garlic and chilli to a plate and reserve for later.

Leave the oil to cool for five minutes or so. Ideally the temperature should be about 50°C/122°F degrees. Now put in the cod, skin side down. (Lots of people put it in skin side up, so I don't think it makes too much difference.) The oil should nearly cover the fish, but not drown it. If there's too much just drain it off and keep for something else. Return the pan to a low to moderate heat.

Now comes the magical part. Holding the pan by the handle, or the *cazuela* by its edge, start to swirl the oil round and around the fish with smooth, regular, circular movements, supposedly always in the same direction. Very soon little spots of the fish juices will appear in the sauce. Keep swirling and swirling for at least 10 minutes and gradually you will see the oil become thicker and more opaque. Do not try to turn the fish over. It is done when firm to the touch, which hopefully coincides with the sauce reaching a reasonably thick consistency.

Return the garlic and chilli to the pan and that's it. The easiest thing is to put the pan in the middle of the table and let everyone dip in as they wish. No salt should be needed. Left over sauce will still be delicious next day with some bread.

If the sauce does not behave as it should, remove the fish to a plate and give the sauce a good go with a hand-held electric whisk. Another trick people use is to whisk it with the rounded base of a sieve. Even if it doesn't oblige completely the sauce will still taste fine.

**Note:** this is also a good recipe for the gelatinous little bits of fish chin called *kokotxas* (see page 203).

# Tortillitas de bacalao con miel de caña

Salt-cod fritters with cane honey (see recipe for *gachas* page 133). This sounds like a marriage made in hell, but give it a try – it is startlingly successful.

280g/10oz salt-cod, soaked
550g/1¼lb peeled potatoes
2 eggs, separated
1 tablespoon chopped parsley
2 cloves garlic, crushed
pepper and salt
oil for frying
cane honey

Poach the cod for about 10 minutes, drain and leave it to cool. Then remove all the skin and bones. Boil the potatoes until tender, drain and mash. Pound the cod in the mortar until you have a fairly smooth pulp. Add to the potatoes, along with the egg yolks, about a tablespoon of parsley, the crushed garlic, pepper and some salt if needed. Beat the egg whites to the soft peak stage, then fold them into the cod mixture. (You may think the latter too stiff for this operation, but enough air is incorporated into the mixture to make the end result light and fluffy.) This should only be done at the last minute.

Heat about 2.5cm/1in of oil and drop in rounded spoonfuls of the mixture, turning them over when one side is done. Drain well on kitchen paper, then drizzle a thin stream of cane honey over them. This thins down with the heat, is absorbed into the crispy coating of the fritters and produces a meltingly delicious crust with a savoury interior.

# Almejas a la marinera

There are any number of versions of this dish of clams and wine. This one is particularly savoury.

125ml/4fl oz white wine
550g/1¼lb small fresh clams, washed
3 tablespoons oil
4 cloves garlic, chopped
2 teaspoons paprika

Put the wine in a *cazuela* or wide frying pan and add the clams. Bring to the boil and cook until most of the clams are opened. Set aside. Heat the oil in a small pan and fry the chopped garlic until brown. Remove from the heat, sprinkle in the paprika and tip the mixture over the clams. Mix well, heat through and serve.

# Chocos con habas

*Chocos* are small cuttlefish, and in this classic Andalusian dish they are combined with broad beans. Avoid large, flabby cuttlefish and big starchy broad beans: rather, use smaller specimens of cuttlefish (or squid) and the first young broad beans that come into the shops, with only three or four little beans per pod. Cut up the pods and add them, too, if you like – when young and immature they are tender and delicious.

3 tablespoons oil
1 onion, finely chopped
3 cloves garlic, chopped
1 tablespoon chopped parsley
2 teaspoons paprika
1kg/2¼1b small cuttlefish or squid, cleaned
1kg/2¼lb young broad beans, shelled
1 bay leaf, torn into 3 or 4 pieces
salt

In a wide *cazuela* or similar, heat the oil and soften the onion with the garlic and parsley. Add the paprika, mix in well and add the cuttlefish or squid. Fry, stirring occasionally, for 5 minutes so that the fish change colour. Add the beans, bay leaf, a little salt and barely cover with water. Leave to simmer, uncovered, until the cuttlefish and beans are cooked and just coated in sauce.

# Conchas de mariscos

A seafood gratin which makes an elegant starter. If you cannot get uncooked prawns and fresh clams you will need to make a good fish stock flavoured with white wine: poach several fish heads and bones, in enough water to cover, with onion, carrot, herbs, etc. for half an hour. You also need, ideally, some scallop shells, but ordinary small oven proof dishes will do.

280g/10oz fresh clams (or about 45g/1½oz tinned)
125ml/4fl oz white wine
120g/4oz fresh prawns (or about 60g/2oz peeled)
280g/10oz red mullet
60g/2oz butter
90g/3oz mushrooms, thinly sliced (or, even better, oyster mushrooms)

60g/2oz Manchego cheese, grated (or use fresh Parmesan)
1 heaped tablespoon flour
30g/1oz breadcrumbs

Cover the base of a saucepan with water and a dash of white wine, bring to the boil and throw in the clams. Remove them as they open. If after about 5 minutes there are still some obstinately resisting, discard them. Cook the prawns in the same broth for about 5 minutes. Then poach the red mullet very gently until just done – again, about 5 minutes. (You will need fish stock for this if you haven't used fresh clams and prawns; see above.)

Now remove the clams from their shells, peel the prawns and chop them roughly, and remove all the flesh from the red mullet, making sure you discard all the bones.

Melt half the butter and gently fry the mushrooms for 5 minutes. Stir in a good tablespoon of flour and let this cook gently for a couple of minutes. Now gradually add 3½-4oz/100-120g of the broth. You need a very thick sauce. Stir the fish and shellfish into it. Butter four scallop shells and divide the mixture between them. Sprinkle lightly with cheese and breadcrumbs, dot with the remaining butter and bake in a very hot oven until browning.

I prefer this to be left to cool down quite a bit before it is eaten, since straight from the oven it can burn your mouth and prevent you noticing what the food tastes like. Also, the flavour actually improves as it cools. The leftover stock makes an excellent base for soup.

# Pescado en adobo

Marinated and fried fish. The best fish of all for this is skate, but the marinade is also commonly used for fish like monkfish (*rape*), tope (*cazón*), pompano (*palometa*) and Ray's bream (*japuta*). Like many tapas it is perfectly feasible to serve in larger quantities as a main course. This, for instance, would be delicious as part of a mixed fry of fish. However, it is very rich and strongly flavoured and I prefer it in small quantities. Start preparing it 24 hours before you need it.

1 wing of skate, about 450g/1lb
salt
2 teaspoons oregano
2 teaspoons paprika
1 clove garlic, crushed
red wine vinegar

oil for deep frying
flour

You must first remove as much of the skin as possible from the skate; this is tricky, and requires a very sharp knife. Chop the skate into small pieces about 5cm/2in long – remember this is finger food. Place in a non-metallic bowl. Sprinkle lightly with salt, then with the dried oregano and paprika. Add the garlic and enough vinegar just to cover. Leave for 24 hours for the flavours to mingle.

Heat 5cm/2in of oil in a frying pan. Have some plain flour ready on a dish. Thoroughly drain the pieces of fish, and press them firmly into the flour, covering them well. Shake off the excess. Fry them in batches in the hot oil until they are well browned and crisp. Drain on kitchen paper. This holds the heat very nicely without spoiling.

There is a knack in eating these to avoid crunching on the cartilaginous 'bones' of the skate: hold by the thick end and pull the flesh away through your teeth.

# Calamares con brandy

An exquisite dish of squid in a rich almond sauce flavoured with brandy and a last-minute boost of garlic and parsley.

3 tablespoon oil
60g/2oz almonds, blanched and peeled
550g/1¼lb small squid, cleaned and sliced (see page 220)
salt
95ml/3fl oz Spanish brandy
2 cloves garlic, finely chopped
2 tablespoons chopped parsley

Heat the oil in a frying pan and fry the almonds briskly until they are well browned all over. Remove them to a mortar. In the remaining oil fry the squid, stirring, until it has changed colour. Sprinkle it with a little salt and pour in the brandy. Cover the pan and leave to simmer for about 20 minutes.

Meanwhile, pound the almonds to a smooth paste in the mortar. Thin it to a cream with a little water.

Uncover the squid and let any liquid evaporate. Stir in the almond cream and let it heat through. Stir in the garlic and parsley and serve at once.

# Calamares a la Enriqueta

This delicious recipe was given to me by my friend and neighbour Cristina. It's simplicity itself, but really lets the marvellous sea taste of squid shine.

6 tablespoons oil
6 cloves garlic
450g/1lb small squid, cleaned and sliced (see page 220)
3 tablespoons chopped parsley

Heat the oil with two sliced cloves of garlic. Cook gently for a minute or two without browning. Add the squid, turn up the heat and fry briskly until it has all changed colour. Season with salt, reduce the heat to a minimum, cover tightly and simmer for about 25 minutes. Chop the remaining garlic. Remove the lid from the pan and strew the chopped garlic and parsley over the squid. Let it all sizzle for a minute or two but no longer, for the garlic and parsley should remain fresh-tasting. Eat piping hot.

If you want to make this ahead of time, prepare everything until the stage when you add the garlic and parsley. When you are ready, add a little water to the pan and reheat until it's all boiled away. Then proceed as above.

# Rollitos de caballa

I have never been absolutely sure what rissoles are, but I think these might be they – little fried rolls of finely chopped mackerel flavoured with bacon, garlic and parsley. They make a lovely tapa or can be eaten cold on picnics. You could substitute bonito for the mackerel if you wish. Having read the recipe you may be tempted to make the whole thing in a food processor but I think that would be a mistake; you are not making fish paste, after all. The quantities below will make about a dozen rolls.

1 large or 2 medium mackerel: ask your fishmonger to fillet it (and skin it too if possible)
You need about 340g/12oz mackerel flesh. completely free of bones
120g/4oz unsmoked bacon
½ onion
salt and pepper
3 cloves garlic, crushed
2 tablespoons finely chopped parsley
1 egg, beaten
2–3 tablespoons dried breadcrumbs

3 tablespoons oil
a little flour
95ml/3fl oz white wine (about a small glassful)

Using a very sharp knife chop the mackerel flesh finely. Do the same with the bacon and onion. Mix them well in a bowl, season with salt and pepper and add the garlic, parsley, egg and breadcrumbs. Mix very thoroughly and leave to stand for half an hour so the flavours can develop. Using your hands, form small tablespoonfuls of the mixture into roll shapes. Heat the oil in a wide frying pan. Flour the rolls lightly and fry them gently, covered, for about ten minutes. Turn them over, pour in the wine and cook, uncovered, until it has evaporated – about 10 minutes more.

# Albóndigas de atún

Little balls of tuna fish in tomato sauce. These quantities make 16-20 balls.

225g/8oz tinned tuna
2 egg yolks
5 tablespoons cream
1 clove garlic, crushed
2 tablespoons chopped parsley
2 tablespoons dry sherry
50g/1½oz dried breadcrumbs
salt and pepper
flour for coating
3 tablespoons oil
250ml/9fl oz tomato sauce (see page 131)

Drain and mash the tuna. Mix it thoroughly with the egg yolks, cream, garlic, parsley, sherry and breadcrumbs. Season. Form the mixture into little balls and roll them in flour.

Heat the oil in a wide pan and fry the *albóndigas*, turning them over when they are well browned on one side. Pour the tomato sauce over them and simmer for 10 minutes.

# Revuelto de morcilla

Scrambled eggs with morcilla, pine-nuts, apple and currants. A deliciously rich dish of satisfying flavours.

4 tablespoons oil
60g/2 oz pine-nuts
225g/8oz morcilla
½ an acid apple, diced
30g/1oz currants
8 eggs

Heat the oil over a low heat in a wide non-stick frying pan. Gently cook the pine-nuts until they start to brown. Slit open the morcilla and scrape the contents into the pan. Gently fry the morcilla for five minutes. If it gives off a lot of fat, sponge it away with kitchen paper. Add the apple and currants and cook a couple of minutes more.

Now beat the eggs with a pinch of salt and add them to the pan. Cook as you would for scrambled eggs, in other words gently, stirring occasionally and without overdoing it. Finally check for seasoning. Eat as soon as possible.

# Lomo adobado

Marinated pork loin. The longer the pork sits in the marinade the better the flavour will be. Once fried it can be served hot, warm or chilled. Lovers of bread and dripping will find that the chilled fat and juices are quite delicious.

Get about 450g/1lb of thinly sliced boned loin, preferably *ibérico*. Make a marinade of 2 tablespoons vinegar, 6 tablespoons oil, 3 cloves of garlic (crushed), 2 teaspoons paprika, 2 teaspoons oregano, 4 cloves, 1 bay leaf and salt and pepper. Leave the pork in it overnight or if possible a couple of days. Try not to put it in the fridge. Drain it. Melt some clean lard and fry the pieces of meat gently in it until cooked (about 10 minutes). It is best if left to cool in the juices.

# Habas con jamón

Broad beans with serrano ham. Very commonly found as a tapa, these also make a delicious side dish. Don't bother to remove the inner shells of the beans – they don't spoil one's enjoyment of the dish.

4 tablespoons oil

thick slice (1.25cm/½in or so) serrano ham, in 1.25cm/½in dice

450g/1lb shelled broad beans (roughly three times that in their pods)

4 large spring onions, roughly chopped

salt (optional)

Heat the oil in a wide frying pan. Fry the diced ham quickly, then remove and reserve. Add the beans and spring onions, give a good stir, add about ¼ pint/150ml water, cover and leave over a medium heat for about 15 minutes. Return the ham to the pan and add more water if the mixture seems very thick. Cover and cook for another 15 minutes. Remove the lid and boil off any excess liquid, until the beans are enveloped in a rich greenish sauce and very tender. Add salt if necessary (it shouldn't need much – the ham provides plenty). Don't serve them boiling hot.

Any leftovers make an excellent tortilla.

# Habas a la bilbaína

From Bilbao. The same as above but with parsley and a couple of sliced red peppers (these may be of the reconstituted dried kind called *pimientos choriceros)* added to the beans and onions, and decorated with sliced hard-boiled egg.

# Habas a la catalana

A Catalan dish of broad beans in a rich sauce flavoured with *butifarra negra*, bacon, garlic, mint and aguardiente. The latter means literally 'burning water', and was the name originally used to describe any sort of distilled wine before the word brandy achieved wider usage. In the sixteenth century people started to take it medicinally in the morning in order to *matar el gusanillo*, to kill the worm, and thus to take the edge off one's appetite. It was often sold by street vendors along with *naranjada*, now the word for orange juice or squash but in those days a sort of marmalade of orange peel and honey which it was believed was good for treating bile. The name aguardiente also came to be used for aniseed spirits which have always been enormously popular in Spain, so that nowadays an aguardiente can mean either a fiery spirit similar to Italy's grappa or an aniseed spirit, dry or sweet.

2 tablespoons oil

2 cloves garlic, crushed

1 onion, chopped
95ml/3fl oz aguardiente (or grappa)
450g/1lb shelled broad beans (see *habas con jamón*, page 55)
2 *butifarras negras* (or chorizo if you can't get it) thinly sliced
3 rashers unsmoked streaky bacon, sliced
2 tablespoons white wine
1 sprig mint
salt (optional)

Heat the oil in a *cazuela* and fry the garlic until it starts to brown. Add the onion and let it soften. Pour over the aguardiente and set it alight. When the flames die down stir in the beans, *butifarra*, bacon, the white wine and mint. Add enough water just to cover the beans and cook steadily until the beans are tender and the liquid reduced to practically nothing. The *butifarra* and bacon will probably provide enough salt, but check for seasoning nonetheless.

# Habas a la asturiana

An Asturian variation on the broad beans and ham theme, cooked this time with potatoes, carrots and wine.

120g/4oz serrano ham, diced
2 cloves garlic, crushed
4 tablespoons oil
1 onion, chopped
4 carrots, peeled and sliced
1 teaspoon paprika
4 tablespoons white wine
450g/1lb shelled broad beans (see *habas con jamón*, page 55)
600ml/1 pint water
salt
450g/1lb small new potatoes, scraped

Fry the ham and garlic briskly in the oil until the garlic starts to brown. Add the onions and carrots and cook over a moderate heat until they start to soften. Stir in the paprika, beans, wine, water and a little salt. Cover and simmer for about 20 minutes. Add the potatoes, top up with liquid if necessary and continue simmering for about another 25 minutes, by which time the potatoes should be tender and the liquid reduced to practically nothing. If not, boil hard until it's very thick, shaking the pan to stop it sticking. Check the seasoning and let the dish cool a little before serving.

## Habas a la rondeña

Ronda in Andalucía must be one of the most spectacular towns in Spain, as well as one of the most beautiful. The town is divided by a tall arched bridge over a canyon, the *tajo*. The fearless *rondeños* have built houses on the edge of the drop; having no head for heights I feel they must be quite mad.

This is a version of how they cook broad beans in Ronda:

120g/4oz serrano ham, diced
1 onion, finely chopped
2 cloves garlic, crushed
1 tomato, peeled and chopped
450g/1lb shelled broad beans (see *habas con jamón*, page 55)
1 teaspoon paprika
salt
3 tablespoons breadcrumbs
2 tablespoons chopped parsley
1 hard-boiled egg, chopped
3 tablespoons oil

Fry the ham, onion and garlic in the oil until soft. Add the tomato, beans and paprika and cook until pulpy. Cover with water, season with a little salt and simmer uncovered until the beans are tender and the sauce quite reduced. Stir in the breadcrumbs and parsley and sprinkle over the chopped egg. Leave to cool a little before serving.

## Setas al Jerez

*Seta* and *hongo* are Spanish for fungi or wild mushrooms. The only kind seen with any regularity in the market where I live is the oyster mushroom, or at least a cultivated version of it. It is of a most subtle pearly-brown colour, its cap undulating, its gills a pale, delicate, finely lined sponge. It is as pleasing to eat as to look at, for it maintains its meaty texture in the pot and doesn't ooze itself away into nothingness like some of its cousins.

450g/1lb fungi of your choice
3 tablespoons oil
2 cloves garlic (at least), chopped
2 tablespoons chopped parsley
60g/2oz butter
95ml/3fl oz fino sherry
salt and pepper

Wipe the fungi clean and divide up any that are enormous. (With oyster mushrooms remove their tough stalk.) In a wide frying pan heat the oil and add the fungi so that they more or less lie in a single layer. Let them colour, then add the garlic and parsley, stirring well. After 2 more minutes add the butter and sprinkle well with sherry and some salt and pepper. Leave it to bubble away for about 15 minutes. Serve hot.

## Setas a la crema

Fungi with cream. This dish has never struck me as being particularly Spanish in style, containing, as it does, butter and cream. However, it is extremely good, if rich, and makes a fine tapa or first course.

60g/2oz butter
450g/1lb fungi, cleaned and sliced
2 cloves garlic, chopped
1 tablespoon chopped parsley
2 egg yolks
2-3 tablespoons meat juices or gravy
150ml/¼ pint cream
juice of ½ lemon
salt and pepper

Melt the butter in a wide pan and add the fungi. Cook rapidly for 2 minutes, then add the garlic, parsley and meat juices. Cover and simmer for about 15 minutes. Beat the egg yolks with the cream and lemon juice and, off the heat, gradually stir this mixture into the fungi. Reheat very gently (so as not to scramble the eggs) until the sauce is thick, creamy and hot. Season to taste and serve as soon as possible.

# Cazuela de setas y piñones

A beautiful combination of fungi and pine-nuts, flavoured with brandy, garlic and parsley. Ordinary field mushrooms work perfectly well if you can't get hold of any more unusual fungi.

3 tablespoons oil
900g/2lb fungi of your choice, cleaned and sliced (try not to wash them)
2 cloves garlic, crushed
salt and pepper
150ml/¼ pint Spanish brandy
120g/4oz pine-nuts
3 tablespoons chopped parsley

Heat the oil in a *cazuela* or frying pan. Add the fungi, garlic and a little salt and pepper. As soon as the fungi start to throw off their juices add the brandy and pine-nuts. Continue cooking rapidly until all the liquid has evaporated and you are left with just the oil coating the fungi. Stir in the parsley and serve at once.

# Setas a la navarra

450g/1lb fungi, cleaned and sliced
60g/2oz lard
12 almonds, blanched and peeled
2 cloves garlic
150ml/¼ pint white wine
1 teaspoon paprika
Salt

Fry the fungi quickly in the lard until they throw off their juices. Pound the almonds and garlic to a paste and add it to the fungi with the wine, paprika and some salt. When the sauce has reduced to a coating consistency the dish is ready.

# 'Champis' a la plancha

The region of La Rioja is the biggest producer in Spain of cultivated mushrooms and other funghi. A very popular tapa in the capital, Logroño, are these mushrooms (called affectionately *champis*), cooked on the *plancha* and served with a dressing, for which each bar has its own secret recipe. This is my version.

12 medium-sized mushrooms
1 clove garlic
½ teaspoon salt
1 tablespoon lemon juice
1 tablespoon chopped parsley
3 tablespoons extra virgin olive oil
A little extra oil for brushing the mushrooms
12 peeled prawns (optional)

Remove the stalks completely from the mushrooms (use them for stock). Make sure the mushrooms are absolutely free of grit.

Pound the peeled garlic to a paste with the salt. Add the chopped parsley and pound it well in. Pour in the lemon juice and stir well to make sure all the salt is dissolved. Stir in the olive oil.

Get a non-stick frying pan or griddle very hot over a medium to high heat. Brush the bottom edges of the mushrooms with oil and place them in the hot pan. Leave them alone for five minutes to brown. Brush the tops of the mushrooms with oil and turn them over. Season with a tiny pinch of salt. Leave the mushrooms another 5 minutes, then carefully pour into each mushroom about a teaspoonful of the dressing. Leave a minute longer, then serve, either skewering them onto toothpicks or as they are. Top them with a peeled prawn if you like, and eat while still very hot.

## Champiñones al ajillo

*Ajillo* is the diminutive of *ajo*, garlic, but the quantities one usually finds in dishes described thus would not lead one to think so. Much the same ingredients as the previous recipe, mushrooms, garlic and so on, but a different style altogether

900g/2lb mushrooms, washed
4 cloves garlic, finely chopped
6 tablespoons oil
juice of ½ lemon
salt
a small bunch of parsley, chopped

If the mushrooms are large cut them into pieces; if not, leave them as they are. Fry the garlic in the oil until it starts to brown, add the mushrooms, lemon juice and some salt and give a good stir. The mushrooms will quickly start leaking their copious juices. Continue cooking over a high heat until these have all but evaporated. Sprinkle in the parsley, mix well and serve.

# Coctel de aguacates

Avocado cocktail. A refinement, and a good one, of the once ubiquitous prawn cocktail. The combination of avocado, hard-boiled egg and prawns is a particularly pleasing one, both in taste and texture.

Avocado is not a traditional food in Spain, so this is a comparatively recent addition to Spanish cuisine. One comes across all shapes and sizes there, ranging from monsters the size of small melons, to tiny elongated ones like green fingers.

225g/8oz mayonnaise (see page 188)
salt and pepper
brandy, lemon juice, tomato ketchup, Worcester sauce
1 medium avocado, flesh scooped out and roughly chopped
120g/4oz peeled prawns
2 tablespoons roughly chopped parsley
2 hard-boiled eggs, roughly chopped
shredded lettuce

Season and colour the mayonnaise with the brandy, lemon juice, tomato ketchup and Worcester sauce, but do try to be discreet: the sauce can become very theatrical if you're not careful. Mix in the avocado, prawns, parsley and eggs. Chill and serve on the shredded lettuce.

# Huevos rellenos

Stuffed egg. Hard-boiled eggs are a favourite tapa, often simply served with mayonnaise, which I find a little dull after a while, good though they can be. This recipe is slightly more elaborate, but if you have all the ingredients to hand you can prepare it in the blink of an eye.

4 hard-boiled eggs
about 4 tablespoons mayonnaise (see page 188)

salt and pepper

60g/2oz slice of serrano ham *or* home-cooked boiled ham, diced small, *or* drained tuna

8 large cooked prawns, peeled

8 parsley sprigs (optional)

Halve the eggs lengthways. Scoop out the yolks and mash them to make a paste. Stir the paste into the mayonnaise along with the chopped ham or tuna. Pile the mixture into the egg whites and decorate each one with a prawn. Garnish with parsley sprigs if you wish.

# Ensaladilla rusa

Russian salad. Why Russian? Supposedly it was the invention of a French chef, who made it popular at a fashionable Moscow restaurant in the mid-19th century, though we have no record of what was actually in it. It has become one of the most popular tapas in Spain, with a great many variations.

340g/12 oz potatoes

1 large carrot, peeled and diced

120g/4oz frozen peas

120g/4oz green beans, cut in small lengths

1 small can tuna

12 anchovy-stuffed olives, halved

½ quantity of mayonnaise (see page 188)

2 hard-boiled eggs

Boil the potatoes in their skins until tender, adding the carrots towards the end of the cooking time. Boil the peas and beans in salted water until tender. Peel and dice the cooked potatoes and mix with the carrots, peas, beans, olives and tuna. This is best done after the first rush of hot steam from the vegetables has evaporated. Stir the mayonnaise in carefully while the vegetables are still warm. Decorate with the sliced eggs.

**Note:** One can use the oil from the tuna towards making the mayonnaise. Try using small cubes of serrano ham instead of or as well as the tuna. Peeled prawns are another option. A very agreeable meal consists of *ensaladilla rusa* accompanied by a selection of Spanish *embutidos*, *chorizo de lomo* and *salchichón*, for example.

# Arroz en ensalada

Spanish rice salad.

1 tomato
1 small onion
6 anchovy fillets
1 tin tuna
225g/8oz rice
1 tablespoon fresh thyme, chopped
oil, vinegar

Peel, seed and dice the tomato quite small. Chop the onion and anchovies finely. Drain and flake the tuna.

Cook the rice in boiling salted water until just tender. Drain and rinse away any stickiness under the hot tap. Mix the rice, still warm, with the other ingredients, seasoning it with thyme and with oil and vinegar to taste. Serve at room temperature.

# Arroz al copo

This can be made with leftover rice and tomato sauce, but is best made from scratch: freshly boiled rice is stirred into some hot tomato sauce (see page 131). Spread it out on a plate and cover the whole thing with mayonnaise (page 188). Decorate with pieces of hard-boiled egg and thin strips of roasted red pepper. Serve warm or cold, but not refrigerated.

# Pimientos fritos

Fried green peppers. These may sound rather dull and unimaginative, but they are hugely popular and wickedly delicious. The first time I ate them was at the April *feria* in Seville, where they appeared piping hot from huge cauldrons of boiling oil.

Unfortunately giant bulbous peppers are less than ideal for frying in this manner. You need the very much smaller, tapering kind that are shiny and gnarled, like bright green roots. Allow about four per person as a tapa.

6 tablespoons olive oil or sunflower oil, for frying
16 small green peppers, whole but seeded, and salted inside

Cover the base of a frying pan with oil. When hot, add the peppers and cover with a lid. Turn the peppers occasionally as they caramelise and collapse. When they're tender remove them to a suitable dish with some or all of the oily juices, and leave covered until required.

Try adding any leftovers to the basic tortilla mix on page 158.

# Espárragos y papas en adobillo

An Andalusian dish of asparagus and fried potatoes in a spicy sauce of garlic, saffron, paprika, oregano and vinegar, the whole bound together with breadcrumbs.

340g/12oz fresh asparagus, trimmed and cut in 2.5cm/1in lengths
(frozen asparagus works well too)
oil for deep frying
450g/1lb potatoes, peeled and cut in smallish chunks
salt
2 cloves garlic
6 peppercorns
good pinch of saffron
1 teaspoon dried oregano
1 teaspoon paprika
1 tablespoon vinegar
2 tablespoons dried breadcrumbs

Separate the asparagus into stalks and tips. Cook the stalks in boiling salted water for 5 minutes, then add the tips and cook 5 minutes more. Drain, reserving the cooking water.

Heat the oil. Sprinkle the potatoes with salt and fry them until brown. While doing so pound the garlic, peppercorns, saffron and oregano in a mortar with a little salt until you have a paste. Stir in the paprika and then the vinegar. Add the breadcrumbs and thin the mixture down to a thickish sauce with some of the asparagus water.

Drain the potatoes well on kitchen paper. Place the sauce and asparagus in a pan and heat through gently. Pour over the potatoes and serve.

## Ensalada de patatas y gambas

Potato and prawn salad. Allow about four small new potatoes and two or three large prawns (raw if possible) per person. Cook the unpeeled potatoes in salted water until tender, adding the prawns just before the end if using raw ones. Peel the prawns and potatoes; mix with some chopped parsley and finely chopped garlic, and dress with oil and vinegar.

## Perdices de capellán

Literally 'the chaplain's partridges', although, with that charming perversity so often found in cooking, these little rolls from the Balearic Islands are actually made with beef rolled round a filling of ham and *sobrasada*, the savoury paste of pork and paprika so popular in the islands. Allow one per person as a rich tapa, two as a main course. The quantities given will make 8 'partridges'.

150g/5oz serrano ham
170g/6oz *sobrasada*
4 x 120g/4oz steaks, cut in half, *or*
8 x 60g/2oz very thinly sliced steak
(*or*, perhaps better, veal escalopes)
flour
2 tablespoons lard
2 cloves garlic
1 teaspoon paprika
salt
pinch each of thyme and oregano
small glass white wine

Divide the ham and *sobrasada* into 8 roughly equal portions. Place each steak between 2 sheets of greaseproof paper and very gently bat it out with a rolling pin or similar, until very thin but without tearing it. Place a piece of ham and a piece of *sobrasada* at the end of a steak, tuck in the side and end of the meat, and roll the whole thing up neatly. Secure with cocktail sticks, or sew it up. Repeat with the remaining steaks and roll them in flour.

Heat the lard in a frying pan large enough to hold all the 'partridges' in a single layer. Brown the meat rolls all over. Pound the garlic to a paste with the paprika and a very little salt. Add a pinch of thyme and oregano, dilute it with the wine and a small glass of water and pour it over the meat. Simmer the rolls in this sauce for about 15 minutes, by which time they should be cooked and the sauce reduced to a small quantity of rich flavour.

Take out the cocktail sticks before serving. This dish is also excellent cold for picnics.

# Salchichas al Jerez

Sausages with sherry. The best type of sausage for this is the thin red chipolata type, slightly hot, from Spanish butchers. Failing these, use any well-flavoured chipolata, preferably from a butcher who makes his own.

about ½ tablespoon lard
450g/1lb salchichas
4 cloves garlic, sliced
small glass of dry sherry (about 4-5 tablespoons)

Melt the lard in a large, wide frying pan. Fry the sausages gently until coloured on all sides. Add the sherry and garlic, let it bubble a moment or two, then cover tightly and simmer for about 20 minutes.

This needs plenty of bread to mop up the juices, or alternatively a few fried potatoes.

# Butifarra con judías

Fried sausage with bacon and beans from Cataluña, where it's known as *butifarra amb mongetes*.

225g/8oz dried white beans, soaked overnight
150g/5oz green streaky bacon (optional)

1 large white *butifarra or* 450g/1lb good-quality Italian or English sausages
2 tablespoons chopped parsley

Cook the beans in boiling water until tender (add no salt – plenty comes later on). Chop the bacon into small cubes and dry fry them until they have thrown off their fat and are reduced to a crispy brown. Fry the *butifarra* or sausages in the bacon fat until browned and cooked through. Remove both bacon and sausage and slice the latter. Keep warm.

Drain the beans thoroughly. Add them to the fat in the pan and fry over a high heat for a few minutes, stirring occasionally, so that the beans start to brown and take on some of the flavoured fat. Remove the beans to a warmed plate, draining them well, then sprinkle with the parsley and decorate with the slices of sausage and bacon. Serve at once.

## Albóndigas a la calle Pintada

Once, after a particularly disastrous evening, trying to fry stuffed courgettes, I found myself with some of the stuffing left over. I nearly threw it away but in the end consoled myself by turning it into meatballs and pouring myself a large gin and tonic. I made half with Manchego cheese and half without, and I don't know which I prefer. I leave it up to you.

1 onion, finely chopped
1 tablespoon oil
120g/4oz minced beef
2 tablespoons white wine
salt and pepper
1 or 2 cloves of garlic, crushed
30g/1oz stoned green olives, finely chopped
30g/1oz currants, soaked until soft in hot water
1 hard-boiled egg, finely chopped
1 beaten egg
1 tablespoon grated Manchego or Parmesan cheese (optional)
breadcrumbs
flour
oil to cover the base of the frying pan

Fry the onion in the oil until soft. Add the mince, let it lose its raw colour, moisten it with white wine and add salt and pepper. Simmer until the wine has disappeared. Leave it to cool.

Stir in the crushed garlic, olives, currants and chopped egg. Add the beaten egg, the cheese if you're using it, and enough breadcrumbs to bind it roughly together (don't make it too dry). Form it into little balls, roll them in flour and fry them in hot oil until well browned. These are nice dipped into mayonnaise.

# Pinchitos

Nowhere are the flavours and scents of Islam so instantly evoked as with *pinchitos*, kebabs of pork (presumably of lamb originally) marinated in spices, then grilled. This should preferably be done over charcoal in a brazier, as they do during *feria* time where I live.

The combination of spices given is one that I have arrived at after considerable experiment, but you should tinker with them to suit your own taste. I once included some roasted coriander and cumin left over from a recipe of Madhur Jaffrey's and found myself eating *pinchitos* with a distinct flavour of India.

2 teaspoons paprika
1 teaspoon turmeric
1 teaspoon crushed coriander
1½ teaspoons ground cumin
1 teaspoon oregano
¼ teaspoon ground ginger
⅛ teaspoon cayenne
1 clove garlic, crushed
1 bay leaf, crumbled
a pinch or two of cinnamon and nutmeg
black pepper, salt
450g/1lb boned loin of pork, preferably ibérico, in 2.5cm/1in cubes
2 tablespoons oil

Mix all the herbs and spices together in a bowl, then rub them into the pieces of meat with your fingers. Stir in the oil and leave the meat to marinate for 12 hours. Thread the meat on to small skewers, brush with more oil and grill, giving the meat about 5 minutes each side. Or you can gently fry the meat in a little oil, which also works well.

**Note:** *Especias para pinchitos* can be bought in Spain and it is far more common to use them than to mix your own. They are perhaps worth buying while on holiday, though you need a large amount to get the right flavour.

# Flamenquines

These are fried stuffed rolls of pork. They can be filled with cheese, serrano ham or both. I prefer both, as the cheese prevents the *flamenquines* becoming too dry. They are more filling than they appear, and the recipe below makes about 10 rolls, enough for five or more, depending on appetite or greed.

450g/1lb boned loin of pork, sliced thin (your butcher should do this)
120g/4oz very thinly sliced serrano ham
120g/4oz any good cooking cheese
1 beaten egg
dried breadcrumbs
sunflower oil for frying
salt and pepper

Between two sheets of greaseproof or waxed paper gently flatten out the pork slices with a meat mallet or the heel of a sturdy bottle. Go carefully or you might tear holes in the meat. Separate the ham and cheese into as many piles as there are slices of meat.

On each piece of pork place a slice of ham and a slice of cheese. These should not overlap the edges of the meat. Season very lightly and roll up tightly along the length of the meat, tucking in any protruding pieces as you go, so that you have a cigar-shaped tube about 15cm/6in long. Roll the tubes in the beaten egg, then in the breadcrumbs, pressing the crumbs gently on to the meat to form a good coating. Leave the *flamenquines* to rest in the fridge for about an hour: this allows the coating to settle and harden slightly.

Heat about 2.5cm/1in of oil in a frying pan, and when very hot but not smoking, slip in 3 or 4 of the *flamenquines*. Fry until well browned on all sides. Drain on kitchen paper and keep warm while you fry the remainder. Serve hot.

# Caracoles a la madrileña

A spicy dish of snails in the Madrid style. I follow the recipe of the late Ignacio Doménech, the influential Catalan cook, with slight alterations. Pieces of chorizo and morcilla can also be added.

3 tablespoons oil
1 onion, finely chopped
75g/2½oz serrano ham, diced
½ dried red chilli, crumbled
2 tablespoons tomato purée
½ teaspoon ground cumin
1 teaspoon paprika
450g/1lb prepared snails in their shells (little ones, preferably)
about 1 litre/2 pints stock or water
2 cloves garlic
salt

Heat the oil and soften the onion and ham with the chilli. Stir in the tomato purée, cumin and paprika. Add the snails and enough stock or water to cover them. Cook for 10 minutes, uncovered. Pound the garlic to a paste with a little salt, stir it into the snails and cook for 5 minutes more.

Serve with cocktail sticks to extract the snails from their shells.

# Croquetas de pollo y jamón

A hugely popular cheap food, *croquetas* are commonly made to use up leftovers. The word comes from the French *croquer*, to crunch, though one wouldn't think so judging by the soggy, glutinous travesties that are offered in too many Spanish bars nowadays.

When properly made, however, and eaten within minutes of being fried, croquetas are delightful, if time-consuming and tricky to get right, with a crunchy crust yielding to a creamy well-flavoured interior. The difficulty lies in binding the ingredients together with a sauce thick enough not to disintegrate on contact with very hot oil, but not so thick as to be stodgy. Following the instructions below, you should achieve about 40 *croquetas*, enough for at least 8 tapas or 4 main courses.  Start preparations the day before you need them.

2 tablespoons oil
250g/9oz raw, lean chicken breast or thigh meat, finely chopped or minced

60g/2oz serrano ham, finely chopped
45g/1½oz butter
½ onion, finely chopped
90g/3oz flour, plus extra for moulding the *croquetas*
525ml/18fl oz stock or milk
1 egg yolk
2 whole eggs
salt and pepper
120g/4oz dried breadcrumbs (home-made are much the best for this)
about 300ml/½ pint sunflower oil for frying

Heat the 2 tablespoons of oil in a frying pan and fry the minced chicken and ham for about 10 minutes. Meanwhile, melt the butter in a saucepan and soften the onion in it. Add the flour, mix well to form a thick roux and cook gently for 5 minutes. Gradually add the stock or milk, stirring well between additions, until you have a thick sauce. Bring it to the boil, add the chicken and ham and simmer for 15 minutes, stirring frequently. Add the egg yolk, mix in thoroughly and simmer a couple of minutes more. Check for seasoning but salt may not be necessary. (If you are using cooked leftover meat, from a joint for example, add it to the sauce without frying it first.) Pour the mixture into a large, shallow dish and leave it to go cold before refrigerating it overnight.

When you are ready to make the croquettes, take three small bowls. In the first put 3-4 tablespoons of flour. In the second beat the 2 remaining eggs with a pinch of salt. In the third put the dried breadcrumbs. Take a heaped teaspoonful of the mixture and mould it with your hands into a fat little sausage shape. Flour it, then drop it into the beaten egg. Lift it out with a fork, letting the excess egg drain off. Now roll the croquette in the breadcrumbs and transfer it to a large chopping board or tray. This is a messy and quite time-consuming business. Do not pile the croquettes on each other. They can now be refrigerated until you need them, or frozen.

When all the croquettes are made, heat the sunflower oil in a saucepan. There should be enough oil to cover them. Fry the croquettes four or five at a time until well browned all over. Drain them on kitchen paper while you fry the rest.

This recipe is also suitable for fish or shellfish, substituting an appropriate stock. With prawns for example, make a stock from the shells and heads. For salt-cod croquettes, cook the chopped fish with the onion (add some garlic and parsley too) and use milk to make the sauce.

If you make croquettes often you will realise that they never seem to turn out the same way twice. One possible problem area is if the mixture is not thick enough, which will become apparent when you try to mould them and significant quantities of mixture adhere to your hands. Rather than add more flour, the best solution seems to me to persevere, but to do the egg-and-breadcrumbing twice so as to prevent the croquettes from cracking. This obviously produces a thicker crust, but the inside will be nice and creamy.

# Empanadillas

These are little turnovers or pies, like miniature Cornish pasties. Instead of being baked they are usually fried, which gives them an attractive blistered finish: this means that you must use a lower proportion of fat to flour than you would normally. In Spain you can buy packets of the dough already stamped out into thin rounds (called *obleas*), but they can be made at home quite easily. These quantities make about a dozen *empanadillas*.

60g/2oz lard
225g/8oz strong flour
salt to taste
about 2 tablespoons boiling water
fillings (see below)

Rub the fat into the flour and salt, then add enough boiling water to make a coherent but fairly firm dough. If the dough is too soft the pies will break, so add more flour if necessary. Roll out thinly and cut into roughly 10cm/4in circles. Put a teaspoonful of filling on one half of the circle, leaving a border. Dampen the edges, then fold over the other half to form a semicircle. Press the edges together, then seal by marking them with the prongs of a fork. Fry the pies in very hot oil until crisp and brown on both sides. Eat very hot, perhaps with a garlicky green salad.

## FILLINGS

One of the most popular fillings in Spain is a simple one of tinned tuna mixed with tomato sauce. There are many other possibilities, and often the best ones are those you invent yourself. The one important rule to follow is that the filling should be moist and well flavoured. Here are some personal favourites:

## De espinacas

From Cataluña, where the local name for their slightly larger pies is *panadoms*.

about 1.35kg/3lb fresh spinach
2 cloves garlic, crushed

90g/3oz seedless raisins
salt and pepper
4-5 tablespoons oil

Thoroughly wash the spinach, removing all stalks. Boil it with just the water clinging to its leaves until it collapses. Drain it, and when it's cold squeeze it as dry as possible. Chop it roughly, then mix with the garlic, raisins, plenty of seasoning and enough oil to make the mixture moist.

# De calabaza

Another Catalan favourite. Like the previous recipe these pies used to be a Holy Week favourite when meat was forbidden. Start preparations the day before.

675g/1½lb pumpkin
2 cloves garlic, crushed
90g/3oz seedless raisins
1 tablespoon chopped parsley
1 tablespoon oil

Cut the peeled pumpkin flesh into small dice and sprinkle well with salt. Leave for 24 hours to drain in a colander. Mix with the garlic, raisins, parsley and oil.

# De bacalao y almejas

Start preparations the day before.
A deliciously savoury combination of salt-cod and clams.

250g/9oz fresh, very small clams or 30g/1oz shelled tinned clams
½ onion, finely chopped
2 cloves garlic, crushed
120g/4oz chopped tomato
2 tablespoons oil
175g/6oz boned salt-cod, soaked and chopped

If using fresh clams, cook them in a little boiling water until they open and remove the flesh. Reserve the strained cooking liquor. Soften the onion, garlic and tomato in the oil. Add the chopped salt-cod and moisten with the clam liquor or a little water. Simmer for 20 minutes until very thick. Stir in the clams, then leave to cool before filling the pies.

# Empanadas

These are full-scale pies, particularly famous in Galicia in the north-west, where they are often enormous. Their variety of *empanadas* has achieved national fame, and practically anything is considered suitable as a filling. The most popular fillings consist of fish or shellfish such as small sardines (*xoubas*), cockles, scallops, eel or lamprey; or else of pork (*raxo*) flavoured with chorizo, or game. The fillings are mixed with a sauce (*la zaragallada*) for moistness – plenty of oil, onions, peppers and so on.

The pastry can be plain bread dough (which can be rather stodgy) sometimes enriched with egg, or a plain shortcrust, or a dough made with a mixture of cornmeal and rye flour, the latter being preferred for pies of sardines or clams.

# Masa de millo

Cornmeal and rye dough for *empanadas*.

280g/10oz cornmeal
120g/4oz strong wheat flour
60g/2oz rye flour
salt
30g/1oz fresh yeast
1 quantity filling (see below)
1 egg (optional)

Mix the flours together with a good seasoning of salt and warm them through in a low oven. Dissolve the yeast in some warm water, then stir into the flour. Add more warm water until you have a manageable dough, though it will be somewhat crumbly. Knead it briefly, cover with a damp cloth and leave in a warm place, the switched-off oven for example, for 2-3 hours. It won't rise much. Knead it again, divide it in half and roll out each half thinly. There should be enough for a 30cm/12in pie plate. Line the plate with half the dough, spread your filling over it, then cover with the other half of the dough. Seal the edges carefully. Cut a slit in the lid, cover and leave to rest for an hour. Paint with beaten egg if you wish, then bake until crisp – about an hour in a hot oven (425°F/220°C/Gas 7).

# FILLINGS
## De pulpo

Octopus pie. Use the pie dough as above.

1kg/2¼lb fresh octopus *or* about 300g/11oz cooked octopus (see page 209)
1½ onions, chopped
1 green and 1 red pepper, chopped
6 tablespoons oil
2 cloves garlic, crushed
salt
2 teaspoons paprika
¼ teaspoon (or more) cayenne

Cut the octopus into small pieces. Stew the onions and peppers in the oil until soft, then add the garlic and the octopus. Season well with salt and cook for a few minutes so that the flavours mingle. Add the paprika and cayenne and leave to cool before filling the pie.

## De bonito

Bonito or tuna-fish pie. Use the cornmeal dough on page 75, or a plain shortcrust.

2 onions, finely chopped
2 red peppers, chopped
2 tablespoons oil
2 tomatoes, peeled and chopped
150g/5oz tinned bonito *or* tuna

Soften the onion and red pepper in the oil, adding that from the fish as well. Stir in the tomatoes and simmer until very thick; there must be no trace of wateriness. Stir in the flaked fish and leave to cool before filling the pie.

# De pollo

Chicken pie. Use a shortcrust or plain bread dough.

salt and pepper
½ chicken, cut in small pieces
3 tablespoons lard or chicken fat
3 cloves garlic, chopped
1 onion, sliced
60g/2oz serrano ham, diced
1 red pepper, roasted, peeled and sliced (*or a tinned one*)
4 tomatoes, peeled and chopped

Season the chicken and fry it in the hot fat until browned, adding the garlic halfway through. Remove the chicken to a plate and add the onion and ham to the pan. Let them soften before adding the red pepper, tomatoes and fried chicken. Half-cover with water and simmer for a good half-hour, uncovered, turning the chicken occasionally. The sauce should be quite thick. Let it cool, then remove all the meat from the bones, cutting it into smallish pieces. Mix with the sauce and check for seasoning before filling the pie.

# Ensaladas
## SALADS

To those used to typical British salads the Spanish versions will come as a revelation. On a blazing hot day in a Spanish summer the appetite can wilt; then the Spanish salad comes into its own. The wise Spaniard will open a meal with a salad, awakening the palate with its clean flavours and crisp textures. It may be no more than quarters of fresh, firm lettuce hearts (*cogollos* or *cogollicos*) cut lengthwise and seasoned with oil and vinegar; or it could be lettuce with a few rough chunks of tomato and onion, a spartan combination to those used to salads with a cast of thousands. However the salad comes, you are grateful for the refreshment and realise that perhaps you were hungry after all.

There are no recipes for such simple salads, so those that follow are for more unusual dishes which can act as tapas, first courses or accompaniments. You put them on the table at the beginning of the meal and people help themselves as they wish.

A Spanish salad dressing is olive oil, wine or sherry vinegar, and salt. In restaurants these are provided in a cruet for diners to dress their own

salad. Fussy additions which might mask these pure flavours are rare and unnecessary. It is no coincidence that those countries such as Britain and the United States which lack a traditional oil are the greatest consumers of all manner of bottled dressings and sauce which they use to swamp their salads with gluey artificiality.

# Ensalada de lechuga al ajillo

To make this lettuce and garlic salad, tear up lettuce leaves into a salad bowl and season them with salt. Dress with a little vinegar, then oil. Mix well with your hands. Leave the salad a little dry at this stage as you are going to add more oil shortly.

Heat a tablespoon or two of oil in a small frying pan. Add two chopped cloves of garlic per person. Let the garlic sizzle over a high heat until it turns a pale brown colour. Remove from the heat and stir the garlic and hot oil into the salad. Mix well and serve immediately.

Another lettuce and garlic salad has water added, and is a refreshing cross between a salad and a soup. Shred the lettuce finely and add finely chopped garlic, oil and vinegar. Add enough iced water to cover, season with salt and place a few ice-cubes in the bowl as well. Serve at once, before the lettuce has a chance to go soggy.

# Escalivada

A salad of roast vegetables from the Catalan countryside. *Escalivar* is a Catalan word meaning to roast over embers, and originally the vegetables – usually just aubergines and peppers – were roasted among the embers of an open fire, and then peeled and dressed with oil and salt, and sometimes with vinegar and chopped garlic too. It is now common to add tomatoes and onions for which such a cooking method is not practical, and they are cooked on a griddle or under a grill. Personally I prefer the simpler version, especially if cooked in the original way, for the hot embers impart a special flavour to the vegetables. Nonetheless, a perfectly acceptable *escalivada* can be made with a conventional cooker.

4 aubergines
2 large red peppers
salt
4 tablespoons oil
garlic and vinegar to taste

Heat the grill or griddle until very hot. Cook the unpeeled vegetables until they are charred black all over – this takes a good half-hour. Place them in a large bowl and cover with a lid or plate. Leave the vegetables to sweat in their own steam for 20 minutes or so. The burnt skins will now peel off easily. Cut them into thinnish strips and season thoroughly with salt. Dress with good oil and finely chopped garlic and vinegar if wished.

## Piriñaca, Pipirrana

These two popular Andalusian salads consist of diced tomatoes, chopped green peppers and onions, oil and vinegar. Cucumber is often added too.

## Ensalada de pimientos asados

Roast pepper salad: the perfect accompaniment to fried fish.

8 small peppers, green or red or both
4 tomatoes
1 onion, peeled
salt and pepper
vinegar and oil

Heat the griddle or grill until very hot. Cook the vegetables until they are charred – the tomatoes will soften and peel if you are doing this on a griddle. Put them in a large bowl, cover and leave for 20 minutes. Peel and seed them, then slice them thinly. Season well with salt and pepper, and dress with vinegar and your best oil.

This is best eaten warm. Have plenty of bread to hand to mop up the dressing.

## Ensalada de judías verdes (1)

Green bean salad.

450g/1lb green beans, topped and tailed
½ clove garlic
salt
1 tablespoon vinegar
4 tablespoons oil
1 hard-boiled egg, roughly chopped

1 tablespoon chopped parsley

Cook the beans in boiling salted water until just tender – about five or six minutes. While they are cooking pound the garlic with a little salt. Stir in the vinegar and oil. Drain the beans well and place in a serving dish. Sprinkle with the egg and parsley, then stir in the dressing. Set the salad aside for a while for the flavours to mingle before you serve it. Do not refrigerate it.

## Ensalada de judías verdes (2)
about 225g/8oz potato, unpeeled
450g/1lb green beans, topped and tailed
½ clove garlic
salt and pepper
juice of ½ lemon
4 tablespoons oil
1 tablespoon chopped parsley

Boil the potato in salted water for 15 minutes. Add the beans and boil for 5 minutes more. Drain well and peel the potato. Make a dressing as above with the garlic, salt, lemon juice and oil. Dice the potato roughly while still warm and mix with the beans and dressing. Season, and leave the salad to go cold before eating it. Do not refrigerate.

## Patatas aliñadas
Boil 450g/1lb of potatoes in their skin. Skin and cut them into chunks. Mix with two chopped hard-boiled eggs, a chopped green pepper (half if it's very big), half a chopped onion and a chopped tomato. Season with salt, oil and vinegar.

# Remojón

This salt-cod, orange and olive salad is commonly eaten during the winter in Andalucía, especially with fried fish or *migas* (see page134). It is particularly good with whitebait (or *chanquetes*, see page 198, should you be so lucky). The salt-cod is not soaked beforehand but merely browned on a griddle and pulled into shreds away from the skin and bones. The oranges should in theory be Seville oranges and the olives *aliñadas*, that is not tinned or bottled in brine but those that are cracked and kept in a marinade with garlic and herbs. However, more widely available versions of these ingredients still work well. In fact I find Sevill oranges too bitter. The important thing is the contrast between the saltiness of the fish, the faint bitterness of the olives and the sweetness provided by the oranges and tomatoes.

3 oranges
120g/4oz green olives
6 spring onions
2 tomatoes
450g/1lb salt-cod, prepared as described above
vinegar and oil

Peel the oranges, divide them into segments and then halve the segments. Stone the olives if you wish, and slice the spring onions thinly. Peel and chop the tomatoes. Mix all these with the shreds of salt-cod and dress well with vinegar and oil.

# Xatonada

The Catalans like starting their summer meals with salt-cod salads, and there are several versions. This makes a good meal with a tortilla of some description alongside.

200g/7oz salt-cod, unsoaked (salted tuna was originally used as well)
2 large tomatoes, preferably on the green side, peeled and cut into chunks
8 anchovy fillets, roughly chopped
2 teaspoons paprika

2 cloves garlic

about 2 dozen green olives, preferably the small Catalan ones called *arbequinas*

pinch *or* two of cayenne pepper

salt

about 2 tablespoons vinegar

about 10 tablespoons oil

curly endive leaves

Wash the cod thoroughly and dry it on kitchen paper. Pull thin strips of flesh away from the skin, leaving behind all the bones. Wash these strips in a colander under the tap, then leave them to soak in fresh water for about an hour. Don't leave them too long or their flavour will be insipid – test a piece if you're unsure. Drain them well and mix with the tomatoes, anchovies and olives.

Pound the garlic to a paste with the paprika, cayenne and a very little salt. Dilute with the vinegar and oil. This sauce is called *xató* and gives the salad its name. Pour the *xató* over the cod strips and leave for half an hour. Mix with some torn-up *frisé* leaves and serve.

*For another version of this dish see my book *The Festive Food of Spain*.

# Poti-poti

This is another summer salt-cod salad from Cataluña.

120g/4oz salt-cod

3 potatoes

1 tomato

½ onion

1 red pepper, preferably peeled

90g/3oz olives, green or black, it doesn't matter

3-4 tablespoons oil

Prepare the cod in strips as in the recipe for *xatonada* and leave it to soak. Boil the potatoes in their skins, then peel and slice them thickly. Peel and roughly chop the tomato, slice the onion and red pepper, and stone the olives if you wish. Mix them all with the drained strips of cod and dress with good oil. (Vinegar is not used in this salad.)

# Ensalada arriera

This is a salt-cod salad for summer, when it's especially good eaten with brown bread and cold Spanish beer. Again, the cod is not soaked but merely held over a flame to char it.

4 medium-sized potatoes, unpeeled, preferably new ones
225g/8oz salt-cod, prepared as described on page 84
2 oranges
2 hard-boiled eggs
6 spring onions
120g/4oz green olives
oil and vinegar

Cook the potatoes in boiling water until tender. Meanwhile, prepare the cod, pulling it into shreds or strips. Peel the oranges, cut them in half and slice them. Chop the eggs and onions roughly. Peel the potatoes and cut into largish chunks. Mix them with every-thing else and anoint generously with oil and vinegar. Do not chill.

# L'empedrat

Another popular Catalan salt-cod salad, this one is a speciality of the Ampurdán region. The word means 'flecked with clouds' or 'dappled', and is also used to describe cobbled streets, so one could translate this as 'cobbled salad', the beans being the stones in question.

120g/4oz dried white beans, soaked overnight
200g/7oz salt-cod
1 tomato
½ red pepper, preferably peeled
3 large spring onions
black pepper
1 tablespoon vinegar
4 tablespoons oil
2 hard-boiled eggs
chopped parsley

Cook the beans in lightly salted water until tender. Meanwhile, prepare the cod in strips as on page 84 and soak them.

Drain the beans and cod thoroughly. Roughly chop or slice the tomato, thinly slice the pepper and cut the onion into 3 or 4 pieces. Mix with the beans and cod. Season with black pepper and dress with vinegar and oil. Decorate with the sliced eggs and some chopped parsley.

# Ensalada de zanahorias

A most attractive carrot salad, with a delightful combination of colours, textures and tastes. It should be eaten separately as it's not really suitable as an accompaniment. Quantities are only approximate and will feed about six. Mix it all together only at the last minute.

3 tablespoons oil
1 onion, chopped
450g/1lb carrots, peeled and sliced
120g/4oz serrano ham
3 tablespoons chopped parsley
1 cooked beetroot (not in vinegar)

120g/4oz cooked beef or lamb
120g/4oz *chorizo de Pamplona* (if unavailable try using a garlicky salami)
2 hard-boiled eggs
some crispy lettuce leaves or curly endive
salt
juice of ½ lemon

Heat the oil and fry the onion, carrot, ham and parsley, covered, for about 15 minutes – the carrots should still be slightly crunchy. Leave to cool.

Slice the beetroot thinly, then into strips. Do the same with the cold meat and chorizo. Slice the eggs. Shred the lettuce or endive. When you're ready to serve the salad, mix all the ingredients together, season with salt and dress lightly with lemon juice.

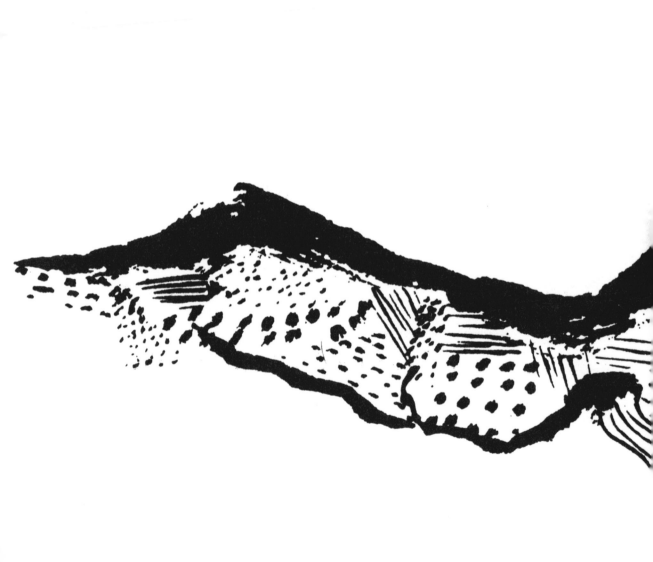

# Sopas

## SOUPS AND RELATED DISHES

There is such diversity among the soups of Spain that the term seems barely adequate to describe what a Spaniard will often call *comida de cuchara*, spoon food. *Sopa* literally means a piece of bread soaked in liquid, and many of the simplest and commonest Spanish soups have their origins in sops: the many varieties of garlic soup are all thick with bread, and Andalucía's gazpacho started life as a few pieces of stale bread soaked in water, vinegar and oil.

Soup is a vital part of the average Spaniard's diet, since the point of Spanish soups used to be to kill the appetite so that the frugality or frequent absence of anything to follow would not matter too much. Thus many Spanish soups are very substantial indeed, and it is often difficult to distinguish between a soup and what we would call a stew. A fantastic variety of pulses – dried beans of all colours, shapes and sizes, chickpeas and lentils – feature prominently, and a large number of ingenious recipes were invented to try to disguise the fact that you were eating more or less the same thing day after day.

It is neither practical nor wise to think of these heavy dishes as soups in the conventional English sense of starter. They were invented for people who burned up calories by the thousand, not for sedentary people in the early 21st century, and so they should be thought of as a meal in themselves, needing only something light and refreshing to follow – salad and fruit are ideal.

# COLD SOUPS

In *Don Quixote*, Sancho Panza's dignified leave-taking of his governorship carries one final barb against the doctor who had made his stay on his 'isle' such a misery, and also contains the first literary reference to Spain's great cold soup:

> *I mean that everyone is best practising the trade for which he was born. A reaper's hook comes better to my hand than a governor's sceptre. I prefer stuffing myself with* gazpachos *to being at the mercy of a meddling doctor who kills by hunger.*

This suggests that gazpacho was a well-established if humble food at that time, and Cervantes almost certainly ate it during his years in Córdoba. As tomatoes and green peppers were not an established part of the diet in Spain until the seventeenth century, Sancho's gazpacho would probably have been just bread soaked in water and flavoured with oil, vinegar and garlic.

The origin of the name is a mystery, though the suffix *-acho* is a derogatory one implying that the soup was originally looked down on. Jane Grigson suggests that the name comes from a Spanish Arabic word *kaz*, meaning food or bread eaten from a wooden bowl; Richard Ford, the nineteenth-century chronicler of Spain, thought that it originated from *posca*, the Roman legionnaires' drink of vinegar and water which was offered to Jesus on the Cross; while the Spanish writer José Carlos Capel claims that it goes back via Portuguese to an old word *caspa*, small fragments or leftovers, which now means dandruff.

Not long ago the gazpacho was still made, very laboriously, by hand. A familiar sound throughout Andalucía as the sun went down was the 'chock-chock-chock' of the next day's gazpacho being made in the housewives' mortars. This was hard work, for the gazpacho should be very smooth, but today the ingredients can all go in the blender and the work is done in seconds.

An Andalusian gazpacho can be red, white or green, but the basic ingredients will be the same – garlic, bread, vinegar and oil. Its texture is most commonly that of a fine cream which is still substantial enough to eat with a spoon. There are, however, so many variations throughout Andalucía that it is impossible to make hard-and-fast rules.

Red gazpachos are made with tomatoes, green peppers and sometimes cucumber, though the latter is often kept aside for the plates of garnishes which may also include onion, hard-boiled egg, peppers and bread, all diced and offered in separate bowls. In some places, Córdoba and Jaén for example, the soup often takes a more liquid form as an accompaniment to the meal, and may be garnished with grapes or pieces of apple. In Antequera they reinforce the colour by using red instead of green peppers and by adding paprika.

*Salmorejo* is a red gazpacho without water; it is simply a thick cream of tomatoes, garlic, bread, oil and seasoning, originally from Córdoba but popular in many parts of Andalucía, with the usual number of variations in names and ingredients. Names include *arranque*, *pirri*, *porra*, *pimporrete*, *carnerete* and *zoque*.

White gazpachos are usually given their colour by the use of ground-up nuts or, in one case (from Almuñecar), dried broad beans, instead of tomato. The best known is Málaga's *ajo blanco* which is made with almonds and accompanied by local moscatel grapes, raisins or pieces of fish. In Córdoba they often use pine-nuts. Another white gazpacho called *gazpachuelo* is generally a thinned-down mayonnaise eaten with potatoes or bread.

Green gazpachos are mainly to be found in the province of Huelva. The colour comes from herbs – coriander, mint, parsley or basil – and/or green salad leaves such as lettuce or curly endive.

All these gazpachos are summer dishes, now usually eaten at the beginning of a meal. They were traditionally served after the first course and before the fruit; a typical meal might have been a *potaje* (a thick soup), followed by a refreshing gazpacho and melon. Gazpacho is also an excellent accompaniment to fried fish.

In choosing the ingredients for gazpachos, try to use good-quality oil and vinegar, preferably sherry vinegar. Almonds should be fresh and unpeeled. Tomatoes are a problem: if it proves impossible to find good well-flavoured summer tomatoes then use tinned ones, but only *in extremis*: gazpacho just doesn't taste right with tinned tomatoes. It is perhaps better to wait until you have some good tomatoes before making gazpacho, rather than deciding to make it and then finding you have to make do with inferior materials.

It is important to remember that no single taste, especially that of garlic, should dominate a gazpacho – all must make their presence felt while at the same time blending harmoniously with the rest.

What makes me think that Mrs Grigson is right in tracing the origins of gazpacho back to *kaz* is that there are several other dishes called gazpacho which seem to have absolutely nothing to do with Andalucía's cold soup. But if we remember the common Spanish habit of calling food after the pot in which it was cooked or from which it was eaten, then logically gazpacho could describe any food originally eaten from a *kaz*. This would explain the other varieties of gazpacho, apparently unconnected except in name. The most interesting of these are called *gazpachos de pastor*, *gazpachos pastorales* or *galianos*, and are to be found in parts of Extremadura, Jaén, La Mancha, Murcia and Valencia. They were originally eaten by shepherds who would cook whatever game they had caught (most commonly rabbit or partridge) with water, garlic and anything else that came to hand – wild mushrooms, herbs, snails and so on. While the gazpacho was cooking they made *tortas*, flat unleavened bread of flour and broth from the pot, which were baked on stones heated in the fire or else on a goat-hide placed among the embers. These *tortas* would either go into the stew to thicken it or act as a sort of primitive spoon. The alternative name *galianos* is derived from the word *cañadas*, the trails along which shepherds drove their flocks to fresh pastures. These gazpachos are also cooked after a day's hunting, when pieces of the day's catch can make a sustaining and restorative end to the exertions.

## Gazpacho

4-5 tablespoons sherry vinegar

60g/2oz stale French bread, crusts removed

about 780g/1¾1b fresh tomatoes

1 or 2 green peppers, depending on size

2 cloves garlic

salt

150ml/¼ pint oil

300ml/½ pint water

Pour the vinegar over the bread and leave it to soak in. Peel and chop the tomatoes roughly. Chop the peppers. Peel and slice the garlic.

Place the bread, garlic, tomatoes and peppers in the liquidiser with some salt and process until smooth. With the motor running gradually pour in the oil. Then do the same with the water. Taste and adjust the amount of salt and vinegar if necessary. Pour the soup into a bowl, cover it and leave it to chill for at least 6 hours or overnight. Add more water if it seems too thick.

For an even smoother soup sieve it before chilling. Serve with some or all of the following: finely diced cucumber, onion, green peppers, tomatoes, hard-boiled egg, cubes of bread (fried if you wish).

## Salmorejo

900g/2lb fresh tomatoes

generous 30g/1oz dry French bread

3-4 tablespoons sherry vinegar

salt

2 cloves garlic

125ml/4fl oz oil

1 egg yolk

Peel and roughly chop the tomatoes, removing the seeds. Soak the bread with the vinegar. Process everything together in the liquidizer along with some salt, and more vinegar if necessary. *Salmorejo* should be quite thick – it is often used as a sauce.

## Porra antequerana

This is a very thick *salmorejo* from Antequera. It is very rich and perhaps best served in small quantities.

450g/1lb fresh tomatoes
1 green pepper
2 cloves garlic
3-4 tablespoons sherry vinegar
60g/2oz stale French bread
salt
250ml/8fl oz oil

Peel, chop and seed the tomatoes and peppers. Liquidise them with the garlic, vinegar, bread and some salt. Gradually beat in the oil. Check for seasoning and chill thoroughly.

Serve this in small bowls with a jug of vinegar to hand and the following garnishes: chopped tomato, diced serrano ham, quartered hard-boiled eggs and flaked tinned tuna. It is also customary for each person to add a final spoonful or two of oil to their *porra* at the table, but I find the soup rich enough without it.

## Ajo blanco a la malagueña

Also spelt as one word, *ajoblanco*. Peeled and seeded moscatel grapes are its traditional accompaniment when in season. Chunks of melon are good too.

90g/3oz stale French bread
450ml/¾ pint water or milk
120g/4oz almonds, blanched and peeled
3 cloves garlic
salt
150ml/¼ pint oil
2-3 tablespoons sherry vinegar

Soak the bread in the water or milk, then liquidise with the almonds, garlic and some salt until fairly smooth. Gradually beat in the oil and then season well with the vinegar. Thin the soup down with more water if it seems too thick. Chill well before serving, with a little extra vinegar if liked.

# Gazpacho de piñones

A delicate, if rich, white gazpacho made with pine-nuts. The flavour can be improved with home-made brown or oatmeal bread.

120g/4oz pine-nuts
1 egg
1 clove garlic
salt
225g/8oz stale bread
about 150ml/¼ pint oil
about 5 tablespoons vinegar

Liquidise the nuts, egg, garlic, and some salt until you have a smooth paste. Add a little bread and oil and liquidise again. Continue in this manner until all the bread and oil are used up. Add water from time to time if it gets too thick. Thin the soup to a cream with more water and vinegar to taste. Taste and add more salt if necessary. Chill well and serve in small quantities with extra vinegar to hand.

# Gazpachuelo

Also known as *sopa de huevo*, egg soup, this is an absolutely gorgeous soup for summer, though not really a true white gazpacho – hence the modification of the name. Its depth of flavour depends entirely on the quality of the olive oil used in the mayonnaise, so use the best oil you can afford.

6 medium potatoes, peeled and cut into large dice
about 750ml/1¼ pints water
salt
mayonnaise made with 2 egg yolks, 300ml/½ pint oil and vinegar to taste (see page 188)
2 egg whites, baked until set and roughly chopped
chopped parsley for garnish

Cook the potatoes in the water with some salt. Drain, reserving the water, and leave until tepid. Thin the mayonnaise to the consistency of single cream with a little of the potato water, then add it to the potatoes. Add the egg whites. Sprinkle with a little chopped parsley and serve as it is, tepid, with a jug of vinegar on the table so that everyone can add a little to taste if they wish – half a soup spoonful is about right.

# SOPAS DE AJO

Garlic soups. A Spanish garlic soup is an object lesson in making the best out of next to nothing; in its basic form it takes the most fundamental items in the Spanish kitchen – garlic, bread and oil – and turns them into something not only nourishing but delicious as well. Water is normally used as the liquid but there are of course several variations, and stock or the water from cooking vegetables like cauliflower may be used. If there are eggs to spare, they can go in too – sometimes beaten into the broth, sometimes poached in it. If there is a little ham or chorizo around, they can both be added as well, and the soup will be all the better for them. In Andalucía tomato is sometimes added, and the soup may be spiced with cumin. In Castilla garlic soup has become part of their culinary folklore; they call it *sopa castellana*, and special earthenware soup bowls from which to eat it are available there.

An excellent variation on the basic theme is to use shellfish – clams or prawns, or both. The shellfish are boiled, the broth used as the liquid for the soup and the shelled meat added at the end. Whatever form you choose to make the basic method is always the same:

6 tablespoons oil
4 (or more) cloves garlic, thinly sliced
8 slices stale French-style bread
about 1.2 litres/2 pints water seasoned with salt, or stock
1 heaped teaspoon paprika

Heat the oil in a frying pan and fry the garlic until it browns. Remove the garlic and add it to the water or stock. In the same oil fry the bread until brown on both sides, then set it aside. If any oil remains stir the paprika into it and then add these to the water also. Bring the water, garlic and paprika to the boil. Place two pieces of fried bread in each soup bowl and ladle the soup over them.

## VARIATIONS

**1.** Break one egg per person into each bowl before adding the broth; or poach the eggs in the broth beforehand.

**2.** Fry 120g/4oz diced serrano ham with the garlic and add it to the broth. Even better, add 120g/4oz thinly sliced chorizo as well when you fry the ham. Peeled and diced tomato can be fried with them too. Add an egg at the end as above if you wish.

**3.** Cook 225g/8oz fresh clams and the same of unshelled prawns in the water first. Strain the broth before you make the soup, and shell the clams and prawns. Stir them in at the last minute.

**4.** In Yeste in the south of La Mancha the soup *costrada*, with a crust, may be served. This is formed by pouring beaten egg into the soup and baking it in the oven for a few minutes. The egg rises to the top and sets into a soft crust.

**5.** In *sidrerías* (cider bars) of the Basque country, a popular soup is *zurrukutuna*, a garlic soup with salt-cod. The name is supposedly onomatopoeic, *zurruk* meaning snore and by extension the sound one makes when noisily dispatching the soup. Personally I find salt-cod too much of a distraction in garlic soup, but it's worth trying *in situ*.

**6.** Garlic soups are considered ideal for sustaining the elderly or for weaning young children. *Maimones*, an Andalusian garlic soup made with much more bread than usual and without the paprika, has long been used for this purpose. Sometimes egg or ham are added, or it may be eaten as a pudding with cane honey or sugar. In effect such soups are a close relative of *gachas* – see page 133.

## HOT SOUPS

First, the stockpot that you can often smell boiling away as you pass Spanish houses in the morning. It provides broth and boiled meats for a number of meals. This is the local version where I live, but of course there are any number of regional variations.

## Caldo de puchero

200g/7oz chickpeas (soaked overnight with 1 teaspoon salt in plenty of cold water)
225g/8oz approximately shin of beef, or a similarly flavourful cut
(stewing pork can be used instead)
½ a boiling hen
180g/6oz *tocino salado* or panceta, in one piece with rind
360g/12oz approximately beef bones, preferably from the leg or ribs, sawn in pieces
180g/6oz salted bones (use a piece of serrano ham rind as an alternative)

Trim the meats of skin and excess fat. Wash any loose salt off the pork and bones, then put the meats, bones and drained chickpeas into a large pot. Cover well with water, put a lid on the pan and bring to the boil. Skim very thoroughly.

Boil briskly for about 20 minutes, then reduce the heat to medium. Have a kettle of boiling water to hand to top up as necessary. Local cooks, for whom the kettle is a source of bafflement, invert the lid so that it sits upside down on the pot. They fill the cavity of the lid with water, which then heats as the broth cooks. When the need arises they simply tip the water into the pot. Everything should be ready after about an hour and a half's boiling.

Skim the fat from the broth (see recipe for *fabada asturiana* page 121) and discard the bones and rind. You now have a number of options:

**1.** Serve the chickpeas and some broth as a first course, adding a little rice if the mood takes you. A sprig of mint in each bowl gives a lovely herbal lift, and a squeeze of lemon doesn't come amiss, either. Follow with a plate of the meats (called the *pringá* where I live) and bread.

**2.** Make *sopa de picadillo*: cook a fistful of fine noodles per person in the broth, along with some diced serrano ham and bits of the hen too, if you want. Stir in a chopped hard-boiled egg or two just before serving, and a sprig of mint. Croutons can be served as well – it's a very flexible feast.

**3.** Serve the broth on its own, very hot, with a slug of *fino* sherry.

The beef can be used up in things like *ropavieja* (page 287) or *ensalada de zanahorias* (page 86) or *croquetas* (page 71).

# Sopa mahonesa

Chicken broth with dumplings from Mahón, the capital of Menorca. The dumplings are made with stale bread, milk, butter and eggs, and are beautifully light. Be sure to use only good home-made stock for this, and add chopped pieces of any meat from the carcass.

about 150ml/¼ pint milk
60g/2oz stale French bread, sliced, crusts removed
60g/2oz butter
2 egg yolks, beaten
salt
1 egg white, stiffly beaten
about 1.35 litres/2¼ pints chicken stock

Sprinkle the milk over the bread – the idea is to moisten it but not enough to make it disintegrate. Melt the butter in a frying pan and fry the pieces of bread very gently, without browning, until the butter is absorbed. Remove it to a bowl and break it all up with a spoon. When it has cooled a little stir in the egg yolks and some salt, and fold in the egg white. The mixture should not be sloppy; if it is, the dumplings won't hold together.

In a wide pan bring the chicken stock to a slow boil. Add a teaspoonful of the mixture to test it. If it falls apart you'll need to add some breadcrumbs to the mixture to tighten it. If it seems all right continue adding small spoonfuls of it to the stock. Cook the dumplings for about 10 minutes and serve.

# Sopas perotas

Tomato soup. This one is slightly unusual – it's lightly flavoured with mint and very thick because of the stale bread used to make it. It is eaten with chopped cucumber, a most pleasant combination, or with moscatel grapes when in season. Its name comes from *perotes*, the name of the people who live in and around Alora. This is a small town in the spectacular countryside to the north-west of Málaga, nestling snugly in the mountains and guarded by the hilltop ruins of a castle, now used as the municipal graveyard. The name *perotes* comes from the town's old Latin name Perosia.

1 cucumber for the garnish

salt

2 onions, sliced

4 cloves garlic. sliced

4 green peppers, sliced

2 tablespoons oil

about 1kg/2½1b tomatoes, skinned and chopped

2 tablespoons paprika

1 litre/1¾ pints water

1 sprig mint

60g/2oz very stale bread (preferably from a good brown loaf)

tomato concentrate (optional)

wine vinegar (optional)

Peel and dice the cucumber quite small. Sprinkle it with a little salt and set aside to drain.

Fry the onion, garlic and peppers in the oil until softened. Add the tomatoes and cook until pulpy. Stir in the paprika. Liquidise or sieve the mixture. Add the water, some salt, the mint and the bread, torn into pieces. Now taste: if you think the flavour of the tomatoes needs help add a teaspoon or two of tomato concentrate and wine vinegar. Bring to the boil and let it simmer for a few minutes until really thick. Serve with the drained cucumber in a separate bowl.

# Sopas de pescado y mariscos

Mixed fish and shellfish soups. As one would expect in a country so enamoured with seafood, Spain is rich in recipes for such soups. Often these started life on the fishing boats or in seafront restaurants, where the fishermen would eat a soup or stew of whatever they'd caught. The most basic formula is simply to boil everything together, adding a little wine for flavour and perhaps some chopped vegetables, herbs or saffron. For extra flavour the fish can be boiled in a broth previously made from heads and bones (hake or monkfish heads are particularly favoured for this purpose). Many people first make a *sofrito* of onion, garlic and peppers to add to the soup, and serve it with fried bread. Andalusians like to add a sprig of mint at the last minute, and often enrich their soups with a final addition of mayonnaise (sometimes flavoured with garlic), in which case the soup is not, indeed cannot be, served boiling hot. Cándido, who gave his name to the famous restaurant near the Roman aqueduct of Segovia, recommends the addition of absinthe.

However you decide to make your soup (I give two examples below), try to use a mixture of firm-textured fish of good flavour (monkfish, hake, John Dory, conger, swordfish, red gurnard, etc.), with squid and shellfish (various prawns, clams and mussels). It is important to season the fish lightly with salt before you start.

## METHOD I

(quantities given for fish are approximate)

### FOR THE BROTH:
fishheads and bones (see overleaf)
about 1.2 litres/2 pints water
½ onion, sliced
½ teaspoon black peppercorns
few parsley stalks
pinch dried thyme
bay leaf
salt

### FOR THE SOUP:
1 small clove garlic
pinch saffron
salt
1 red pepper, peeled (if possible) and chopped

4 tablespoons oil
1-2 tablespoons white wine
juice of ½ lemon
1 teaspoon Pernod (optional)
120g/4oz squid, cleaned (see page 220) and cut into rings, the tentacles chopped
120g/4oz swordfish, cut into smallish chunks
225g/8oz hake, thickly sliced
225g/8oz fresh prawns
120g/4oz fresh clams

First make the broth: bring the fish carcasses and water to the boil and skim off all the scum that floats to the surface. Add the remaining ingredients (you can also add the prawn shells) and simmer, covered, for a maximum of 30 minutes. Throw your kitchen windows wide open while this is going on, or the smell that fills the house will do its best to ruin your appetite. Strain the broth thoroughly.

Now make the soup: pound the garlic with the saffron and a little salt in a mortar. Add the paste to the broth along with the red pepper, oil, 1 or 2 tablespoons of white wine and the lemon juice. Add the merest *hint* – say, a teaspoon – of Pernod if you like. This is not 'authentic' but it does bring out the flavour of the fish if used with care. Bring the broth to the boil and add the squid. Boil for five minutes, then add the swordfish and boil another five minutes. Add the hake and boil for 2 minutes. Finally, add the prawns and clams and cook for another 2 minutes. Add salt if necessary. Serve in big bowls with some pieces of fried bread and perhaps a small sprig of mint in each.

## METHOD II

### (a la malagueña – Málaga style)

This involves enriching the soup with mayonnaise just before serving. You *must* let the broth cool down for a few minutes before adding the mayonnaise or it will curdle. It is thus obvious that the soup is served *templado* – warm. Serves 6.

12 mussels
1.5 litres/2½ pints fish broth (see Method I)
150g/5oz fresh clams
120g/4oz frozen peas
225g/8oz potatoes, peeled and diced
½ onion, finely chopped
1 clove garlic, crushed

2 tablespoons oil
225g/8oz monkfish, boned and cut into small cubes
150g/5oz hake, sliced
12 very large prawns, in the shell
good pinch saffron, soaked in a little hot broth
salt
mayonnaise made with 1 egg, 150g/5oz oil and lemon juice to taste (see page 188) mixed
with a dash of tomato purée to colour it and a crushed clove of garlic if desired

Trim the beards off the mussels. Bring a small saucepan of the broth to the boil and add the clams and mussels. Remove them as they open and set them aside. Strain the broth and add it to the rest. Add the peas and potatoes and cook rapidly for 15 minutes. Meanwhile fry the onion and garlic in the oil until softened. Add them to the broth. Now add the monkfish and 5 minutes later the hake, large prawns and saffron. Cook for 5 more minutes, then add the clams and mussels (shelled if you prefer). Add salt to taste. Set the soup aside to cool down for about 10 minutes.

Now gradually whisk ladlefuls of the broth into the mayonnaise until you get a thin cream. Gradually stir this cream into the soup and serve.

## Sopa de langostinos y espárragos

*Langostinos* in Spain are very large prawns, not Dublin Bay Prawns (*langoustines* in France). In this Andalusian soup they are cooked with clams and fresh asparagus, and the result is every bit as good as it sounds.

340g/12oz fresh asparagus, trimmed and sliced in 2.5cm/1in lengths
about 1.2 litres/2 pints water
550g/1¼lb fresh clams
550g/1¼lb very large prawns, raw if at all possible
2 large cloves garlic
salt
good pinch of saffron
1 tablespoon flour, toasted in a small frying pan
2 tablespoons chopped parsley
black pepper
2 hard-boiled eggs, sliced

Separate the asparagus into two piles – one of tips, one of stalks. Bring the water to the boil and add the clams. Remove them as they open. Take the meat from the shells and reserve it. Peel the prawns and add the debris to the broth. Cook the shells for 10 minutes, then strain, reserving the broth. Pound the garlic to a paste in a mortar with some salt and the saffron. Work in the flour, then gradually thin the paste to a cream with some of the broth. Pour this cream back into the broth and add salt to taste. Bring it to the boil and add the asparagus stalks. After 5 minutes add the prawns and asparagus tips. Cook for 5 minutes more, then stir in the parsley, clams and a little ground black pepper. Place two or threes slice of hard-boiled egg in each soup bowl and ladle the soup over them.

Serve with croutons of fried bread, if you wish.

# Sopa de rape

A very popular Andalusian soup of monkfish, flavoured and thickened with fried almonds, bread, garlic and saffron. The huge head of the monkfish is essential – as your fishmonger never puts it on the slab you should be able to get one for nothing. He should also skin it and cut it up for you.

1 monkfish head, skinned and chopped in two

about 1.2 litres/2 pints water

salt

2 bay leaves

6 tablespoons oil

60g/2oz almonds, blanched and skinned

3 cloves garlic, peeled

6 sprigs parsley

60g/2oz piece of stale bread, crusts removed

good pinch saffron

2 onions, chopped

2 green peppers, chopped

1 tomato, peeled and chopped

1 large potato, peeled and diced

340g/12oz fresh monkfish

Put the fish head to boil in the water with some salt and the bay leaves. Skim it well and boil for 20 minutes. Strain, reserving both the broth and the fish head. When the latter has cooled a bit, remove all the bits of flesh that you can find.

Heat the oil in a frying pan and fry the almonds and garlic until brown. Transfer them to a mortar or liquidizer. Fry the sprigs of parsley briefly in the same oil (make sure it is thoroughly dry before doing so or it will spit at you venomously) and put it in the liquidiser also. Now fry the chunk of bread until brown all over and add it to the liquidiser, along with the saffron and a ladle of the broth. Liquidise until smooth and stir the purée into the broth.

In the remaining oil fry the onion and peppers until they wilt, then add the tomato and cook for 5 more minutes. Liquidise this *sofrito* and add it to the broth. Bring the broth to the boil and put in the potato. Cook for 15 minutes, then add the pieces of monkfish and some pepper. Add salt to taste. Simmer for 10 minutes before stirring in the pieces of monkfish from the head, and serve, with extra fried bread if you like.

**Note:** It's perfectly possible just to use the monkfish head, in which case you would call the soup *sopa de cabeza de pescado*.

# Porrusalda

A popular Basque leek and potato soup given an unmistakable flavour by the addition of salt-cod. Its name comes from the Basque word for leek.

225g/8oz salt-cod, soaked overnight
1.8 litres/3 pints light stock or water
4-6 good fat leeks
790g/1¾lb potatoes
4 cloves garlic
4 tablespoons oil
salt and pepper

Drain the cod and cover it with some of the stock. Heat it until the liquid starts to foam. Remove the cod, reserving the broth. Remove all skin and bones from the cod, chopping the flesh roughly.

Trim the leeks and slice them into 2.5cm/1in rounds. Wash well and drain. Peel and cube the potatoes. Slice the garlic thinly.

Fry the garlic in the oil until it starts to brown. Add the leeks and let them cook over a minimum heat for 5 minutes, stirring occasionally. Add the potatoes and cook for 5 more minutes. Add the cod and pour in all the stock. Bring to the boil and simmer, covered, for about 45 minutes. Add salt to taste and pepper if you wish.

**Note:** The soup is now eaten just as it is. However, I find it an unappetising sight, good though the flavour may be. I prefer to liquidise half the soup and stir it back in, which gives it a more welcoming look. This is unorthodox, or at least inauthentic, but better, I think.

# Sopa de congrio

Conger eel makes very good soup. (See the notes about it on page 198.) This recipe comes from Guipuzcoa, the part of the Basque country bordering France.

280g/10oz fresh clams
a little white wine and water
3 cloves garlic, peeled
2 tablespoons oil
1 onion, chopped
2 leeks, roughly chopped and washed
1 tomato, peeled and chopped
450g/1lb potatoes, peeled and cubed
2 tablespoons chopped parsley
about 900ml/1½ pints water
30g/1oz rice
450g/1lb conger eel, skinned and sliced
salt and pepper

In a small pan open the clams in a very little white wine and water (see page 49). Remove them from their shells and set aside. Reserve the broth.

Fry the whole garlic in the oil until brown, and pound to a pulp in a mortar. In the same oil gently fry the onion, leeks and potatoes until they start to soften. Now add the tomato and parsley and cook for 5 more minutes. Strain the clam broth and water into the vegetables, then add the rice and the slices of conger. Season with salt and pepper and stir in the pounded garlic. Simmer uncovered for about 20 minutes, then stir in the clams.

Serve with fried bread.

# Sopa al cuarto de hora

A popular quick fish soup originating from Cádiz, though not quite as quick as the name, 'quarter-of-an-hour soup', would suggest. As with all such soups there seem to be as many recipes as there are cooks, the chief differences being in the combination of fish and shellfish used. All contain rice, however, are unmistakably flavoured with serrano ham and are finished with chopped hard-boiled egg.

Here is one comparatively cheap version.

8 mussels
450g/1lb small clams
1.5 litres/2½ pints fish broth, unsalted
3 tablespoons oil
120g/4oz serrano ham, diced
120g/4oz rice
400g/14oz filleted hake or similar white fish, in medium-sized chunks
2 hard-boiled eggs, chopped

Wash the mussels and clams, removing any dead or broken specimens. It is not necessary to scrub the mussels. Place them in a wide pan, cover and place over a medium heat. Very soon the shellfish will open, releasing their juices. Set them aside as they do so. When they are all open remove the flesh from the shells and reserve it. Strain the juices through a fine sieve into the fish broth.

Heat the oil in a saucepan and fry the ham quickly for a couple of minutes. Add the rice and stir it around with the oil and ham until it starts to go transparent. Pour in the broth and bring to the boil. Cover and simmer for 5 minutes before adding the fish. Taste for salt at this stage, though enough should be provided by the ham and shellfish. Simmer for 10 minutes more. Add the egg, mussels and clams and heat through briefly. The rice should be more or less tender, and certainly will be by the time everyone is seated and served.

# Raya en amarillo

This is a substantial soupy version of the Andalusian recipe for grey mullet on page 202, but using skate instead.

900g/2lb skate wings
good pinch saffron
900g/2lb potatoes, peeled

2 slices stale French bread or similar

4 tablespoons oil

1 onion, finely chopped

1 green pepper, chopped

1 tomato, peeled and chopped

2 or 3 cloves garlic

2 tablespoons chopped parsley

4 tablespoons dry sherry

pinch ground cumin

½ teaspoon oregano or marjoram

juice of ½ lemon

Using a very sharp knife separate the thin corrugated fillets of skate flesh from both sides of the wings. Set the flesh aside and make a broth (see page 100) by simmering the wings and some aromatics in water for 20 minutes. You need a good 1.2 litres/2 pints.

Strain the broth, add the saffron and use it to cook the potatoes. While they are cooking, brown the bread in the oil, remove it then fry the onion, pepper and tomato until you have a thick *sofrito*. Use either a pestle and mortar or a liquidiser to purée the *sofrito* with the fried bread, garlic, parsley, sherry, cumin and oregano or marjoram. When the potatoes are almost tender pour in this purée and add the pieces of skate. Cook for 3 minutes more, then, off the heat, add a squeeze of lemon juice to bring out the flavour.

## Caldo de perro, Pescado en blanco

*Caldo de perro* is a soup prepared by the fishermen of Cádiz using small specimens of hake called *pescadillas*. The origin of the name, 'dog broth', seems to be a mystery. The fish, about 675g/1½lb, should be sliced and seasoned well with salt about an hour before cooking the soup – this firms up its rather soft-textured flesh. Apart from the fish, which should be very fresh, you need some oil, 2 cloves of garlic, a large chopped onion, about 1.5 litres/2½ pints boiling water and the juice of 2 bitter oranges. The peeled garlic is browned in the oil and discarded. The onion is softened in the same oil and the water added. When it boils the fish are put in and cooked rapidly for 10-15 minutes, when the orange juice is poured in.

A similar soup, *pescado en blanco*, is more widely cooked in Andalucía. The difference is that the onions and garlic, both sliced, are added to the boiling water without preliminary frying, and cooked until tender. Any cheap white fish, *rosada*, for example, is then added. Once cooked, the soup is finished with an addition of raw olive oil and lemon juice, which whitens the soup – hence its name. I can particularly recommend this soup as a restorative for tired digestions or for the poorly who don't feel like eating.

Another soup with bitter oranges is *sopas cachorreñas*, described by Enriqueta Mapelli di Carrión in *Papeles de Gastronomía Malagueña* (1982):

> Cut the rind of some oranges, that should be thick, in spirals, making sure they stay in one piece. Hang them up to dry from the shelves, window or fireplace of the kitchen, where they also serve as a decoration, like strings of garlic.
> For four people use three rinds. Pound them in the mortar with some peppercorns. When it's all perfectly ground up start adding oil to form a paste which you dilute with water, adding bread cut in small pieces. Boil it all and season it with salt and vinegar or lemon.

# FISH STEWS

Throughout the length of both Spanish coastlines are to be found a number of fish stews which sprang originally from the cooking pots of the local fishermen. Despite regional variations a thread of consistency runs through them all: to sustain themselves the fishermen, or rather the best cooks among them, cooked whatever, if any, of the day's catch they could spare in a communal pot with a few other basic ingredients. These dishes have been taken up by the public and are now popular fare in seafood restaurants.

The dishes are frequently named after the pot they are cooked in, the *caldero*, for example. This cauldron-like pot is also used inland by shepherds for cooking their stews. In Galicia the favourite stew of the local fishermen is *caldeirada* which includes potatoes and a flavouring of garlic and paprika. Along the coast in Asturias their *caldereta* is a rather more elaborate affair, made even more so by the meddling attentions of restaurants.

In Euskadi we find *ttoro*, where the fish is cooked with *txacoli* wine, onions, tomatoes, garlic and red pepper, both paprika and chilli. It may all be eaten together or the broth may be consumed first, followed by the fish. Another local speciality is *marmitako*, a very old dish consisting of tuna or bonito stewed with potatoes, peppers, tomato and garlic. The original *marmitako* dates back to the time before Columbus when of course there were no potatoes, tomatoes or peppers, and probably consisted of any available fish cooked in water with some fat and the very hard bread they took with them on their voyages. The *marmita* from which the dish takes its name is a metal casserole with a lid, like the French *marmite*.

In Cataluña on the Costa Brava we find *el suquet*, (from the verb *sucar*, to dip – your bread in the sauce, for example) which consists of fish boiled in water or broth with various flavourings, potatoes and usually finished with an addition of allioli or *picada*. In Valencia they make an almost identical dish known as *llauneta* with the addition of saffron and paprika. *Suc* is also to be found and is another variant of *el suquet*. Here and in Murcia they cook *calderos* of fish and rice, described on page 168. In Algeçiras in Andalucía we find *abajá* which is eaten like *ttoro*, while in Huelva they make a *calderada*.

# El suquet

1kg/2lb fish, preferably bonito or large mackerel, cut into 12 thick slices

salt

oil

2 onions, thinly sliced

2 cloves garlic, crushed

2 tomatoes, peeled and chopped

about 550g/1¼lb medium-sized potatoes, peeled and thickly sliced

2 tablespoons chopped parsley

about 1.5 litres/2½ pints light fish broth

Season the fish well with salt. Heat enough oil in a large, wide *cazuela* or similar to cover its base. Make a *sofrito* of the onion, garlic and tomato, then add the potatoes, parsley and enough broth just to cover. Simmer for 20 minutes or so, uncovered, until the potatoes are more or less tender. Add the fish slices in a single layer and simmer for 10 more minutes, turning the slices over carefully after 5 minutes if they're not quite covered by liquid. Check seasoning, and either serve as it is or:

**1.** Enrich the broth with 2 teaspoons of allioli (see page 188). This is my favourite way. Put the allioli in a bowl and gradually stir in spoonfuls of broth from the *suquet* until the allioli is thinned down. Stir this back into the *suquet* and serve.

**2.** Enrich it with 1-2 tablespoons of *picada* (page 190) in the same way.

# Marmitako

400g/14oz fresh tuna or bonito, cut in large chunks

salt

4 tablespoons oil

1 onion, finely chopped

3 cloves garlic

2 tablespoons chopped parsley

2 tomatoes, peeled and chopped

4 medium-sized potatoes, peeled and thickly sliced

1 small dried red chilli, finely chopped
1 bay leaf
fish broth or water
1 red pepper, roasted, peeled and sliced

Season the fish with salt. Heat the oil in a large *cazuela* and fry the onion until it softens. Meanwhile, pound the garlic in the mortar with a little salt and the parsley. Add the paste to the onion along with the tomato and cook until pulpy. Add the sliced potatoes, chilli, bay leaf and enough broth or water to cover. Simmer for about 15 minutes, uncovered. Add the pieces of fish and red pepper and simmer for another 15 minutes, when the fish should be tender and the stew very thick.

# Puchero de pulpo

This is an adaptation of an octopus stew which is a speciality of the fishermen of Calpe on the eastern seaboard near Benidorm, many of whom have now abandoned their traditional way of life for the easier money to be had by feeding tourists. The town is famous for the great rock that looms over its beach, the Peñón de Ifach.

1kg/2¼lb octopus (raw weight), cooked as explained on page 209
4 cloves garlic, sliced
6 tablespoons oil
good pinch saffron
2 dozen almonds, blanched and peeled
125ml/4 fl oz white wine
bay leaf
salt

Cut the octopus into smallish pieces. Fry the garlic in the oil until it starts to brown, then add the octopus. Simmer this for a few minutes while you pound the almonds up to a fine paste with the saffron. Mix this paste with the wine and pour it over the octopus. Add a bay leaf and a little salt. Leave the octopus to simmer, uncovered, until its sauce is well reduced and thickened.

# Nuadeta de polp

An old octopus dish from Castellón in Valencia. The recipe is also used for monkfish and a cheap, pink-fleshed fish called *pintarroja*, a sort of dogfish.

4 cloves garlic

salt

2 teaspoons paprika

ground black pepper

pinch cinnamon

1kg/2¼lb octopus, precooked as explained on page 209 and cut into smallish pieces

oil to cover the bottom of the pan

90g/3oz fresh white breadcrumbs

Pound the garlic to a paste with a little salt. Add the paprika, a little ground black pepper and a pinch of cinnamon. Thin the paste to a cream with a little water.

Fry the pieces of octopus briefly in a little oil. Pour over the cream from the mortar and add the breadcrumbs. Mix well and add enough water to make a fairly liquid sauce. Cook the octopus in this for 10-15 minutes, by which time the sauce should be thick. Add more salt if necessary before serving.

# Romescada de pescado

One of the rich fish and shellfish stews to be found on the Catalan coast, in this case around Tarragona. The choice of fish used is up to the individual cook, the only guideline being that it should be fresh and firm-fleshed.

*FOR THE SAUCE*
(a version of romesco – see page 189):

2 *ñoras* (see pages 32-33)

about a dozen almonds, blanched and peeled

6 tablespoons oil

6 cloves garlic

2 slices stale French bread

1 onion, peeled and chopped

1 tomato, peeled and chopped

1-1.25kg/2¼–3lb fish (monkfish, squid, hake, sea bream, grouper and turbot are all suitable)

8 very large prawns or Dublin Bay prawns
16 mussels or large clams

Prepare the *ñoras* as explained on pages 32-33, and scrape the red flesh into the mortar or liquidiser. Fry the almonds in the oil, then four of the whole cloves of garlic, then the bread, removing them once browned. Stew the onion, two remaining cloves of garlic (crushed) and tomato in the same oil (adding a little more if necessary) and then pound to a pulp or liquidise with the other sauce ingredients.

Place the cleaned, sliced and salted fish in a large shallow pan. Pour over the sauce and enough water or fish broth to dilute it to a creamy consistency. Heat gently and simmer for about 20 minutes, shaking the pan carefully from time to time. Add the shellfish after 10 minutes. Don't stir it or you'll break up the fish. The almonds and bread will thicken the sauce to a certain extent. Now leave the dish off the heat for an hour or so for the flavours to develop and impregnate the fish. Reheat gently and serve on its own, preceded by a simple salad.

As this is the sort of dish one reserves for special occasions one should perhaps splash out on a decent wine to go with it. I would recommend a Spanish sparkling wine (*cava*), which sets the *romescada* off very well.

# PISTO, VEGETABLE STEWS AND SOUPS

Pisto, meaning hotchpotch, is one of several similar dishes resembling ratatouille widely eaten in many parts of Spain under different names, consisting of various vegetables stewed together in oil or lard. The vegetables are generally tomatoes, onions, peppers, aubergines and courgettes. The best-known pisto comes from La Mancha where it is popular as a first course, perhaps followed by *queso manchego* (the region's great sheep's-milk cheese) or roast meat; or it may accompany products from the *matanza* (the slaughter of the family pig) such as chorizo or morcilla.

There are several regional variations on the theme. In Albacete, for example, they add pine-nuts and fish preserved *en escabeche*. In parts of Andalucía a common tapa is *alboronía* or *boronía*, which is the basic pisto with an interesting inclusion of chopped quince in season. In Valencia and especially Cataluña the dish becomes *samfaina* or *chamfaina* (roughly meaning 'symphony') and in summer may be eaten chilled as a salad with hard-boiled eggs. Otherwise it is cooked with meat or salt-cod. An Extremaduran *chamfaina*, however, bears no relation to any of the above and consists of lamb's offal stewed in a garlicky sauce. The Basque version, which originated in the region of Zuberoa on the other side of the Pyrenees, is called *piparrada* (*piperade* in France, *piperra* being the Basque word for pepper). It is simply tomatoes, peppers and onions stewed with oil and garlic, and usually finished with beaten eggs.

More elaborate vegetable stews are called *menestras*. Ingredients depend on where you are and on the season, though this is generally a springtime dish and it tends not to include the vegetables used in a pisto. Instead you will find peas, broad beans, artichokes, spring onions, carrots, celery, potatoes, turnips, wild asparagus and lettuce. It is often served with eggs, hard-boiled or poached.

## Pisto manchego

For four as a first course, for two as a main dish.

½ onion, finely chopped
60g/2oz green bacon, diced
60g/2oz lard
2 smallish potatoes, peeled and cut into small cubes
1 large courgette, or 2 or 3 small ones, thinly sliced
salt and pepper
1 red and 1 green pepper, seeded and roughly chopped
2 tomatoes, peeled and chopped

Start with two pans. In one, fry the onion and bacon in half the lard until they soften. Add the potatoes and courgettes, season with salt and pepper, cover and leave simmering over a low heat. In the other pan soften the peppers in the remaining lard. Add the tomatoes and cook for a couple of minutes more. Season and add to the mixture in the other pan. Leave to cook gently, uncovered, until the pisto is very thick and the potatoes tender. If it becomes too thick before the potatoes are cooked add a little water, but remember that wateriness is the arch-enemy of such dishes.

Let the pisto cool for a few minutes, then serve it with some fried bread. Sliced chorizo can be added towards the end, or meat can be cooked with the vegetables from the beginning.

## Pisto riojano

The Riojan version of pisto, with marinated pork and sausages stewed with tomatoes and red peppers. A pared-back but delicious pisto.

2 cloves
2 cloves garlic, crushed
4 peppercorns
salt
1 teaspoon paprika

nutmeg
½ teaspoon dried oregano
450g/1lb boned pork loin, diced
60g/2oz lard
2 tomatoes, peeled and chopped
1 red pepper, roasted, peeled and sliced
8 small, good-quality sausages (or 4 large ones)

In the mortar pound up the cloves, garlic and peppercorns with a little salt. Mix in the paprika, a grating of nutmeg and the oregano. Add a little water to form a cream. Pour it over the pieces of pork and leave for several hours or overnight.

Drain the pork and fry it in the lard for 5 minutes. Add the tomato and let it soften. Stir in the strips of red pepper, check seasoning and simmer, covered, for 15 minutes. Add the sausages and cook uncovered for 15 minutes more.

Other dishes built round a pisto mixture include *ropavieja* (page 287), *cordero al chilindrón* (page 273) and *putaco tarragoní* (page 230).

## LA BORRETA; EL HERVIDO VALENCIANO; GIRABOIX

All these are thick vegetable soups or stews which constitute the main part of the midday meal in homes in many parts of Valencia. The *borreta* is found in the valley of the Vinalopó, the river which runs through Elche. It consists of nothing but potatoes, greens, a little salt-cod flavoured with *ñoras* and garlic, boiled together until thick. It's given a lift at the table by a dressing of raw oil which each person pours over his helping. Poached eggs are sometimes added at the end.

The *hervido*, meaning boiled, is based on potatoes, onions and green beans, sometimes with artichokes or greens, cooked gently together and dressed with oil and vinegar at the table. *Giraboix* consists of various boiled vegetables with salt-cod, eaten after first serving the cooking liquid as a soup. Both soup and vegetables are given savour by the addition of allioli.

## La borreta
120g/4oz salt-cod
3 *ñoras* (see pages 32-33)
900g/2lb spinach *or* chard, *or* both

900g/2lb potatoes
4 cloves garlic
salt

Pull the flesh of the cod away from the skin into thin strips. Rinse them and soak in water for an hour. Pull the stalks from the *ñoras*, shake out the seeds and soak in water for an hour. Wash the greens thoroughly and slice them roughly, including the stalks. Peel the potatoes and cut into even-sized chunks.

Place the greens in a large pot with just the water clinging to their leaves. Cover and leave over a good heat until they have collapsed. Add the potatoes and salt-cod and just cover with water. Bring to the boil and leave to simmer uncovered.

Pound the garlic to a paste with a little salt. Scrape the flesh from the *ñoras* and pound it with the garlic. Add this paste to the pot and continue cooking until the cooking liquid has almost evaporated and the potatoes are tender.

Serve with a jug of good oil to hand round at the table. One poached egg can be placed on top of each helping if wished.

# Menestra de verduras

This version of *menestra* comes from Murcia. It is less time-consuming to prepare if you cut up and peel the vegetables as you fry them. Add vegetables such as peas or asparagus in season. Leave out the artichokes if they are unavailable; the point is to use a wide selection of *fresh* vegetables.

6 tablespoons oil
4 cloves garlic, crushed
60g/2oz serrano ham, diced small
½ onion
2 leeks
2 sticks celery
3 carrots
3 small turnips
2 medium potatoes
3 small artichokes
1 tomato
1 heaped tablespoon flour
1 litre/1¾ pints water or light stock

salt and pepper
280g/10oz green beans

Heat the oil in a large pot and fry the garlic and ham until the garlic starts to brown. Roughly chop the onion and add to the pot, frying it over a lowish heat while you clean and slice the leeks. Add them to the onions and continue in this manner with the sliced or diced celery, carrots, turnips, potatoes, artichokes (in quarters) and tomato. When the latter has been cooking 5 minutes add the flour and mix well. Gradually add the water or stock, season and bring to the boil. Top and tail the beans and add them when it boils. Leave boiling for 10-15 minutes, by which time the vegetables should all be tender.

## POTAJES

These are thick soups using *legumbres*, pulses, as their base. A rich variety of dried beans, chickpeas and lentils are all used, and formerly the dried broad bean too was a staple food for many. While they are good when fresh, they become tiresome and tough when dried, but they were eaten and endured thus throughout the winter until a new crop of fresh beans heralded the arrival of spring. The plethora of popular fresh broad bean dishes reflects the importance of these new beans. Dried broad beans are still sold of course, and although of better quality these days they have been largely supplanted in Spanish diets by other pulses. They are popular, however, fried and salted for nibbling.

The catalyst for change was the arrival from the New World of new varieties of bean. Ordinary people turned gratefully to these beans of all shapes, sizes and colours, and they quickly established themselves in the Spanish diet. Each region now seems to have its own favourite. The Basques, for example, love their red and black beans, *alubias de Tolosa*, to the extent that they now fetch three times the price of ordinary white beans. Varieties of the latter are found all over Spain, as well as black-eyed beans, and pretty 'painted' beans. Their regional names are legion, but the commonest are *judía*, *habichuela* and *alubia*. *Pochas* are white beans that are popular eaten fresh in some northern parts of the country.

Chickpeas (called *garbanzos*, from an Arabic word *arbanco*) are thought to have arrived in Spain with the Carthaginians when they established themselves in Cartagena on the Murcian coast in 200BC. It was perhaps the Carthaginian taste for them that made chickpeas despised by the Romans, who thought that their consumption not only indicated stupidity but also induced it. They became a popular source of daily protein throughout much of Spain.

A *potaje* generally consists of one of the three pulses cooked in water with onion, garlic or a *sofrito*. Vegetables, usually green, are added later, along with fresh meat if affordable or any *matanza* products that can be spared, such as chorizo or morcilla. A completely meatless *potaje* is described sadly as *viudo*, widowed. At times when meat was forbidden, during Lent for example, salt-cod would be used instead. Rice and potatoes are sometimes added for extra bulk, and in a cheap roadside restaurant I once had to face up to a *potaje* laden with beans, chickpeas, rice, potatoes, noodles and little else.

Overnight soaking can be avoided by bringing the beans or chickpeas to the boil, cooking them for a couple of minutes and then leaving them in the hot water for about two hours.

## Potaje de lentejas

Thick lentil soup. Lentils are a comforting food, and if you're lucky enough to be able to eat them by an open fire and in good company, even better. To make a complete meal out of this recipe, add a chorizo or two per person towards the end of cooking, and serve with good sturdy bread.

The lentils should be khaki-coloured, not the bright orange ones that turn into mashed potato after five minutes in the pot. They do not need pre-soaking, unless they are very ancient.

450g/1lb lentils, picked over and washed
water or vegetable cooking water
salt
2 tomatoes, skinned and chopped
2 onions, chopped
2 green peppers, chopped
1 bay leaf
1 good pinch saffron
2 tablespoons oil
6 cloves garlic

Cover the lentils with about 5cm/2in of water and bring to the boil. Add some salt, the tomatoes, onions, green peppers and bay leaf. Cover and leave to simmer gently, topping up with water if it becomes very thick.

Soak the saffron in a little of the cooking liquor. Use a pestle to extract as much colour as possible. Heat a little oil and brown the garlic. Pound it to a paste and add it to the lentils, along with the saffron and oil.

The lentils should be ready in about an hour, and the soup very thick. Eat it steaming hot in generous bowlfuls, and have a jug of good vinegar to hand for each person to season his soup to taste.

# Lentejas con morcilla

Lentils with morcilla. This soup not only has a lovely flavour but is also a most beautiful colour.

450g/1lb lentils, picked over and washed

water or vegetable stock

salt and pepper

1 bay leaf

3 tablespoons oil

4 cloves garlic

2 slices stale French bread

1 onion, chopped

2 tablespoons flour

1 tablespoon paprika

400g/14oz morcilla, in a piece if possible

Cover the lentils with the water or stock, add a little salt and the bay leaf and bring to the boil. Leave to simmer uncovered. Meanwhile, heat the oil in a frying pan and brown the cloves of garlic and the bread. Put them both in the mortar. Add the onion to the oil and let it soften. Pound the garlic and bread with a little salt and pepper until you have a paste. Thin this down with some of the cooking liquor and add it to the pot.

Add the flour and paprika to the onion in the frying pan. Let it cook for a minute or two, then add to the lentils, which may need more water by now.

When the lentils have been cooking for about 45 minutes put the morcilla in with them and continue cooking for about 15 more minutes, or until the lentils are tender, the oil from the morcilla is absorbed and the soup is very thick. Remove the morcilla and slice it up. Stir the slices back into the soup and serve very hot.

# Potaje de frijoles (frigüelos)

A popular *potaje* where I live is this one made with delicious black-eyed beans. It is often eaten with a side-dish of raw spring onions or radishes.

550g/1¼lb black-eyed beans, soaked overnight

water or stock

salt

2 tomatoes, peeled and chopped

2 bay leaves

1 teaspoon ground cumin

4 cloves

1 head garlic

1 onion, chopped

1 green pepper and 1 red pepper, chopped

60g/2oz serrano ham, finely chopped

1 tablespoon paprika

1 good pinch saffron

Cover the beans well with water or stock. Add a little salt, bring to the boil, skim, cover and boil for 30 minutes. Peel off the loose skin from the garlic and trim the root. Using tongs, hold it over a flame until it is charred all over. Add it to the pot along with all the other ingredients except the saffron. Soak the latter in a little of the hot broth. Cook the *potaje* for about another hour, by which time the beans should be tender. Add the saffron and its liquid and cook for 2 more minutes. Add a chorizo or two if you wish. Serve with a jug of vinegar to hand, so that each person can season his or her *potaje* to taste.

## Pote asturiano

Asturias is most renowned for its stew of fat white beans and meat (*fabada asturiana*, page 121); an even older dish is this *pote*, a hefty soup which also contains meat (originally only on feast days) and those lovely buttery beans, along with greens and potatoes, all in a beautifully flavoured saffron-coloured broth.

175g/6oz large white beans, preferably *fabes asturianas de la granja*, soaked

340g/12oz piece of gammon *or* ham *or* (ideally) *lacón*

120g/4oz streaky bacon in a single slice

2 meaty pork ribs

about 2.3 litres/4 pints water

2 morcillas* (*or* one if they are very large)

2 chorizos*

340g/12oz potatoes, peeled and cut into large chunks

780g/1¾lb green cabbage, sliced, but not too thinly

1 good pinch saffron

salt (optional)

*Asturian morcilla and chorizo are smoked. If they are unavailable use ordinary ones and use smoked ham or bacon as well to give the smoky flavour.

Put the beans in a large pot with the ham, bacon and ribs. Cover with the water and bring to the boil. Skim and leave to simmer, the lid slightly askew, for 45 minutes. Add the morcillas, chorizos and potatoes and continue simmering. Remove a ladleful of broth and soak the saffron in it. After 30 minutes add the cabbage and saffron water to the pot. Cook for 10 more minutes, by which time the beans should be tender – continue cooking if not. When ready, slice up the meats and sausages and return them to the pot. Serve in large bowls with plenty of bread. The meats should provide enough salt, but check nonetheless.

# Potaje de alubias blancas

A thick white bean soup from Galicia. The same recipe can be used for lentils.

340g/12oz dried white beans, soaked overnight and drained
550g/1¼lb cheap pork
150g/5oz piece of green bacon or salt pork
2 tomatoes, peeled and chopped
4 cloves garlic, crushed
1 onion, chopped
2-3 parsley stalks
2 tablespoons oil
4 chorizos
4 potatoes, peeled and cut into chunks
salt and pepper

Put everything except the chorizos and potatoes into a large pot and cover well with water. Bring to the boil, skim and simmer with a lid on for 1-1½ hours. Add the chorizos and potatoes and continue simmering until the latter are tender. Add more water if necessary. Season, and slice up the meats before serving.

# Potaje de garbanzos con coles

This recipe uses cabbage with chickpeas, but you can try using spinach or chard as a variation – they are equally good. I urge you to do your best to get a piece of cured ham rind for this, for it makes all the difference to the flavour. Failing this, substitute a piece of ham bone or even some chopped ham.

225g/8oz chickpeas, soaked overnight

1 slice cured ham rind, washed

1 bay leaf

3 tablespoons oil

2 cloves garlic

2 slices stale French bread

salt

1 hard-boiled egg

450g/1lb white cabbage, thickly sliced

225g/8oz potatoes, peeled and cut into chunks

2 tablespoons chopped parsley

Drain the chickpeas, place them in a large pan with the ham rind and bay leaf and cover well with cold water. Bring to the boil, skim, cover the pan and leave to cook at a low boil.

Heat the oil in a small frying pan and fry the garlic and then the bread until brown. Transfer them to a mortar and pound to a smooth paste with a little salt and the yolk of the egg. Chop the egg white roughly.

Once the chickpeas are tender, stir in the cabbage, potatoes, parsley, egg white and the paste from the mortar. Taste for salt, then boil for 15 more minutes until the potatoes and cabbage are soft. If you want your cabbage to have a crisp texture don't add it until 10 minutes after the potatoes.

# Judías blancas guisadas con chorizos

A typical thick *potaje*.

450g/1lb dried white beans (or whatever beans you prefer), soaked overnight in cold water

1 head garlic

120g/4oz serrano ham, diced

1 bay leaf

½ teaspoon peppercorns

salt

1 onion, finely chopped
1 red pepper, chopped
2 tablespoons oil
1 tomato, peeled and chopped
3 chorizos, sliced
1 pinch ground cumin
1 good pinch saffron

Drain the beans, place them in a large earthenware casserole and cover them well with cold water. Bring them to the boil. While they are coming to the boil strip the head of garlic of all loose skin and trim off the root base. Hold the garlic over an open flame (using kitchen tongs) until charred all over. Add it to the pot along with the ham, bay leaf, peppercorns and a little salt. Leave the beans boiling quite rapidly, uncovered. Fry the onion and red pepper in the oil until well softened, then add the tomato and cook for 5 more minutes. Stir this *sofrito* into the beans. Keep topping up the beans with cold water as the level drops. When the beans seem nearly tender (start testing them after about an hour) add the chorizos, cumin and saffron (crumble the latter with your fingers or in a mortar) and continue cooking until the liquid is reduced to a thick sauce coating the beans. Check the seasoning before serving.

## Fabada asturiana

One of Spain's great dishes, one that's ideal for Sundays and holidays, *fabada* is extremely simple in concept – beans are cooked with preserved pork of various sorts – but like all 'simple' dishes it calls for the very best ingredients. Ancient, dried-up little beans and the first sausages that come to hand will give you a dish that wasn't worth the effort. You need Asturian white beans (the best are *fabes asturianas de la granja*) which swell to a considerable size and have a melting, buttery texture with a very thin skin; you need, ideally, Asturian or Galician ham (*lacón*) and smoked Asturian chorizo and morcilla; or you need considerable ingenuity in finding alternatives. It is a difficult dish, then, but unforgettable if made well.

450g/1lb large white beans, soaked overnight and drained
450g/1lb *lacón* or good ham, soaked if necessary
60g/2oz serrano ham, diced, or a piece of serrano ham bone
2 smoked chorizos
1 good pinch saffron
2 smoked morcillas
2 tablespoons oil

2 cloves garlic, crushed

1 tablespoon paprika

In a large, wide casserole put the beans, two sorts of ham and chorizo. Cover with water and bring to the boil, skimming as necessary. Cover and leave to simmer for an hour.

Toast the saffron, pound it to a powder and add it to the *fabada* with the morcilla. Cover and cook for another 30 minutes, by which time the beans should be nearly tender. If not, continue simmering until they are, making sure the beans are always just covered with liquid.

Now skim off as much fat as possible and let the *fabada* cook uncovered until the beans are just coated with sauce. Turn off the heat.

In a small frying pan heat the oil, garlic and paprika until they sizzle. Stir the mixture into the *fabada* and leave for an hour, or until needed. Some of the broken beans can be liquidised with a little of the cooking liquor and stirred back in to thicken it a little. Reheat carefully and slice up the meats (known as the *compango*). The meats can be mixed with the beans or served as a second course with a little bread, the latter being preferable in my opinion.

*If you are in a hard water area some cooks recommend that you use mineral water for cooking the beans.

*Another frequent recommendation is that you 'startle' the beans by turning off the heat or adding a little cold water two or three times during the boiling process, the idea being to encourage the natural enzymes in the beans to tenderise them.

*A variation I now usually adopt is to simmer the chorizo and morcilla separately for 15 minutes or so before I add them (minus their cooking water) to the beans. This seems to make the whole thing a bit more digestible. For the same reason I may omit the final seasoning with the oil, garlic and paprika.

*Skimming off fat is really easy if you just lay sheets of kitchen paper on the surface, let them soak up the fat, then discard. I can't remember where I first read this tip but it's incredibly useful.

# Fabes con almejas

Another Asturian recipe, invented to relieve the tedium of eating beans every day, is to add some cooked clams towards the end of cooking.

780g/1¾lb white beans (*fabes*, if possible) soaked overnight

2 cloves garlic, crushed

1 onion, sliced

1 bay leaf

4 tablespoons oil

2 sprigs parsley

salt

450g/1lb fresh clams

1 large pinch saffron

2 tablespoons dried breadcrumbs

Put the drained beans in a large pot and cover with fresh water. Add the crushed garlic, onion, bay leaf, oil, parsley and some salt. Simmer gently for about 1½ hours or until the beans are tender, topping up the water level if necessary – the beans should always be just covered.

Wash the clams and place them in a wide frying pan with a little water. Cook over a high heat and remove them as they open. Take out the meat from the shells if you wish – this makes the dish less attractive but easier to eat. Strain the liquid from the clams through a fine sieve into the beans. Now pound the saffron to a powder and mix it into the beans with the breadcrumbs. Cook for a few more minutes until the sauce has thickened. Stir in the clams and serve in large soup plates.

Two other variations use hare and chicken. The basic dish is the same but with the pieces of meat cooked with the beans from the beginning.

# Llegumet

A thick concoction of beans, rice, potatoes, greens and snails. A country dish from Alicante province.

2 small turnips

225g/8oz Swiss chard or spinach

225g/8oz potatoes

1 *ñora*

225g/8oz dried beans, soaked overnight

salt

2 dozen small prepared snails

2-3 cloves

6 peppercorns

1 good pinch saffron

2 tablespoons oil

120g/4oz rice

Peel and slice the turnips into rounds or chunks. Wash the greens thoroughly and slice them thinly, stalks and all. Peel and thickly dice the potatoes. Soak the *ñora* as explained on page 33.

Cover the beans and turnips with plenty of cold water. Add salt and bring to the boil. Cook for 45 minutes, covered. Add the snails and potatoes and cook for 15 more minutes. Scrape the flesh from the *ñora* and pound it to a paste with the cloves, peppercorns and saffron. Dilute the paste with the oil and add it to the pot, along with the rice and greens. Add more water if it seems very thick and check the seasoning. Cook until the rice is just tender.

**Note:** If prepared as above, the beans are cooked for only about 1¼ hours, which may be too little if they are old. If you are not sure of their quality, give them a little longer before adding the vegetables.

# Judías blancas con salchichas

A Spanish version of bangers and beans.

450g/1lb white beans, soaked overnight and drained
1.2 litres/2 pints water
4 tablespoons oil
2 onions, quartered
salt and pepper
3 cloves garlic
1 good pinch saffron
3-4 smallish potatoes, cut into thick chunks
340g/12oz good sausages, thickly sliced

Place the beans in a pot with the water, the oil and the onions. Add a little salt. Bring them to the boil and let them simmer for about an hour, uncovered, topping up with water if necessary.

Pound the garlic and saffron with a little salt and pepper. Thin the paste down with some water and add it to the beans along with the potatoes. After about another 30 minutes everything should be tender and the stew quite thick. Add the pieces of sausage and cook for another 10 minutes.

# Judías a lo tío Lucas

There are various stories about the origins of the legendary uncle Lucas. It seems he was of Cantabrian stock but first set up a restaurant about 200 years ago on the quayside at Puerto Real, near Cádiz, catering for seamen. He then moved to Madrid, where he was a great success, and his more popular dishes such as these stewed beans, of which there are several 'authentic' versions, still bear his name.

400g/14oz large white beans, soaked
salt
4 tablespoons oil
2 large onions, finely chopped
2 teaspoons paprika
150g/5oz unsmoked streaky bacon or *tocino*, diced small
1 bay leaf
1 head garlic
2 tablespoons vinegar

Cover the beans with a good quantity of cold water, add a little salt and boil for 45 minutes or until nearly tender. Drain, reserving the cooking liquor.

Heat the oil in a *puchero* or deep casserole and soften the onion and bacon. Add the paprika, bay, beans and the head of garlic (whole, but with all loose skin stripped off and the root base trimmed clean). Just cover with the bean liquor and leave to simmer very gently uncovered, until the stew is thick and the beans very tender. Add more water if necessary and check the seasoning. Stir in the vinegar at the end and leave the beans to rest, covered, for 15 minutes.

Chorizo can be added for a more substantial meal, in which case do not add salt to the beans. Olives or peppers in vinegar are sometimes eaten with it for extra savour.

## Olla de trigo

This uses whole-wheat grains whose pleasant chewy texture contrasts nicely with the crunchier chickpeas.

120g/4oz whole-wheat grains
225g/8oz chickpeas, soaked overnight
225g/8oz green bacon or salt-pork, in a piece
225g/8oz morcilla, thickly sliced
1 handful fennel leaves, chopped
225g/8oz chorizo, thickly sliced
2 slices stale French bread
1 fresh green chilli (removing the seeds will make the dish less fiery)

Cook the wheat in boiling water until tender (about 1 hour). Meanwhile, cover the chickpeas with water and boil them with the bacon and fennel leaves for about 2 hours. Add the wheat and its cooking water, and the sliced sausages.

Fry the bread in oil until brown. Pound it with the chilli and add to the stew. Simmer a few more minutes, until the chickpeas are tender and the sausages heated through. Slice up the bacon or pork, stir it back in and serve.

# Pilongas con chorizo

Dried chestnuts with chorizo and pinto beans. This is equally good either thinned down and served as a soup, or as a thick, enticing stew. Pinto beans (*alubias pintas*) in their raw state are mottled with streaks and patches of violet, delicate and beautiful like little birds' eggs. Unfortunately all that disappears when they're cooked. You can of course use any other similar bean, as well as fresh chestnuts.

This dish will be even better if by some miracle you can get hold of smoky Asturian chorizo. Start preparation the night before.

225g/8oz dried chestnuts
175g/6oz dried pinto beans
1 onion, sliced
salt
6-8 chorizos

The night before, pour boiling water over the chestnuts in a bowl. In another bowl cover the beans with cold water.

The next day drain them off, discarding the water, and put them in a casserole. Cover with water, and add the sliced onion and some salt. Bring to the boil and simmer for about 1½ hours, uncovered, or until they seem almost tender. Top up with water if necessary. Add the whole chorizos and simmer for 30 more minutes, stirring occasionally as the sausages release their juices.

Remove a ladleful of the beans and chestnuts, and either liquidize or sieve them to a purée. Stir this back into the stew, which will now be lovely and thick, a gorgeous colour and ready to eat with good bread and some stout wine.

# Judías blancas guisadas con sepia

A thick, garlicky Catalan stew of white beans and cuttlefish.

400g/14oz dried white beans, soaked overnight

salt

1 onion, thinly sliced

¼ green pepper, diced small

6 tablespoons oil

1kg/2¼lb cuttlefish, cleaned as explained on page 220\ and cut into chunks

2 tomatoes, peeled and chopped

4 cloves garlic

1 good pinch saffron

Just cover the drained beans with water, add a little salt, bring to the boil and simmer uncovered for 30 minutes. Meanwhile, soften the onion and green pepper in the oil. Add the pieces of cuttlefish and tomato and cook until the fish changes colour. Add to the beans and simmer for another hour, uncovered, by which time both the beans and the cuttlefish should be tender and the sauce thick. If not, continue cooking until they are. Pound the garlic and saffron to a paste and stir it into the stew. Taste for salt and simmer for 5 more minutes before serving.

# Potaje de garbanzos con bacalao

A really satisfying and sustaining soup of chickpeas and salt-cod, with some beans to help give body to the broth. This is a typical meal for Holy Week when tradition dictates you go without meat. You don't need the best cuts of salt-cod for this and the soup benefits if you add the cod's tail along with the other pieces of fish. This is not eaten, but its natural gelatin improves the texture of the soup. Make the soup a day ahead of time if you can, so the flavours can mature. Some chopped spinach can be added towards the end if wished.

400g/14oz chickpeas

400g/14oz salt-cod

100g/3½oz small dried white beans

1 whole head garlic

4 extra cloves garlic, peeled and sliced

2 bay leaves

12 black peppercorns
4 tablespoons olive oil
saffron colouring (optional)
chopped parsley

The night before you want to make the soup, put the chickpeas and beans in a big bowl. Rinse the salt from the cod and add it to the bowl. Cover everything with plenty of cold water and leave to soak overnight. If the cod is very thick allow a few more hours and change the water half way through.

Next day, drain everything and put the beans and chickpeas in a large pot. Put the cod back in the water to carry on soaking.

Strip all the loose skin from the head of garlic, then grip it with tongs and hold it over a medium gas flame until it is thoroughly scorched all over. Brush off any burnt bits and put the garlic into the pot along with the extra sliced garlic, bay leaves and peppercorns.

Pour in the olive oil and swirl it around so that everything gets coated, then pour in 1.5 litres/2¾ pints of water. Cover the pot and bring to the boil, skimming as necessary, then reduce the heat to medium so that the soup cooks at a lively boil. Continue in this way for an hour, topping up the soup with boiling water every twenty minutes or so.

Now check to see if the chickpeas and beans are tender. If they are, add the drained pieces of cod and a little saffron colouring (it looks a bit drab otherwise). Cook for ten minutes more, then check for salt, though it shouldn't need any. Turn off the heat and leave to cool. Refrigerate until the next day if that fits in with your plans, then gently reheat it and sprinkle in some chopped parsley.

This is really nicest if you take the trouble to remove all the skin and bone from the fish before you serve the soup. Make sure everyone gets a bit of the head of garlic. Best with a strong red wine to accompany it.

## THE OLLA PODRIDA

Sancho Panza, recently installed as governor of his isle, and having astonished observers with his sagacity in its court of justice, sits down to what promises to be a great feast that has been laid out in front of him. He has just started to eat when the dishes are whisked away from under his nose on the orders of the attendant physician, one of Cervantes' most amusing creations. According to this good Dr Pedro Recio de Agüero he had the fruit removed for being too moist for his master's good. Another dish was too spicy. There are still some partridges on the table but these too are forbidden, likewise the stewed rabbits and pickled beef, because they might upset the royal digestion. Sancho's hungry gaze lights on something else:

*That great smoking dish further over, said Sancho, looks to me like an* olla podrida *and seeing what a lot of different things there are in these* ollas podridas *we can't fail to find something in it tasty and wholesome for me.*

But Dr Pedro will have none of it:

*There is nothing in the world less nourishing than an* olla podrida. *Leave your* ollas podridas *for canons or rectors of colleges or for country weddings. And let them be banished from Governors' tables, at which every delicacy and refinement must preside.*

And he prescribes Sancho a meal of a hundred wafer rolls and some thin slices of quince, but he doesn't even get to eat these as important business intervenes requiring his wisdom. Eventually a meal is forthcoming, albeit a poor one, after which he requests that they bring him *ollas podridas* in future, 'for the rottener they are, the better they smell'.

*Olla podrida*, a dish at the heart of traditional Spanish cooking, means rotten pot, and one theory about the name is that the food was cooked so slowly that it almost decomposed. It may also suggest, of course, that its ingredients were not quite fresh. Another explanation is that the name was originally *olla poderida* which would have meant something like 'pot for the powerful', as if it was full of meat only such people could afford it. Whatever the origin, the *olla podrida* contained a wide variety of things, the number depending on the pocket of the cook, and it was a commonly eaten dish among all classes. The dish practically cooked itself, sitting quietly at the side of the stove and requiring just the occasional addition of this or that. Even better, soup, vegetables and

meat could all be cooked in one pot, and more or less anything to hand could go in at some stage.

Its place of origin is difficult if not impossible to pinpoint. Castilla, León, La Mancha and Extremadura all claim it as their own. A large assortment of similar boil-ups are derived from it, their names and ingredients varying from region to region, though known generally as *cocidos*. Dishes called *olla podrida* are still to be found, in Albacete and Burgos for example, where they refer to its three courses as *sota, caballo y rey*, jack, queen, king. All the *cocidos* have certain things in common, not least the affection with which the Spaniard regards the version of his own region. To the Spaniard the eating of a good *cocido* is as comforting a maintenance of tradition as our own Sunday roast lunch. Indeed, the size and composition of a modern *cocido* requires a day free of all work after eating it. It is a Sunday dish or a meal for celebrations between large numbers of family or friends.

There is no one correct recipe for any of the various regional *cocidos*, but one can detect a consistent thread running through them. They start with the big family pot, into which are put chickpeas (or beans in many northern parts); chunks of meat, usually beef and chicken; unglamorous bits and pieces (trotters, pigs' ears, even cow udder); preserved pork fat, *tocino*, maybe in two forms, salted and *rancio*, the latter used for flavour but not for eating; and bones. It is all simmered slowly, with later additions of *pelotas*, a sort of meatball or dumpling, sausages (chorizo, morcilla, *butifarra* and so on) and vegetables. The broth is eaten as a soup, often thickened with rice or noodles or just bread; the chickpeas and vegetables form the second course and the meats the third; or the two courses may be eaten together.

The Madrid version of the *cocido* is well worth seeking out if you are in the city, at places such as the Taberna Buenaventura, but be warned: portions are huge.

# Cocido madrileño (1)

150g/5oz chickpeas
1 pig's trotter, split lengthways
250g/9oz beef shin *or* flank
¼ boiling fowl
10cm/4in piece marrow bone
60g/2oz serrano ham, chopped
120g/4oz piece unsmoked streaky bacon *or* salt pork
½ onion
1 small turnip
1 carrot
1 leek

1 small stick celery

4 small potatoes

1 chorizo

1 morcilla

1 good pinch saffron

340g/12oz green beans *or* cabbage *or* Swiss chard

1 clove garlic, chopped

oil

*FOR THE* PELOTAS *OR* BOLAS:

1 egg

30g/1oz breadcrumbs

½ clove garlic, very finely chopped

1 tablespoon chopped parsley

salt and pepper

1 tablespoon flour

1 tablespoon oil

*FOR THE TOMATO SAUCE:*

2 tablespoons oil

2 tomatoes, peeled and chopped

salt

sugar

tomato purée *or* vinegar

The night before, cover the chickpeas with plenty of cold water. Roll the trotters in coarse sea salt.

The next morning, place in a very large pot with a lid the drained chickpeas, the rinsed trotters, the piece of beef, the chicken, the bone, the ham and the bacon. Pour in enough cold water to cover them by at least 5cm/2in. Add no salt, as enough will be provided by the bacon and ham. Bring to the boil, skim thoroughly and add the onion, turnip, carrot, leek and celery, all whole. Cover and leave to simmer extremely slowly for about 4 hours – just the occasional bubble should appear on the surface of the broth.

After 3 hours add the potatoes, chorizo and morcilla. Remove a little of the stock and soak the saffron in it. Mix together the first five ingredients for the *pelotas*. Divide into four balls, flour them and brown them in a little oil. Add to the pot, along with the saffrony water.

Now make the tomato sauce: heat the oil and add the chopped tomatoes. Season with a little salt, sugar and a dash of tomato purée or vinegar to bring out the flavour if necessary. Leave to simmer until thick.

Now put the beans in a saucepan and cover with broth from the pot. Cook for 10 minutes, then drain the cooking liquid back into the pot. Fry the garlic in a little oil until lightly browned. Dress the beans with this and keep them warm in a low oven.

After the 4 hours are up add the potatoes to the beans. Take out all the meats and slice them into large pieces, removing the bones from the trotters and chicken. Slice the morcilla and chorizo into four. The vegetables are best discarded. Strain the broth from the chickpeas into a soup tureen and season if necessary. Remove all fat floating on its surface. It is common to cook fine noodles in it for the soup, but I prefer to start the meal with the broth on its own – there's quite enough to cope with without adding pasta.

Place the chickpeas in the centre of a large heated platter and arrange the meats and *pelotas* around them. Cover with foil and keep warm in the oven while you eat the soup. Then serve the meats and chickpeas accompanied by the tomato sauce and the green vegetables (and bread and wine, of course).

Any leftover chickpeas, tomato sauce, broth or meat can be used to make a paella. Use the marrow from the marrow bone for spreading on hot toast.

# Cocido madrileño (2)

A slimmed-down version which is perhaps more suitable for days when you can't collapse into bed afterwards. It was this version that was once eaten on a daily basis by many of Madrid's workers.

340g/12oz chickpeas, soaked overnight
225g/8oz piece green bacon *or* salt pork
450g/1lb piece beef flank *or* shin
10cm/4in piece marrow bone
1 onion
900g/2lb potatoes
1 pinch saffron
120g/4oz thin noodles *or* rice

Boil the chickpeas, bacon, beef, bone and onion with plenty of water, skimming as necessary. After 3 hours add the potatoes and saffron soaked in a little of the hot broth. Remove most of the broth, leaving just enough to cook the potatoes. Cook the noodles or rice in this broth and serve it as a soup, followed by the cut-up meats and chickpeas.

Some regional variations are known as follows: *Escudella i carn d'olla* (Cataluña) which is served with very large pasta shapes called *galets*; *La olla de tres abocás* (Valencia); *Bullit* (Baleares); *Presa de predicador* – 'preacher's pot' from Aragón, ie a dish fit for a religious worthy. The broth was traditionally boiled down and given to invalids; and *Berza* (Andalucía).

# Gachas

*Gachas*, meaning porridge or thick gruel, are used today mainly as baby food or nourishment for the sick or elderly. Once, though, they were a common winter lunch. Their history may go back to before the invention of bread. *Gachas* were (and still are) often called *puches* and gave their name to Spain's large cooking pot, the *puchero*, where they would be cooked in copious quantities.

If forced to eat them on a daily basis, one would tire of *gachas* very quickly indeed, but as an occasional change they are a warm, comforting food on wet winter days – if well made. But, like semolina, porridge or Italy's polenta they can be unsurpassed in their ghastliness if done badly. However, you have to be an extremely incompetent cook to make bad *gachas*, and following these uncomplicated instructions you should have no problems.

1 level teaspoon aniseed
5 tablespoons oil
500ml/18fl oz milk
500ml/18fl oz water
1 level teaspoon salt
1 large strip lemon peel
1 good pinch cinnamon
240g/8½oz coarse white wheat flour *or* cornmeal

Heat the aniseed gently in the oil for a few minutes; it must flavour the oil without burning. Put the milk and water in a large saucepan together with the salt, lemon peel and cinnamon. Strain into the oil and sprinkle in the flour. Bring to the boil, stirring continuously with a wooden spoon. Reduce the heat so that the *gachas* bubble thickly, and stir for 20 minutes, taking care that they don't burn. Add more salt if necessary – they will taste fairly unpleasant at this stage, but don't worry.

Ladle the *gachas* into warm soup plates and serve them with a plate of croutons (fry these before you make the *gachas* and keep them warm) and a bowl of sugar or, much better, a jar of black *miel de caña*, the cane honey made in Frigiliana, Andalucía. (This incidentally is sugar cane juice cooked down to a delicious syrup, not molasses or black treacle, which are by-products of the sugar-making process.) Each person then helps themselves.

**Variations:** Needless to say, there are many. They can be made with all water, in which case milk would be added at the table. They can be eaten with savoury foods such as sausages or bacon. In La Mancha you may find the dish made with flour from the wild grass pea plant (*harina de almortas*). In some places they make their *gachas* extra thick and fry them as a sort of tortilla with potatoes or sweetened with sugar. In the far north-west in Galicia they are known as *papas* and are often made with the water left over from cooking turnip greens (*grelos*), in which case they are called *papas pegas*, 'magpie porridge', because the dark blotches of the greens mixed with the white of the *gachas* are said to resemble the bird's plumage. *Papas afreitas* are made with barley and eaten for breakfast.

# Migas

One Sunday, shortly after arriving in Spain to live, I was told by my friends that we were going to eat *migas* for lunch. My Spanish was still at a very primitive stage so I had to look up the word in the dictionary. 'Crumb. Fried breadcrumbs', it told me. That didn't sound very exciting but everyone was talking about the *migas* as enthusiastically as if they were paella. Out came a deep iron frying pan. Large quantities of sliced garlic were fried in oil. Coarse flour and water were added. It was explained to me that *migas* were a favourite winter-weather dish, originally eaten by the very poor but now, like so many Spanish dishes born in poverty, eaten out of choice rather than necessity.

The *migas* were perfect: they rather resembled mashed potato in appearance, though slightly granular in texture like couscous, and very light. We ate them sprinkled with pomegranate seeds, a delightful touch, and accompanied by fried *jureles* (scad), fried marinated anchovies (see page 195) and a roast pepper salad (page 81). I discovered that *migas* were a very filling but delicious change from potatoes, rice or bread as the carbohydrate element in a meal.

I later found out that *migas* vary a great deal from place to place. As with *gachas*, different flours can be used. It is, however, most common to use stale bread (it needs good country bread to work well) instead of flour. It is chopped into small squares and fried in olive oil with garlic. *Migas* can be eaten with more or less anything, on condition that it be flavourful. Fried bacon, fried fish, ham, chorizo or other sausages, salted sardines, grapes, even hot chocolate (no garlic needed in that case), are all good with *migas*. fried eggs above all in my opinion.

oil
6 cloves garlic, peeled and thinly sliced
500ml/18fl oz water
340g/12oz coarse-ground wheat *or* maize flour
salt

In a large, wide frying pan, non-stick to be on the safe side, heat enough oil to cover its bottom quite generously and fry the garlic until well browned. Add 2 tablespoons of the flour and let it sizzle briefly in the oil. Pour in the water, add some salt and bring it to the boil. Pour in the rest of the flour and mix well. Still over a high heat, fry the *migas*, stirring and lifting them continuously with a large metal spoon (a flat, round one is ideal) as if you were stir-frying. On no account must they burn. Break down any large lumps as you go. Fry the *migas* for about 10 minutes, remove from the heat and test for seasoning. There should be no taste of raw flour.

Serve very hot, either immediately or heated up later once the accompaniments (see above) are ready.

# Verduras
## VEGETABLES

With our own history of cruelty to vegetables, perhaps we should not scoff when we try them cooked in many a Spanish household or restaurant. The modern notion of eating vegetables when tender but still firm and tasting of something has yet to get firmly established with many Spanish cooks. However, things are improving, something that struck me a few years ago when a bar in Altea in Alicante province served us up some simple artichokes and asparagus crisp, golden and hot from the griddle, dressed with good oil and salt. I don't think either vegetable has tasted as good before or since.

So some Spaniards do know how to cook vegetables, and many Spanish recipes are worthy of their efforts. Such dishes should be good enough to perform on their own, not as supporting cast, and should be eaten as a first course, as a salad is in Spain.

### SWISS CHARD
*(Acelgas)*

Chard leaves are interchangeable for culinary purposes with spinach. Although they have slightly more body, they collapse as drastically as spinach when cooked. The large white stalks, resembling celery, have what is often described as a 'delicate' flavour, in this case a kind way of saying practically

tasteless, but it is wasteful not to use them, so cook them with the leaves (sliced roughly first). They will still be slightly crunchy when you eat them.

## Acelgas a la malagueña

900g/2lb Swiss chard, well washed

salt

4 tablespoons oil

4 cloves garlic, sliced

2 tablespoons paprika

black pepper

vinegar

Cook the chard in a large covered saucepan over a medium heat with some salt and just the water clinging to its leaves until it collapses – just a few minutes. Drain it well, and when cool enough to handle squeeze out as much residual water as you can. Slice the chard roughly.

Heat the oil in a wide frying pan and throw in the garlic. When it starts to brown add the chard, paprika and a good grinding of black pepper. Stir it until it's heated through, then sprinkle with vinegar and serve – the vinegar serves as a seasoning and should barely be noticeable.

## Acelgas al Sacromonte

One of the obligatory stops on the tourist route of Andalucía, indeed of all Spain, is Granada, a city sprawled over a wide plain and guarded by the snowy peaks of the Sierra Nevada. Everyone goes there to see the Alhambra, the elegant palace which was the Moors' last stronghold in Spain. From its great bell tower one can see the charming old quarter of the town on a hill below the walls, and further over the gypsy quarter of the Sacromonte, the Holy Hill, so called because human bones were found there, supposedly of St Cecil, the patron saint of the city, whose monastery sits atop the hill. Dotted over the hillside are the black mouths of the caves where the bones were found, and where there is a thriving industry of Flamenco music and dancing aimed at the tourist market.

This dish of chard in a sauce of almonds, garlic and saffron is named after Granada's holy hill (as is an omelette, see page 160).

120g/4oz almonds, blanched and peeled

3 large cloves garlic

4 slices stale French bread
6 tablespoons oil
1 good pinch saffron
1 tablespoon sherry vinegar
60g/2oz raisins
900g/2lb Swiss chard, washed
salt

Fry the almonds, garlic and bread in the oil until brown. Pound to a paste in the mortar, along with the saffron. Stir in the vinegar, raisins and any leftover oil. Cook the chard in a large covered pan over a medium heat with just the water clinging to its leaves and a little salt. When it collapses drain it well. Do not wring it dry – the water it retains helps to form the sauce. Slice the chard roughly, place it in a pan and stir in the sauce. Heat through gently and add more salt if necessary.

## Acelgas a la magdalena

The *Magdalena* market gardens of Pamplona, fed by the waters of the river Arga, produce fine vegetables, especially lettuces, and chard for this recipe with potatoes, ham and tomato.

450g/1lb potatoes, peeled
780g/1¾lb Swiss chard, washed
3 tablespoons oil
120g/4oz serrano ham, diced
1 quantity tomato sauce (see page 131)

Boil the potatoes until nearly tender, adding the sliced stalks of the chard a couple of minutes before the end of the cooking time. Heat the oil and lightly fry the diced ham. Add the drained potatoes, chard stalk and the shredded chard leaves. Give it all a good stir, then add the tomato sauce, enough to give the vegetables a good coating but without drowning them. Simmer uncovered for 10-15 more minutes, by which time the vegetables should be tender and the sauce reduced.

# ARTICHOKES
## *(Alcachofas/Alcauciles)*

In Spain artichokes are picked small – about 10cm/4in long or less – and there are often no fiddly bits of choke to worry about when the artichokes are so young. Do not throw away the stalk; cut it off at the base, peel it, and cook it with the rest.

## Alcachofas estofadas

Artichokes stewed in white wine. This recipe from Navarra makes a good light tapa, and is also excellent with roasts. Try to buy reasonably small ones.

about 9 artichokes
lemon juice in water
3 tablespoons oil
1 onion, finely chopped
3 cloves garlic, crushed
250ml/8fl oz white wine
salt

To prepare the artichokes: have a bowl of water to hand, acidulated with lemon juice. Rub your fingers with lemon too. Cut off the stalk of each artichoke just below its base (see above about not discarding it). Now ruthlessly strip away the tough outer leaves, then cut off the top half (or more if it's on the big side) and trim away any green bits around the base. Don't be shy about it, you are removing all that is inedible. Now cut the artichoke into four. If there's some hairy choke to be removed, do it with a small, sharp knife. Drop the pieces into the bowl of water. When they are all prepared – it doesn't take nearly as long as it sounds – drain and rinse them well to get rid of any stray wisps of choke.

Heat the oil in a *cazuela* or sauté pan and add the onion, garlic and artichokes. Let them all fry over a fairly high flame until the onions start to brown. Pour in the wine, a little salt and enough water nearly to cover. Put on a lid and simmer for about 10 minutes. Remove the lid and let the liquid practically evaporate before serving.

## Alcachofas a la cordobesa

Artichokes and potatoes with saffron and garlic, from Córdoba.

3 cloves garlic

4 tablespoons oil

12 small *or* new potatoes, peeled

1 good pinch saffron

salt

1 tablespoon flour

about 300ml/½ pint stock

12 artichokes, prepared as above

Fry the whole cloves of garlic in the oil until well browned. Remove them to the mortar. Add the potatoes to the hot oil and let them colour lightly all over. Pound the garlic and saffron to a paste with a little salt. Mix in the flour, then stir in the stock. Add the artichokes to the potatoes and fry them, stirring, for 2 minutes. Pour over the stock, cover and simmer for about 20 minutes. Remove the lid and cook uncovered until there's just a small amount of thick sauce left coating the vegetables.

# Alcachofas con jamón

Artichokes stewed with ham and bacon.

3 tablespoons oil

½ onion, finely chopped

120g/4oz serrano ham, roughly chopped

120g/4oz unsmoked bacon, roughly chopped

3 cloves garlic, crushed

12 small artichokes, trimmed and quartered as explained opposite

juice of ½ lemon

2 tablespoons chopped parsley

salt and pepper

Heat the oil in a *cazuela* or sauté pan and fry the onion, ham and bacon for 5 minutes. Add the artichokes and garlic. Cook for 2 more minutes, stirring, then add the lemon juice and parsley, and some seasoning. Cover and simmer for 12-15 minutes. Remove the lid and boil off any excess liquid – the artichokes should be more or less dry.

# Zarangollo

A simple little dish of fried courgettes and onions, from Murcia. There you can eat it mixed with scrambled or fried eggs. Potatoes may be added too, either fried with the courgettes or separately.

Thinly slice equal quantities of courgettes and onions (about 675g/1½lb is enough for four), or chop them. Season with salt. In a large frying pan heat 6 tablespoons of oil and fry the vegetables over a medium high heat. They will be rather piled up at first but they gradually collapse. Turn the vegetables frequently as they brown and soften. Once they are tender and well coloured drain them with a slotted spoon and add salt if necessary.

# Calabacines en pisto

A richer version of zarangollo which is very good as a tapa. In addition to courgettes and onions, you need two or three egg yolks and a large tin – 200g/7oz – of tuna or bonito. Once the vegetables are tender add the fish, broken into chunks, and let it heat through. Beat the egg yolks and, off the heat, stir them into the courgettes so that they go creamy with the heat and bind everything together. Serve at once.

## THE CALÇOTADA

The *calçot* is a large sweet Catalan spring onion grown principally in the area around Valls, a few miles north of Tarragona in the region known as Alt Camp. It is in season from December to April. The *calçotada* is typical of the simple, rustic cooking to be found there and consists of an informal meal in the open air around the fire or barbecue. Over the latter are cooked *butifarra* sausages and lamb chops, but more important are the huge quantities of *calçots* that are roasted and eaten with a sort of *romesco* sauce called *salbitxada* and accompanied by plentiful draughts of local red wine or cava drunk from the *porrón*.

Roasted spring onions may not sound special, but I urge you to try them. As the outer skin slowly chars, the inner onion becomes meltingly tender without a trace of fieriness. In fact the *calçotada* perfectly demonstrates the spirit behind the best of Spanish culinary occasions: no fuss, no standing on ceremony, just plenty of good food and wine consumed against a background of uproarious conversation. Anyone going to Spain should try and get themselves invited to at least one such meal – a paella, a *cocido*, a *calçotada*, even *migas*; you will enjoy yourself enormously, even if you can understand little or nothing of what is being said at such volume all around you.

It is not difficult to have your own *calçotada*, and you needn't wait for a fine day because very passable roast spring onions can be produced on a griddle or under the grill. Allow at least a dozen large onions per person. (How large? The white part should be at least 15cm/six inches long and 2.5cm/an inch or so thick, according to my rough interpretation of local regulations.) This may sound a bit loopy but I can assure you that they will disappear in the blink of an eye. With a largish party you need to cook them in batches, but this doesn't matter in the least because you can all busy yourselves putting one lot away while the next is cooking. Alternatively wrap the cooked onions in newspaper to keep warm.

Apart from the spring onions you need good sausages (white *butifarras* for preference), small lamb chops and a dish of *romesco* sauce (page 189) mixed with a chopped sprig of mint. Have the grill or griddle hot but not at its maximum, or the onions will char without cooking through. Cut off most of the green leaves of the onions and trim off any little roots, making sure that the base remains intact. Wipe off any dirt but don't remove any of the skin (unless you can see dirt trapped inside). Now place them on a rack over the griddle or in the grill pan (lined with foil) which should be quite close to the heat. The onions soon start to brown. Turn them over as they do so, and when well browned all over remove them. They will have shrunk and gone rather floppy. One can attempt to peel them but it's much easier (and tastier) to eat them whole, dipped in the sauce. However, if they are very thick, or you're doing it all on a barbecue, the outer skin will end up black by the time they are done, in which case peeling is recommended. Hold them vertically by the leaf end and pull the skin off downwards.

Make space to cook the sausages and chops as you go. Have plenty of bread and wine to hand. And wear a napkin round your neck.

## CARDOONS
### (Cardos)

These are large, edible thistles and a popular winter vegetable in some parts, particularly Aragón and Navarra. They are distinctly bitter and taste similar to artichokes, another member of the thistle family. The bitterness can be overpowering if the cardoons aren't blanched before use, but this also removes much of the artichoke flavour, so a balance has to be struck. Prepare cardoons as you would celery, which it resembles in appearance: cut off the root base and separate the stalks. Cut them up if they are enormous and wash them. Drop them in boiling water for a maximum of 5 minutes and drain. When they are cool, peel off the strings and thorny projections with a potato peeler. They are now ready for use in the following recipes.

# Cardos a la aragonesa

1 tablespoon chopped parsley
2 cloves garlic, crushed
3 tablespoons oil
a dozen toasted almonds
1 good pinch saffron
1 heaped tablespoon flour
275ml/9fl oz water (*or* the cooking water from the cardoons if you don't object to the bitterness; try it and see)
450g/1lb blanched cardoons, cut into 5cm/2in pieces

Fry the parsley and garlic in the oil until the garlic starts to brown. Pound the almonds to a paste with the saffron. Stir the flour into the garlicky oil, cook for a couple of minutes and then stir in the water, the almonds and the saffron. Bring to the boil, add the cardoons, season and simmer for 10 minutes or until the cardoons are tender.

# Cardos a la castellana

2 cloves garlic, sliced
60g/2oz serrano ham, diced
3 tablespoons oil
½ onion, finely chopped
½ teaspoon paprika
450g/1lb prepared cardoons, cut in 5cm/2in pieces

Gently fry the garlic and ham in the oil until the garlic starts to brown. Add the onion and let it soften. Stir in the paprika and the pieces of cardoon. Season and moisten with a little water. Cook, uncovered, until the cardoons are tender and the water evaporated.

# Revoltijo de espárragos

This is one of the most common ways of serving asparagus in Andalucía, where the first bundles of thin, spiky wild asparagus appear in the markets after heavy rain as from late February. It is unlikely that you will be able to obtain wild asparagus in Britain, but this recipe works very well with the cultivated variety, especially the thin green kind.

*FOR 1KG/2LB ASPARAGUS:*
1 tablespoon oil
4 cloves garlic, peeled
2 slices stale French bread
1 good pinch saffron
1 pinch ground cumin
1 tablespoon flour
120g/4oz white wine

Slice the asparagus into 2.5cm/1in lengths, keeping the heads separate from the stalks. Cook the stalk pieces in boiling salted water for 5 minutes, then add the heads and cook for 3-4 more minutes. Drain.

Heat the oil in a small frying pan, and fry the whole cloves of garlic and bread until well browned. Remove them to the mortar. Add the saffron and cumin and pound to a paste. Add the flour to the remaining oil and let it brown. Add this to the paste in the mortar, mix it well, then thin it down with the wine. Return this mixture to the frying pan and let it cook for a few minutes until very thick. Stir in the asparagus and let it heat through.

# Espinacas con pasas y piñones

Spinach with raisins and pine-nuts. Of all the recipes that I have come across for this, the method below is for me the best. The secret seems to lie in the anchovies. Be sure to squeeze the cooked spinach as dry as you can, otherwise the dish will be soggy. This recipe is also suitable for Swiss chard.

60g/2oz seedless raisins
900g/2lb spinach
salt
4 tablespoons oil
2 cloves garlic
4 anchovy fillets, chopped
60g/2oz pine-nuts

Pour boiling water over the raisins and leave them to soak. Wash the spinach thoroughly, sprinkle it with salt and pack it into a large saucepan. Cover it and leave it over a medium heat for a few minutes.

Remove the lid and you'll now see that the spinach has collapsed dramatically. Drain it in a colander and leave until cool enough to handle (longer than you think). Press out all the water and slice it up.

Heat the oil in a large frying pan. Gently sauté the crushed garlic and the anchovies for a few minutes. Add the pine-nuts and drained raisins and leave to sizzle for a couple of minutes. Add the spinach and stir it over a low heat until heated through. Serve at once.

# Guisantes y alcachofas a la catalana

A Catalan dish of artichokes and peas.

4 small fresh artichokes
100g/3½oz green bacon, diced small
60g/2oz lard
1 onion, chopped small
1 tomato, peeled and chopped
340g/12oz shelled fresh peas (about 1kg/2¼lb in the pod)
1 small glass aguardiente *or* grappa (say 45ml/1½fl oz)
1 pinch each thyme, oregano, cinnamon
1 bay leaf
1 sprig mint
2 cloves
salt and pepper

Trim the artichokes as explained on page 140; fry the bacon in the lard until the fat from the meat starts to run. Add the onion and let it soften before adding the tomato, peas, artichoke quarters, aguardiente and enough water or light stock just to cover. Add the thyme, oregano, cinnamon, bay leaf, mint and cloves. Season with salt and pepper. Cook uncovered until the vegetables are tender and the liquid somewhat reduced.

# Guisantes a la valenciana

An ingenious idea from Valencia combining fresh peas with a light flavouring of aniseed. It sounds strange but is very successful. Try to use fresh peas if possible.

2 tablespoons oil
1 onion, finely chopped
3 cloves garlic
450g/1lb shelled peas (about 1.35kg/3lb in the pod)
250ml/8fl oz white wine
3 tablespoons dry anis (not Marie Brizzard which is too sweet)
2 tablespoons chopped parsley
1 bay leaf
1 teaspoon thyme
salt and pepper
1 pinch saffron
1 pinch ground cumin

Heat the oil and fry the onion and one clove of crushed garlic until softening. Add the peas and stir for a couple of minutes so that they start to absorb the oil. Pour over the wine and anis, and add the parsley, bay leaf, thyme and some salt and pepper. If the peas aren't covered by liquid add some water until they are. Cover the pan and leave to simmer.

Pound the remaining garlic with the saffron and cumin to make a paste. When the peas are practically tender (this can take at least an hour with the cannonballs you sometimes get in Spain), stir in the paste. Leave to finish cooking uncovered. Boil hard if the sauce is thin – the finished product should be very thick. Let it cool a little before eating.

# Guisantes con jamón

Perhaps the simplest Spanish way with peas is also the best: for about 450g/1lb freshly cooked peas you'll need about a 120g/4oz slice of serrano ham, preferably with a decent quantity of its own delicious fat, and a clove or two of garlic. Melt a little bacon fat or similar, fry the sliced garlic until it starts to brown, then add the ham (cut into pieces) and let it cook for a couple of minutes. Add the peas and cook, stirring, for 2-3 more minutes. Serve sprinkled with parsley.

# Hinojos con jamón

A delightful way with fennel from Aragón, and a popular dish there especially on Holy Tuesday. The fennel is boiled until just tender, briefly sautéed with serrano ham and chorizo, and finished with beaten eggs.

4 medium-sized heads of fennel

salt

120g/4oz chorizo, thinly sliced

175g/6oz serrano ham, diced (it should theoretically be local Teruel ham)

3 tablespoons oil

4 eggs

Cut off any stems from the fennel and remove the outer skins if they seem tough. Otherwise peel them with a potato peeler to rid them of strings. Quarter the fennel, cut out the hard core at the base and slice the quarters quite thickly. Cook them in boiling salted water for a few minutes until just tender. Drain, reserving the cooking water for soups or stews.

Gently fry the chorizo and ham in the oil for a few minutes. Add the fennel and stir it until it is covered with the flavoured oil. Pour in the beaten eggs and continue cooking over a low heat until they are nearly set. Serve at once on warmed plates.

**Note:** Do not season the eggs. The ham and chorizo should provide enough salt.

# Judías verdes a la andaluza

Green beans cooked simply with tomato, onion and garlic; they are also seasoned with vinegar, not enough to taste vinegary but just enough to bring out the flavour of the tomatoes.

2 tablespoons oil

1 onion, sliced

2 cloves garlic

450g/1lb tomatoes, peeled and sliced

225g/8oz green beans, trimmed and cut in half

2 tablespoons vinegar

salt and pepper

Heat the oil in a wide frying pan and fry the onion and crushed garlic until soft. Add the tomatoes and fry until a sauce starts to form. Add the beans, vinegar and some salt and pepper. Cover and simmer for about 15 minutes. Remove the lid and reduce the sauce to a good thick consistency.

# Judías verdes con ajo y aceite

Green beans with oil and garlic: the simplest Spanish way of dressing cooked beans.

450g/1lb green beans, trimmed and cut into 2.5cm/1in lengths
salt
3 tablespoons oil
4 cloves garlic, sliced

Add the beans to boiling salted water and cook for 6-7 minutes at most. Drain them before they are completely tender, and run them under the cold tap.

Heat the oil in a frying pan and fry the garlic until it starts to brown. Add the well-drained beans and a little salt and fry gently, stirring, for a couple of minutes so that the beans heat through.

# Judías verdes a la madrileña

The *madrileños* add paprika to the oil (about a teaspoonful), having first let it cool a little to prevent the paprika burning.

# Judías verdes con champiñones

Green beans sautéed with mushrooms.

450g/1lb French beans, topped and tailed
salt and pepper
2 tablespoons oil
2 cloves garlic, chopped
1 tablespoon chopped parsley
225g/8oz mushrooms, wiped and thickly sliced
1 tablespoon lemon juice
2 tablespoons home-made tomato sauce (see page 131), *or tomato purée*

Cook the beans for about 5 minutes in boiling salted water, drain and quickly refresh them under the cold tap.

Heat the oil in a large frying pan and fry the garlic until it browns. Add the mushrooms, parsley, lemon juice and some salt and pepper. Let them cook gently for about 5 minutes, then add the beans and tomato sauce. Let it all simmer for another 5 minutes or so, and serve.

## POTATOES
### *(Patatas)*

Also known colloquially as *papas*, a word originally borrowed from the Quiche Maya Indians of Guatemala. *Patatas* to a Spaniard means fried potatoes, the usual accompaniment to meat dishes and fried eggs. The Spanish are every bit as fond of them as we are but generally cook them rather better. They season the potatoes with salt before they fry them, and this seems to produce a much better-tasting chip than when they are seasoned afterwards. Many Spanish housewives are ignorant of the 'double cooking' method of making chips, which involves a preliminary cooking of the potatoes in oil, followed by a final crisping in much hotter oil. The chips are simply put into hot oil in an ordinary frying pan and left to fend for themselves, with an occasional stir so they can brown evenly. This method does not produce a perfectly crisp chip, but they taste excellent.

## Patatas en salsa verde

Potatoes in 'green sauce', of which there are many versions. In this one the colour comes from the asparagus, peas and parsley garnishing the potatoes. If allowed to get cold (but not refrigerated) this also makes a good salad.

450g/1lb fresh green asparagus
900g/2lb new potatoes, washed but unpeeled
salt
1 onion, finely chopped
2 cloves garlic, crushed
6 tablespoons oil
225g/8oz peas, fresh if possible
3 tablespoons chopped parsley

Cut the tough ends off the asparagus spears and slice them into 2.5-5cm/1-2in length. Boil the potatoes in salted water until tender. Meanwhile, soften the onion and garlic in the oil. Add the asparagus and some salt, cover and cook gently for 5 minutes. Add the peas and cook for another 5 minutes. The idea is that the vegetables should be *just* tender. If not, cook them a little longer.

Drain the potatoes and peel off their papery skins. Cut up any large ones and add them to the pan with the vegetables. Stir them into the sauce over a low heat until they have absorbed the oil. Add more salt if necessary and stir in the parsley.

Some fresh, raw oil may be added at the table if you like.

# Joecas

Potatoes in garlic sauce with chorizo. This is an old winter dish from the countryside around Córdoba, where it was eaten by olive pickers when lodged for the night in remote farmhouses far from their wives' cooking pots, or on rainy days with no work. Being packed with calories and very cheap, it was ideal. It is for garlic lovers only, but for them a real treat.

oil for deep frying
900g/2lb potatoes, peeled
salt
1 tablespoon flour
4 cloves garlic
1 pinch saffron
3 tablespoons chopped parsley
2-3 tablespoons vinegar
120g/4oz chorizo, sliced

Heat the oil. Slice the potatoes into thick rounds. Season them well with salt and fry until they start to brown. Remove and drain well.

Place the flour in a small dry frying pan and put over a high heat. Stir it round until it's toasted a good brown colour. Place it in the mortar with the garlic, a little salt, the saffron and parsley, and pound it to a paste. Stir in 2 tablespoons of the oil from the potatoes and the vinegar. Place the potatoes in a pan and pour the sauce over them. Add a little water to make the sauce thoroughly coat the potatoes, and heat through gently until very thick and hot. Add more salt and vinegar if necessary.

Dry fry the slices of chorizo until heated through. Add them to the potatoes and serve.

# Patatas a la malagueña

Potatoes in olive sauce from Málaga.

4 tablespoons oil
1 onion, sliced
2 cloves garlic, crushed
1 celery stalk, thinly sliced
1 tomato, peeled and chopped
½ tablespoon paprika
2 tablespoons chopped parsley
450g/1lb potatoes, peeled and cubed
60g/2oz stoned and halved green olives
salt and pepper
2 hard-boiled eggs, chopped

First make a *sofrito*: heat the oil and fry the onion, garlic and celery until they soften. Add the tomato and cook until pulpy. Stir in the paprika and parsley. Add the potatoes, olives and about 600ml/1 pint water. Season with salt and pepper and leave to simmer for at least 20 minutes, or until the potatoes are tender. If the sauce is still runny let it boil quite hard until it's very thick. Sprinkle with the chopped eggs.

Not at its best when eaten boiling hot, so wait until it has cooled somewhat before serving.

# Papas a lo pobre

Poor man's potatoes. They may well be eaten by the badly off, but are probably the best way of enjoying potatoes in Spain and an excellent accompaniment to all sorts of meat dishes. They also make an excellent tapa.

675g/1½lb potatoes, peeled and thinly sliced
salt
oil
4 thick rashers bacon, diced, *or* 120g/4oz slice serrano ham, diced (optional)
1 onion, thinly sliced (sliced green peppers can also be added)

Season the potatoes with salt. Heat enough oil to cover generously the base of a large frying pan (non-stick makes life much easier). Add the bacon or ham and fry briskly until the fat runs. Remove. Add the potatoes and onion to the oil, mix, then cover the pan and leave them to cook gently. Unless they start to catch, they shouldn't be stirred too much or they will turn to mush. When the potatoes are absolutely tender return the bacon (if using) to the pan. Some cooks stop there but they are a bit pale for my liking. I increase the heat to brown some of the potatoes, shaking the pan to stop them sticking – it doesn't matter if they break up a bit. When they are well browned you can add beaten eggs, or put some fried eggs on top. There may be some excess oil: tilt the pan and drain it off.

## PATATAS PANADERAS

These are a similar concept but done in the oven and rather easier to get right. You basically pile sliced potatoes, onions and oil into a roasting dish with some seasoning (I like chopped garlic and parsley as well) and bake until tender and attractively tinged with brown. Don't make the layer of potatoes too deep.

See also *patatas al montón*.

# Papas en ajopollo

A popular Andalusian way with potatoes; they are cooked in a rich sauce of pounded almonds, garlic, saffron, parsley and fried bread, then seasoned with a little lemon juice. The same sauce is also very good with meatballs.

5-6 tablespoons oil
4 cloves garlic, peeled
120g/4oz almonds, blanched and peeled
1 small bunch parsley, washed and well dried
4 slices (about 60g/2oz) stale French bread
1 large pinch saffron
6 peppercorns
900g/2lb potatoes, peeled and cut into smallish chunks
salt
½ lemon

Heat the oil and fry the garlic and almonds until they are browned all over. Transfer them to a mortar or liquidiser (the latter is preferable for this sauce). In the same oil fry the parsley for a few seconds before adding to the ingredients in the blender. Now fry the pieces of bread until brown on both sides. Place them in the blender together with any remaining oil. Add the saffron, peppercorns and 3-4 tablespoons of water. Blend until smooth. Place the potatoes in a saucepan and pour the sauce over them, plus just enough water to cover. Season with salt. Bring to the boil and simmer, covered, for about 15 minutes. Remove the lid and continue cooking gently until the sauce is very thick, shaking the pan frequently to prevent sticking. Season lightly with a squeeze or two of lemon juice and serve.

## Buñuelos de patatas

Mashed potato fritters flavoured with lemon rind and cinnamon. Be sure to use a very light hand with the cinnamon: like cumin, it packs an enormous punch and can leave your taste buds reeling. In this recipe you should hardly notice it.

900g/2lb potatoes, peeled
salt and pepper
90g/3oz butter
2 eggs, beaten
¼ teaspoon (maximum) ground cinnamon
finely grated rind of 1 lemon
4-6 tablespoons flour
oil for frying

Cook the potatoes in boiling salted water until tender. Drain, dry well and mash them. Mix in the butter, eggs, cinnamon, lemon and enough flour to form a fairly stiff mixture. Season with salt and pepper. Heat about 1.25cm/½in of oil and fry a small spoonful of the mixture to test it. If it starts to disintegrate after a little while stiffen the mixture with more flour. Fry small spoonfuls of it until golden-brown on both sides. Drain well on kitchen paper.

## Puré de patatas con setas

Mashed potatoes with fungi and bacon – a marvellous combination of flavours. Use ordinary mushrooms if no fungi are available.

900g/2lb potatoes, peeled
salt and pepper

2 tablespoons oil
225g/8oz smoked bacon, thickly diced
4 cloves garlic, crushed
675g/1½lb fungi (*or* mushrooms), cleaned and thickly sliced
150ml/¼ pint Spanish brandy
butter

Put the potatoes on to boil in some salted water. While they are cooking heat the oil in a wide frying pan and fry the bacon and garlic until they start to brown. Add the fungi, season with salt and pepper and let them cook until all their liquid has evaporated. Pour in the brandy, set it alight and cook until it has evaporated. Mash or sieve the potatoes, season with salt and pepper and add a good lump of butter. Pile them neatly on to a serving dish and pour the mushroom and bacon sauce over and around them. Serve at once.

# Remolachas a la sevillana

Beetroot cooked with sherry. While surely nobody's favourite vegetable, beetroot is sturdy and dependable, and does not require a lot of fuss. Its outrageous colour certainly brightens up the plate, and it makes a nice change once in a while.

2 or 3 large beetroots, stalks and roots intact
salt
1 onion, sliced
1 tablespoon oil
1 tablespoon flour
225ml/8fl oz oloroso sherry

Trim the stalks off the beetroot, leaving a good 2.5cm /1in or so. Rinse the beetroot under the tap, taking care not to break the skin. Cook them in plenty of boiling salted water for about 1½ hours. Drain. When they are cool enough to handle, top and tail them and peel off their skins. Chop into largish cubes (unless you want a purple work-surface don't do this on anything porous).

Fry the onion in the oil until it softens. Add the flour and cook for a minute or so. Gradually stir in the sherry to form a sauce. Add the beetroot and salt and pepper, and simmer for about 15 minutes. Depending on the sweetness of the sherry you may need to add a pinch or two of sugar.

# Huevos
## Eggs

An egg to a Spaniard means a fried egg, just as potatoes signify fried potatoes – *huevos con patatas*, egg and chips, is standard fare for hungry children. The taste for them never leaves the Spaniard and adults often consider
them among their favourite meals. As is so often the case, Spanish cooks ignore all conventional theory and not only cook fried eggs fast but in plenty
of oil as well. They also season them first, and having tried them like this I
think I prefer them to a more traditional egg slowly fried in just a little fat.

Spain's great egg invention is, of course, their tortilla, meaning little cake,
and although there is nothing little about it, a tortilla is cake-like in that it is
solid enough to cut into segments and eat with the fingers. The flavour of a
tortilla is completely different from that of a normal omelette, *tortilla francesa*
as the Spanish call it, mainly because it is cooked more slowly. Nor should
you eat a tortilla hot from the stove; its taste improves as it cools.

My first taste of tortilla was at an impressionable age at a long-deceased
Hampshire prep school. As I wandered through the kitchen one day, my attention was caught by a delicious smell and I asked María, the Spanish lady
who prepared our meals, what she had cooked for her supper. 'Tortilla', she
replied, and gave me a piece from her plate. It was so good, so unlike

anything I had tasted before, that I always asked for 'Spanish omelette' whenever I saw it on a menu, but with decreasing optimism; none of them at that time had anything to do with María's tortilla. It wasn't until I visited Spain for the first time many years later that I finally ate a proper potato tortilla again, and once more I was back at María's elbow in that Hampshire kitchen.

The Spanish are not great boiled-egg eaters: *un huevo pasado por agua*, an egg passed through water, is how they clumsily describe them. However, they enjoy poached eggs in soups and have some wonderful recipes for scrambled eggs. They also have many more complicated ways with eggs, but I have to admit that I'm not a fan of these dishes of fried or baked eggs with sauces and garnishes – the joy of an egg is its delicacy and simplicity.

## Tortilla española/Tortilla de patatas

Spanish omelette, and a reflection of the Spanish genius for creating the most delectable food from the most mundane ingredients – in this case eggs, potatoes and onions. That is all the standard tortilla contains, (though argument rages about including onion or not) and it is usually eaten as a tapa or between hunks of bread as a *bocadillo*, but is lovely with salad or taken on picnics. Eat it lukewarm or at room temperature (but not cold from the fridge). It is incredibly popular in Spain and one never seems to tire of it. It is also very filling. Serves 8 as a tapa, 4 or less as a main course

Approximately 300ml/½ pint olive oil
2 large potatoes, in small, but not tiny, dice
(by large I mean total weight of very roughly 675g/1½lb)
1 large onion, roughly chopped (about 225g/8oz)
salt
4-5 large eggs, well beaten with a pinch of salt

Heat the oil in a medium-sized frying pan (non-stick will help to reduce stress levels) and add the potatoes and a good seasoning of salt. Mix well, cover and cook fairly fast for five minutes, then add the onion and mix in (with a silicone spatula is gentlest). After ten minutes remove the lid. Stir occasionally so that the vegetables cook evenly.

After about fifteen minutes the potato mixture should be tender and have an attractive colour. Put a sieve over a bowl and drain the potatoes and onions into it (keep the oil). Let the hot steam dissipate for five minutes or so, add the hot vegetables to the eggs, mixing in quickly. I now like to let them sit together for a while before continuing. Check for salt. Wipe the pan clean and cover the base with a little of the oil. Heat it over a medium flame and pour in the egg mixture. Leave it to cook quite gently until the bottom has set, shaking the pan every now and then (this helps with the shape and reassures you that it hasn't stuck). Using a palette knife or spatula check that the bottom of the tortilla is completely free of the base.

Now comes the tricky (and often messy) bit: invert a plate or flat saucepan lid over the pan. With one hand on the plate turn the pan upside down with an abrupt movement. The omelette should come away cleanly on to the plate. Return the pan to the heat, add a little extra oil and when it's hot slide the omelette back in. The raw part will now be on the underside but will have left some mess on the plate. Scrape it back into the pan too, pushing it underneath if you can. Keep shaking the pan every now and then so that the edge of the omelette is curved rather than straight. Press the top too so that it's uniformly flat. When the omelette is loose in the pan and its bottom a good colour, slide it out on to a serving plate. The inside should, in an ideal world, still be slightly gooey. Let it cool down for at least ten minutes before eating it, maybe with some fried peppers on the side, a simple salad, some *embutidos ibéricos*...

If all this sounds a bit hair-raising, practice makes perfect, and there is a cheat's way of doing it, though the end product is the wrong shape: instead of inverting the half-cooked omelette on to a plate, place the pan under a hot grill – this cooks the top very efficiently. Then turn out as normal.

In some places, León for example, they take things a stage further, by simmering the cooked omelette in a little sauce of onion, garlic, paprika and so on, and they call it *tortilla guisada*. In Seville you find it finished off with whisky (better than it sounds).

**Note:** the potato mixture can be served as it is, as an accompaniment to meat dishes such as *cochifrito* (page 274) or simply with some fried eggs on top. It is similar, really, to *papas a lo pobre* but known as *patatas al montón*.

# Tortilla campestre

There are lots of versions of this 'country' omelette. This one is very sturdy as the potatoes are mashed before being added to the eggs. The vegetables used are a matter of choice. Peas and sweetcorn are good, but diced carrots and green beans would do very well too.

2 tablespoons oil
1 large onion, sliced
6 eggs
1 tablespoon milk
salt and pepper
4 medium-sized potatoes, peeled, boiled and mashed
about 225g/8oz cooked vegetables

Heat the oil and fry the onion briskly until well browned. Beat the eggs with the milk and some salt and pepper, and stir in the potatoes (still warm if possible). Add the vegetables and drained onions. Cook the omelette in the remaining oil, as for *tortilla española*.

# Tortilla con chorizo

Chorizo omelette with peas and potatoes. This is perhaps the most gorgeous Spanish omelette of all. It is sometimes referred to, mistakenly, as *tortilla sacromonte*. The authentic version of the latter, which comes from Granada, contains lamb's brains, testicles, puppy-dog tails, and so on. For each person allow:

2 small potatoes, diced

oil

salt

½ chorizo, sliced

about 120g/4oz peas

2 beaten eggs

Fry the potatoes in 1.25cm/½in of oil with some salt until tender. Add the chorizo and peas and cook for 5 more minutes. Drain, reserving the oil, and add to the beaten eggs. Heat a little of the oil in the frying pan, add the eggs and continue cooking as for *tortilla española*.

You may think it disgraceful, but this omelette is even nicer spread with some freshly made English mustard and Heinz tomato ketchup.

# Tortilla de alcachofas

Artichoke omelette from Madrid. I was somewhat startled when I first tried this: I thought I knew what artichokes tasted of. But by the simple expedient of frying pieces of fresh artichoke heart with little chunks of serrano ham and then adding them to eggs, the *madrileños* show us that artichokes are at their best if they don't go anywhere near boiling water.

I think this is one of the most beautiful dishes in the Spanish repertoire, and would recommend it as ideal for small fresh artichokes.

120g/4oz serrano ham
10 small artichokes
6 tablespoons oil
salt
6 large eggs

Cut the ham into small dice. Trim and prepare the artichokes as explained on page 140. Cut the hearts into four, remove any choke and cut the quarters in half. Heat the oil in a large frying pan. Add the ham, artichokes and a little salt. Let them fry quite gently, covered, for 15 minutes. Add extra oil if necessary – the ham and artichokes should have a good bath in it but without being submerged. Test a piece of artichoke. When it's just tender, drain off the oil.

Beat the eggs thoroughly and add the warm artichokes and ham. Taste for salt. Heat a little of the oil and cook the omelette as for *tortilla española*. Eat while it is still hot.

## Torta de formigos

*From my childhood years I remember the* torta de formigos *that we used to make in the family hearth as a light supper. It amounts to a tortilla of bread crumbled into milk, then fried in the pan with lard. You add beaten eggs and then form the tortilla . . . In this case the* formigos *resemble a French omelette more than a Spanish one, though more substantial seeing as the bread used was of wheat and called* molete.

Cipriano Torre Enciso, *Cocina Gallega 'Enxebre'*

## Tortilla murciano

The combination of vegetables in this omelette can be varied according to what is available.

1 small aubergine, diced
3 tablespoons oil
1 onion, chopped
½ green pepper, diced
60g/2oz serrano ham, diced

1 small courgette, diced
1 tomato, peeled and chopped
6 eggs

Salt the pieces of aubergine and leave them to drain for an hour or two.

Heat the oil and soften the onion, pepper and ham. Add the aubergine and courgette. When they too have softened, add the tomato. Stew until very thick. Season.

Beat the eggs, add the warm vegetables and make the tortilla in the usual way.

Although I prefer the ones described above, tortillas can be used to make almost any small amount of something go further – sausage, cooked white beans or fish, for example. Care should be taken, however, not to empty six different little pots of leftovers from the back of the fridge into your tortilla. It will taste of nothing in particular and will end up being a leftover itself.

## WILD MUSHROOMS

### (Setas, hongos)

The people of many rural parts of Spain, especially the Basques and Catalans, have always appreciated the wild mushrooms of their lush woodlands and fields. Opinions differ between regions on the merits of various mushrooms, but among the most popular are the *níscalo* or *rovellón* (the saffron milk cap) which is almost the Catalan's national fungus, the *perretxiko* or *moixernó*, (the St George's mushroom), the *negrilla* (grey knight), the *rebozuelo* (chanterelle), the *oronja* (Caesar's mushroom), the *senderuela* (scotch bonnet), the *boletus* (cep), the *gurumelo* (amanita ponderosa), the *parasol* (same in English) the *seta de cardo* (king oyster mushroom), the *trompeta de la muerte* (horn of plenty) and the *lengua de vaca* (the cow's-tongue mushroom). Black truffles are also available – at a price. Come December they have their own fair in the Valdorba region of Navarre. Beware the truffles you see in little jars in Spanish supermarkets, however. They are not the genuine article, have no taste and are a waste of money.

## Revuelto de setas

Scrambled eggs with wild mushrooms. This is a common way of serving fungi in the Basque country and elsewhere, but whereas in other parts of the country cooks often feel the need to embellish the dish with onion and garlic, I like the way the Basques leave the dish's stars, good fresh eggs and delicate fungi, to fend for themselves. The mushrooms are wiped clean, torn into pieces by hand (cutting with a knife can ruin some species), stewed gently in a little oil and then mixed with eggs. All you can taste are eggs and mushrooms, with nothing to distract the attention from such pleasures. This wisdom in simplicity makes a wonderful starter or lunch dish with a plain salad. For each person allow:

3 tablespoons oil
90-120g/3-4oz wild mushrooms
salt
2 large, very fresh eggs

Heat a little oil in a frying pan or *cazuela*. Add the mushrooms, prepared as above, season them with salt and let them stew slowly, stirring occasionally, until the liquid they throw off has disappeared, through evaporation and re-absorption. Break in the eggs and with the heat at a minimum stir gently with a fork until most of the egg has set. Serve at once on warmed plates – the residual heat will finish cooking the eggs.

## Revuelto de grelos y cigalas

Scrambled eggs with turnip tops and scampi. The use of turnip tops indicates the dish's Galician origins, but if they are unobtainable spinach makes an acceptable alternative. I am also rather loath to use fresh scampi in this – as explained elsewhere, I prefer to enjoy these precious things on their own – so I use very large prawns instead.

340g/12oz fresh turnip tops *or* spinach
salt and pepper
450g/1lb fresh scampi *or* large prawns
8 large eggs
2 tablespoons milk
2 tablespoons oil
1 small clove garlic, crushed

Wash the greens thoroughly in two or three changes of water, keeping an eye out for slugs and snails. Cook them with a little salt and the water that clings to their leaves in a covered saucepan over a high heat, turning occasionally, until they are collapsed and tender. Drain thoroughly, then slice roughly.

Peel the tails of the prawns and chop them into three or four pieces. Use the heads and debris to make a broth for fish soup. Beat the eggs well with a little salt, pepper and milk. Heat the oil and gently fry the garlic until it's lightly coloured. Add the prawns and stir for a couple of minutes, then add the greens and let them heat through before pouring in the eggs over a gentle heat. Finish cooking in the normal way, serving the eggs on heated plates garnished with triangles of fried bread. Serve at once.

# Huevos revueltos con bacalao

There are few things more sensuous than a dish of perfectly cooked, creamy scrambled eggs. They seem to me cooking's answer to velvet. In this recipe they're mixed with sticks of cooked potato and fragments of salt-cod. A fine dish for lunch.

175g/6oz salt-cod, not pre-soaked
675g/1½lb potatoes, peeled and sliced into thick matchsticks
oil
1 onion, very finely chopped
10 eggs

Bring the cod almost to the boil in some water. Remove it and let it cool a little. Remove all skin and bones, and chop the flesh quite small. Fry the potatoes in deep oil until tender but not browned. Drain well.

Heat enough oil to cover the bottom of a large frying pan. Add the onion and let it soften. Add the cod and the potatoes and stir until they're thoroughly heated through. Beat the eggs well with a little salt and a good seasoning of pepper. Pour them over the cod and potatoes and leave over a very low heat, stirring quite frequently until the eggs are nearly set but still very creamy. Pile on to warmed plates and eat at once.

# Revoltijo de setas y gambas

Scrambled eggs with fungi and prawns. Lightly flavoured with brandy this is a subtle dish of great quality. Use the best fungi you can lay your hands on. Serves 2.

400g/14oz fresh, uncooked prawns
2 tablespoons oil
225g/8oz fungi, cleaned and sliced

salt and pepper
1-2 tablespoons Spanish brandy
4 eggs, beaten with a little salt

Peel the prawns. (Use the debris to make the broth for a soup.) Heat the oil in a wide frying pan and add the fungi. Sprinkle them with a little salt and the brandy. Cook them rapidly until all their liquid has evaporated. Add the prawns and cook for 2 more minutes, stirring. Pour in the beaten eggs and add a grinding of pepper. Stir occasionally over a low heat until the eggs are nearly set but still creamy. Serve immediately on warmed plates.

## Huevos fritos a la cubana

Although I usually find the acid of tomato sauce too overpowering for fried eggs, this recipe of fried eggs, bananas, rice and tomato sauce is enjoyable, in the child-like way one sometimes enjoys a messy hotchpotch, or the children's tea-time fish fingers instead of that evening's 'proper' food. In fact, instead of tomato sauce I prefer a little stew of pork in tomato. The sweetness of the banana seems to take care of the acidity. Eating this all chopped up and mixed together so that you get a taste of everything at the same time is rather fun, though not, I suppose, ideal for formal dinner parties.

The trick when cooking this is to have everything ready and hot at the same time, leaving the fried eggs until last. First prepare a dish of *lomo con tomate* (page 268). When that's ready boil about 60g/2oz of rice per person. While it's cooking prepare the bananas, one not-very-ripe one per person (very ripe ones will disintegrate). Cut them through the middle, then lengthways. Dip them in milk and then flour. Fry the pieces briefly in oil until lightly browned. Drain them on kitchen paper and fry the eggs, quantities according to appetite.

Arrange everything on individual plates and serve piping hot.

# Arroz

## RICE

Possibly the Moors' greatest contribution to Spanish food was the rice they brought with them in the eighth century, at the beginning of a dominion that was to last, to a greater or lesser degree, for seven hundred years. Although no one can say for certain that they introduced it to Spain, their word for rice, *ar-ruz* or *ar-ruzz*, is almost identical to the Spanish word. The Ancient Greeks called it *oriza* and it was they who first brought it to the Mediterranean in the fourth century BC, after Alexander's invasion of India. From Greece it spread to Egypt, Morocco and thence Spain, where the Moors established rice fields in Andalucía, Murcia, Valencia and Cataluña, with immense growing areas in Calasparra, Hellín and round the Albufera lagoon, 'the little sea' just south of Valencia.

The Spaniards realised the grain's potential and its adaptability, and an enormous variety of rice dishes was born, often out of economic necessity. Rice can be cooked to advantage with either very few or a great many ingredients, depending on the pocket of the cook, who would try to make something interesting with whatever she could spare. This could be gleanings from the marshes like wild duck or frogs or eels, maybe some snails or a rabbit. Some days it might just be leftovers from a *puchero*, or some cheap vegetables as in *arroz sabater*, a dish eaten by the shoemakers of the Alcoy area of Alicante on their days off, or when they simply couldn't afford meat. However, it was preferable to find at least a little meat or fish for the rice, which would nearly always have a *sofrito* as its base flavoured with *ñoras* (see page 32), or paprika in more southerly areas.

There are 'dry' and 'wet' (or 'juicy') rice dishes, *arroces secos* and *arroces caldosos*. If the rice is somewhere in between it is called *meloso*, smooth-textured, literally 'honeyed'. The wet dishes have to be cooked with great care (hence their rarity in restaurants) as the idea is that the rice, once cooked, should still have a reasonable quantity of its cooking liquid left as a sauce. They have to be served promptly, since the heat from the cooking dish means that the rice continues to cook after it leaves the stove, and too much delay will lead it to burst and go mushy, when really it is all but inedible.

I was given an illustration of this at Casa Pepa, a restaurant famous for its rice hidden away down a country track near Ondara in Alicante province. The waiter hovered, his agitation increasing as we took too long over our starters. "¡El arroz está ya!" he repeated nervously about our rice with rock fish, "The rice is ready! The rice is ready!" To his great relief we tucked in just in time.

On the Murcian and Valencian coasts a common *arroz caldoso* is called a *caldero*, after the copper or cast-iron cooking pot in which it's made. *Calderos* were invented by the local fishermen, who prepare them either on board their boats or in a sheltered spot on the beach. They consist of rice cooked with oil, garlic, water and *ñoras*; and nothing else if the day's catch is bad. On a good day, though, plenty of fresh fish will be added and the whole thing eaten with a garlic sauce.

Another *caldoso*, the *perol*, is made in Córdoba in the mild spring and autumn months, when groups of friends or family often go out into the hills with their *perol*. The most popular day of all for this is October 24, the feast day of San Rafael (he's not their patron saint, at least officially, but he did save them from the plague in the Middle Ages). The *perol* is a very deep frying pan and in it will be cooked a wet rice with whatever you fancy – game, shellfish or wild mushrooms for example.

Generally though, *arroces caldosos* are made in *cazuelas* and are often simply called *cazuelas de arroz*. Exceptions, apart from the *caldero* and the *perol*, are the hefty dishes of inland Valencia, such as *arros amb fesols i naps*, a gloriously rib-sticking dish of rice with beans, turnips, wild duck, shin of beef, morcilla, and a pig's ear, snout and trotter. Or *llegumet*, (see page 123) a mixture of rice, vegetables, snails, chard and potatoes. These are cooked in the *olla* or *puchero*. Many of the 'wet' dishes are dressed towards the end of their cooking time with a mixture of paprika gently heated with some oil. This is a most effective touch, and the Asturians do something very similar to their *fabadas* (see page 121).

*Arroces secos* are dishes in which all the cooking liquid has been absorbed by the rice, and include paella. These are also commonly cooked in *cazuelas*, but shallower ones (also called *rossejadoras*), and often in the oven.

*Arros rossejat*, browned rice (it is basically toasted in the oil before the stock is added) is another common form of 'dry' rice. It is frequently made to use up leftovers from a *cocido*, but there are many variations. In Valencia's Marina Alta region, they grow famous muscat grapes, and put the dried fruit into their baked rice (*arròs amb panses*). Another popular dish is *arros engravat* or *arroz empedrado*, a charming name meaning 'cobbled' rice, some beans being the cobbles in question (see also the salad *la empe-drada* on page 86). A famous variation which I tried in Elche is to cook the rice *amb costra*, with a billowing crust of beaten egg added at the end, the rice arriving at the table looking like a giant soufflé.

And then there's paella, a cliché of Valencian and Spanish cooking which has the most awful things done to it, as much by Spanish restaurants as by foreigners trying to imitate it. Perhaps this is the place to try and disentangle some of the mystery and confusion surrounding paella.

*La paella* is a cooking utensil, traditionally of carbon steel but also widely available in polished and black enamelled steel. I am not mad about the stainless steel ones. The base of the *paella* is flat and should be of a good thickness. The pan is circular and shallow, and has two round handles on opposite sides. It is commonly called a *paellera* ('dish for making paella'), although strictly speaking this is incorrect, for the pan gives its name to the food cooked in it, not vice versa. The word itself is old Valencian and probably has its roots in the Latin *patella* (a flat basket in Galicia). The Castilian *paila* and the French *paele* mean the same thing.

The origins of paella are uncertain, but it seems that during the centuries following the establishment of rice in Spain, the peasants of Valencia, more specifically those in the areas L'Horta de Valencia and Ribera del Xuquer, would use the paella pan to cook rice with easily available ingredients from the countryside: tomatoes, beans of various sorts, onions and snails. On special occasions rabbit or duck might be included, and the better-off could afford chicken. Little by little this 'Valencian rice' became more widely known. By the end of the nineteenth century *paella valenciana* had established itself.

Purists claim that a distinction should be made between paella and dishes cooked in a paella pan, and that the word should only be used to describe rice dishes cooked according to the traditions of the area where paella originated. They say that rice dishes cooked in a paella pan but originating elsewhere should not (as seems logical to me) bear the name of their cooking dish. I detect the whisper of splitting hairs. What is certain is that much of the *paella valenciana* served in Spain is no such thing.

Whatever the terminology, rice cooked in a paella pan has become a dish for special occasions. Whole families will troop off to a restaurant to eat it, or make it at home with all those present lending a hand with the preparations. The whole thing becomes a mixture of party, ceremony and debate, or rather, considering the volume at which it is maintained, argument between the master paella cooks who are present and who are all convinced they know best how to make it.

However, there is nothing more agreeable than a paella picnic, when everyone crams themselves into cars, the boots laden with food and drink, to bump their way down to a favourite beach or up into the mountains. There, wood is gathered for the fire and olives and sausage are nibbled, while discussion rages over the rice, glistening yellow and bubbling in the warm air. It is the most sociable of occasions.

# MAKING PAELLA

## THE PAN

The following is a very approximate guide to the size of pan you will need, depending on the number you are cooking for (and appetite):

for 2-3 people, a pan with a 30cm/12in base.
for 4-5 ” ” ” ” ” 40cm/16in ”
for 6-8 ” ” ” ” ” 50cm/20in ”
for 10 ” ” ” ” ” 55cm/22in ”
for 12 ” ” ” ” ” 60cm/24in ”

Making a good paella requires practice, and it is perhaps better to gain experience by cooking it for small numbers at first, maybe using a large shallow frying pan which will produce a perfectly acceptable dish of rice for two or three people.

If you buy a carbon steel paella pan, clean it carefully before using it for the first time, to rid it of any metallic taste: one method is to wash it thoroughly with a mixture of vinegar and fine sand, then rinse it and wash it again with soapy water. You can get away with just the soapy water. After you've dried it, and this applies to every time you use it, sprinkle it with flour, which will absorb any residual moisture and stop the pan rusting. You can oil it to prevent this but if you don't use the pan again for some time the oil may go rancid and sticky, and taint the metal.

## THE FIRE

Making paella on a conventional stove for a party of any size will mean using all the burners. A decent-sized barbecue can be ideal for making paella, but check your pan fits comfortably before you start. You need firewood of various sizes, for the heat must be intense at first, then more moderate. Pine wood is particularly recommended, and bunches of rosemary and thyme added at intervals will produce a fragrant smoke which subtly flavours the rice. A very practical solution for an outdoor paella is to buy one of the portable gas-fired burners designed specifically for making paella and with easy to control flames. These are now available in the UK.

## THE RICE

Use a roundish medium-grain Spanish rice. The *bomba* variety is perhaps to be preferred if you are new to paella cookery as it is less liable to overcook than the *senia* or *bahía* types. There are several reliable brands, for example the 'Flor de Calasparra' brand from Murcia. Do not wash it before cooking. If the rice is well cooked it is the star of the show, no matter how extravagant the other ingredients. Generally allow about 100g/3½ oz per person.

## THE SAFFRON

You should naturally use real saffron for its subtle flavour. Wrap the threads in silver paper and leave them in a low oven or near a flame for about 10 minutes. This toasts and dries the saffron and makes it easier to pound up, and also means you get the maximum colouring power out of it. *Colorante* (see page 33) can be used to boost the colour, but should never be used as a substitute for the real thing (though it frequently is).

## THE BROTH

You need at least 2½ times the volume of water or broth to rice, though the absorption rate differs from brand to brand. Expert paella makers, of course, do it by eye (traditionally you add enough liquid to reach where the handles are bolted to the sides) but this is risky for the less experienced. The broth should always be boiling when added to the rice. It is best not to add liquid during cooking, but it is not disastrous if you have to. A good tip is to boil a sprig of rosemary for a minute or two in the cooking liquid. This was originally done when snails weren't available and was thought to imitate the taste they would have provided.

## OTHER POINTS

The heat should be high for the first 8-10 minutes after the broth is added to the rice, then be reduced gradually as the rice dries out. The rice takes 18-20 minutes to cook, but must be removed from the heat while it is still firm to the bite and with a light coating of liquid. The pan is then covered with a lid, sheets of foil, large towels or even bunches of herbs to finish cooking in its own heat for 5 minutes. In a perfect paella the rice will be *en su punto* (with exactly the right texture) and will have completely absorbed all the cooking liquid. It's not an easy trick to pull off but practice makes perfect.

Try not to stir the rice while it is cooking. Instead, grip the pan by its handles and shake it. Go very carefully: a large paella for several people could easily tip over – believe me, I've seen it happen. Get someone to help if need be. Do not cover the rice while it is cooking. The *socarrat* or *socarraet*, a layer of lightly scorched and caramelised rice (not burnt, but it happens to the best of us), will ideally form on the base, which is one of the reasons why it's a mistake to stir the rice as you would a risotto. This is delicious, and for some people the most desirable part of the dish.

# La paella nuestra

The standard *paella valenciana* contains chicken, rabbit, snails and a selection of local beans. The recipe I prefer I call *paella nuestra*, our paella, the one my friends and I make, with a mixture of meat and shellfish. It is a lot of work, so get some help. It is for eight people.

2 litres/3½ pints light chicken stock

16 fresh mussels

oil

8 large cloves garlic, peeled

leaves from 1 small bunch parsley

2 good pinches saffron, toasted

1 x 2lb/1 kg chicken, skinned and cut into small pieces

450g/1lb belly pork, cubed

450g/1lb squid, cleaned and prepared as explained on page 220

2 teaspoons Spanish paprika

900g/2lb tomatoes, peeled and chopped

900g/2lb green peppers, chopped

790g/1¾lb rice

450g/1lb raw prawns in the shell

450g/1lb fresh clams

4 lemons, quartered

120g/4oz cooked peas

1 red pepper, roasted, peeled and sliced into long thin strips

A few cooked prawns for decoration

Bring the stock to the boil and drop in the mussels. Remove them as they open. Discard the empty halves of the shells. Strain the stock to rid it of sand and grit.

Heat enough oil in the paella pan to cover its base. Brown four of the garlic cloves, whole, and remove them to a mortar. Quickly fry the parsley in the same oil for a few seconds until crisp. It should be dry or it will spit. Add it to the garlic, add the saffron and pound it all to a paste.

In the remaining oil fry the chicken and pork, previously seasoned with salt, until well browned. Add the squid, tomatoes, peppers and remaining garlic, sliced. Cook until soft. Stir in the paprika, then the rice. Cook, stirring frequently, for a couple of minutes. Now add the boiling stock and the *majado* (the pulp from the mortar).

Let the rice boil rapidly for 8-10 minutes, by which time it will be visible through the surface of the cooking liquid. Now reduce the heat to medium and then progressively lower it over the next 8-10 minutes. Five minutes or so before the end add the prawns and clams. Test a grain of rice. If it is still a little chalky, leave the paella to cook a little longer. If it is firm to the bite remove the pan from the heat.

Now decorate the paella: cut a little way into the rind of the lemon segments, following the line of the flesh, and wedge them round the edge of the pan; this is for people who like to season their rice with lemon juice. Scatter over the cooked peas. Make a spoked wheel pattern radiating out from the centre with the strips of red pepper. Place the mussels and reserved prawns around the surface of the rice at strategic intervals. Cover with a lid (if you have one large enough), sheets of tinfoil or a large clean towel and leave to rest for at least 5 minutes. Now tuck in greedily. It's as well to provide spare plates for the shells, and plenty of napkins.

**Note:** If fresh raw prawns and clams are not available, substitute cooked prawns for the former, peeling them first. Add the heads and shells to the cooking broth and boil them for a few minutes to extract the maximum flavour. Add the peeled prawns to the rice right at the end of the cooking time. Fresh cockles are a possible alternative to clams, or you could use tinned clams, though it's probably not worth the bother.

If you want to eat paella the traditional way, get everyone to sit round the pan and arm them with a spoon (people would have their own well-worn wooden spoon in the old days). Give any children their plateful from the centre of the pan. The gap left is for you to put any bits of meat and so on that you don't want so that others can help themselves. Etiquette demands that you keep strictly to your triangle of rice, starting at the rim and working your way inwards.

**Leftovers:** Fry a chopped clove of garlic in a little olive oil, then add the cold paella. Stir fry until the rice is really spanking hot again. Alternatively, make *croquetas de paella*. Take out all the meat and seafood, chop them finely and mix with the rice, adding a beaten egg to bind the mixture together. Season with salt and pepper and form the mixture into small croquettes. Roll them in dried breadcrumbs and fry in hot oil until well browned. This absolutely delicious way of using up leftover paella is from Penelope Casas' book *The Foods and Wines of Spain* (1985).

## La fideuá/Rossejat de fideus

These are increasingly popular versions of paella made with noodles instead of rice.

# Arroz a la sevillana

A superb paella from Sevilla with a glorious taste of the sea provided by squid, clams and monkfish. The hints of serrano ham and chorizo supply unexpected and delightful contrast.

oil
½ onion, finely chopped
4 cloves garlic, crushed
60g/2oz serrano ham, diced
225g/8oz sliced squid (see page 220)
400g/14oz rice
a good pinch saffron, toasted
225g/8oz fresh clams
225g/8oz monkfish, sliced
2 tablespoons chopped parsley
about 1.25 litres/2¼ pints boiling water
salt and pepper
60g/2oz chorizo, thinly sliced
1 hard-boiled egg
1 red pepper, roasted, peeled and thinly sliced
120g/4oz cooked peas

Heat enough oil to cover the base of a paella pan, and soften the onion and garlic. Add the ham and squid and cook until the squid changes colour. Add the rice and stir until it starts to become transparent. Now add the saffron, clams, monkfish, parsley and most of the boiling water. Season, and cook as described on pages 172-73, adding more water if necessary. Before serving, decorate with the slices of chorizo, hard-boiled egg, red pepper and peas, and cover the pan so that they can warm through.

# Arroz con almejas

Rice with clams. This makes a nice change from more elaborate rice dishes, and in fact the flavour of these clams is so good that it doesn't really need much help – it stands perfectly well on its own, supported only by a *sofrito* and saffron.

about 1.25 litres/2¼ pints water
900g/2lb small clams

1 large pinch saffron
4 tablespoons oil
2 onions, chopped
2 tomatoes, peeled and chopped
½ red and ½ green pepper, chopped
1 tablespoon paprika
400g/14oz rice
3 cloves garlic, crushed
salt

Boil the water and drop in the clams. Remove them as they open, then take the meat from the shells. Strain the cooking liquor and soak the saffron in a little of it.

Heat the oil in a paella pan and soften the onion and peppers in it. Add the tomatoes and cook until they are pulpy. Stir in the paprika and then the rice, cooking until the latter starts to go transparent. Add the saffron, garlic and most of the boiling broth. Add salt if necessary. Continue cooking in the usual way (see page 172), adding the clams towards the end. Add more water if necessary.

# Arroz con atún

A glorious paella of fresh tuna, artichokes and peas.

550g/1¼lb fresh tuna, cut into small cubes (or use swordfish as an alternative)
salt
6 tablespoons oil
2 green peppers, sliced
1 head garlic, the cloves peeled and sliced
400g/14oz shelled peas
400g/14oz rice
8 artichokes, trimmed and quartered as explained on page 140
1 good pinch saffron, toasted
1 ñora, soaked as explained on pages 32-33
about 1.25 litres/2¼ pints water

Season the fish with salt and fry in the oil until it changes colour. Remove and set aside. Add the peppers and garlic and fry until the garlic starts to brown. Add the artichoke hearts and peas, season with a little more salt and fry for 2 more minutes. Add the rice and cook over a fairly high heat until it starts to go transparent. Pound the saffron with the pulp from the *ñora* and add it to the rice with most of the water. Cook the paella in the normal way (see page 172), adding more liquid if necessary.

## Arroz con bacalao

Rice with salt-cod – a 'widowed' paella for Fridays and other fast days.

450g/1lb salt-cod
6 tablespoons oil
2 tomatoes, peeled and chopped
4 cloves garlic
2 tablespoons chopped parsley
3 cloves
1 good pinch saffron
about 1.25 litres/2¼ pints boiling water
400g/14oz rice
black pepper
2 roasted red peppers, sliced in strips for decoration

Toast the unsoaked piece of salt-cod over a flame until scorched. Carefully remove all skin and bones, then chop the meat – there should be about 250-280g/9-10oz. Put it in a sieve and rinse well under the tap.

Heat the oil in a paella pan and fry the tomato, crushed garlic and parsley until soft. Pound the cloves and saffron to a powder and dilute with a little of the water. Add it to the pan along with the rice. Stir the rice until it starts to go transparent. Season with black pepper, add the cod and most of the boiling water. Continue cooking in the usual way (see page 172), adding more water if necessary. Decorate with the strips of red pepper before serving.

## Arroz con cordero

Lamb and rice is not a common combination in Spain, but is delicious nonetheless. I came across it in the *Manual de Cocina*, a modern Spanish equivalent of Mrs Beeton. This is an adaptation of the recipe.

900g/2lb boned leg of lamb, diced
salt and pepper
2 cloves garlic, crushed
1 onion, finely chopped
3 tablespoons oil
150ml/¼ pint red wine
400g/14oz rice
1 good pinch saffron, toasted
about 1.25 litres/2¼ pints light stock

Season the lamb with salt and pepper and mix well with the crushed garlic. Soften the onion in the oil, then add the lamb pieces and fry them, stirring occasionally, until they have changed colour and thrown off some of their juices. Pour in the red wine and let it simmer until it has evaporated, by which time the lamb will be more or less tender. Meanwhile, bring the stock to the boil. Add the rice to the lamb and stir until it goes transparent. Crumble in the saffron and pour in most of the boiling stock. Check the seasoning and finish cooking in the usual way (see page 172), adding more liquid if necessary.

## Arroz con costillas

A plain but good dish of rice and pork.

675g/1½lb meaty pork ribs, cubed
salt
4 tablespoons oil
3 cloves garlic, peeled
1 good pinch saffron, toasted
3 tablespoons chopped parsley
2 red peppers, sliced
2 tomatoes, peeled and chopped
400g/14oz rice
1 teaspoon paprika
about 1.25 litres/2¼ pints water or light stock

Season the meat with salt. Heat the oil and fry the whole garlic until brown. Remove it to a mortar and pound to a pulp with the saffron and parsley. Now fry the meat in the oil until well browned all over. Add the peppers and cook for 5 minutes, then add the tomatoes and cook until they become pulpy. Stir in the rice and let it cook for a couple of minutes until it starts to go transparent. Bring the stock to the boil, add the paprika to the rice and most of the stock. Scrape in the mixture from the mortar and cook in the usual way (see page 172), adding more liquid if necessary.

# Arroz con pollo y setas secas

Rice with chicken and dried mushrooms.

about 45g/1½oz dried mushrooms
about 1.25 litres/2¼ pints hot chicken stock
6 tablespoons oil
1kg/2lb chicken, cut into small pieces and skinned
6 cloves garlic, crushed
1 green pepper, sliced
1 tomato, peeled and sliced
400g/14oz rice
1 good pinch saffron, toasted
225g/8oz green beans, cut into 2.5cm /1in lengths

Soak the mushrooms in some of the hot stock until soft. Strain the soaking liquid back into the stock through a fine sieve.

Heat the oil in a paella pan, add the chicken and garlic and fry gently until they both start to brown. Add the mushrooms, pepper and tomato and let them soften. Stir in the rice and cook until it starts to go transparent. Crumble in the saffron, boil the broth and add most of it with the beans, and check the seasoning. Cook in the usual way (see page 172), adding more liquid if necessary.

# Arroz con habas

A simple Murcian dish of rice and broad beans.

4 tablespoons oil
1 onion, finely chopped
400g/14oz fresh broad beans (about 1.5kg/3lb in the pod)

5 cloves garlic
400g/14oz rice
3 tablespoons chopped parsley
2 tablespoons chopped mint
about 1.25 litres/2¼ pints boiling water
1½ teaspoons coriander seeds
2 teaspoons black peppercorns
4 cloves
1 pinch ground cumin
2 teaspoons paprika

Heat the oil in a *cazuela* and gently fry the onion, beans and three of the garlic cloves, crushed, for about 10 minutes. Stir in the rice, parsley and mint and cook until the rice starts to go transparent. Add most of the boiling water and some salt. Leave to cook while you pound to a paste the 2 remaining cloves of garlic, the coriander, peppercorns, cloves, cumin and paprika. Thin it down with a little water, and when the rice has been cooking for about 10 minutes stir it in. Finish in the usual way (see page 172), adding more liquid if necessary.

## Arroz con garbanzos fritos

Rice with fried chickpeas. This sounds barbarously over the top, but the combination of the light crunchy chickpeas and the softer, slightly resilient rice is a most agreeable one. Depth of flavour is provided by a thick, well-reduced tomato sauce. Some people top it all off with a fried egg or two. Needless to say, it is rather filling.

340g/12oz chickpeas, soaked overnight
salt
225-280g/8-10oz rice
sunflower oil for frying
*FOR THE SAUCE:*
2 onions, chopped
4 cloves garlic, crushed
½ green pepper, sliced
3 tablespoons oil

790g/1¾lb tomatoes, peeled and roughly chopped
1 teaspoon sugar
2 tablespoons chopped parsley
1 bay leaf
¼ teaspoon each oregano and thyme

Cover the chickpeas well with water, add a little salt, bring to the boil and simmer until just tender. The time depends on the chickpeas; start testing them after about an hour. Drain well and set aside.

Meanwhile, make the sauce. Fry the onion, garlic and green pepper in the oil until wilted. Add the tomatoes, a teaspoon of sugar and the herbs. Cook steadily until thick and pulpy.

Cook the rice in boiling salted water. Drain well and place on a warmed serving dish. Cover with the tomato sauce and keep it all warm while you fry the chickpeas in 5cm/2in of very hot oil. They are ready when they go golden-brown in colour and start to smell, strangely, of frying bacon. Drain them on kitchen paper, scatter them over the rice and serve.

**Note:** The above is a good, all-purpose tomato sauce; liquidised, and with the addition of a little white wine, garlic and chilli it becomes *salsa brava*, to be eaten poured over cubes of fried potato for a classic tapa, or tortilla. In this case the sauce must have a very concentrated flavour of tomato and it must be quite fiery. For extra piquancy crush the garlic directly into the sauce. A few skinned and crumbled chorizos added to *salsa brava* and heated through make an excellent sauce for spaghetti.

## Arroz con verduras

Another Murcian rice dish. In this one a wide variety of vegetables produces a beautiful, comparatively light paella, its flavour boosted with fried garlic and almonds. Use fresh vegetables if possible.

about 1.25 litres/2¼ pints water
salt
2 large carrots, sliced
225g/8oz shelled broad beans
4 tablespoons oil
4 cloves garlic
2 dozen almonds, blanched and skinned
a good pinch saffron, toasted
1 onion, finely chopped

2 red peppers, diced
2 tomatoes, peeled and chopped
400g/14oz rice
4 tablespoons chopped parsley
4 artichoke hearts, quartered (see page 140)
225g/8oz green beans
225g/8oz shelled peas
4 hard-boiled eggs, sliced

Bring the water to the boil, add salt and cook the carrots and broad beans for 5 minutes. Drain, reserving the cooking water.

Heat the oil in a paella pan and fry the garlic and almonds until brown. Transfer them to a mortar and pound to a paste with the saffron. Soften the onion and red pepper in the same oil, then add the tomatoes and cook for 5 more minutes. Add the rice and stir until it starts to go transparent. Add the parsley, carrots, artichokes, both sorts of beans and the peas. Pour in most of the hot broth, check for salt and add the pounded garlic and almonds. Cook in the usual way, adding more liquid if necessary and decorating the rice with the egg slices before covering it.

## Cazuela de arroz a la marinera

This 'rice casserole' is an *arroz caldoso*, a dish halfway between a paella and a soup, rather in the manner of Italy's *risi e bisi*. This is a recipe for spring, when the first asparagus appears in the markets. In the south of Spain this would be at the end of February or early March, and the asparagus will often be wild. Use fresh peas too if you can: the combination of these new, young vegetables with seafood is delectable. Cook, or at least serve it, in an earthenware *cazuela* if possible. Serves 6.

450g/1lb fresh clams (*or cockles*)
about 2 litres/3½ pints water
450g/1lb giant prawns (*langostinos*) in the shell
1 onion, chopped
1 green pepper, sliced
4 tablespoons oil
1 tomato, peeled and chopped
1 tablespoon paprika

225g/8oz shelled peas (about three times that weight in the pod)
450g/1lb monkfish, sliced
450g/1lb thin green asparagus, sliced into 2.5cm/1in lengths
4 cloves garlic
1 good pinch saffron
3 tablespoons chopped parsley
salt
550g/1¼lb rice

Open the clams in some of the water over a high heat. Remove and shell them. It's worth persevering with those that appear unwilling to open – clams often have an understandable reluctance to give up the ghost. However, if there are still some unopened after about 10 minutes they were almost certainly dead when you bought them and should be discarded.

Peel the prawns, then put the shells and heads into the clam broth and boil them for ten minutes or so, skimming as necessary, then strain, discarding the debris.

Soften the onion and pepper in the oil in the *cazuela*. Add the tomato and paprika and cook until pulpy. Add the peas and asparagus to the pan and pour in the broth and prawn juices. Add more water to cover if necessary. Cover and simmer until nearly tender.

Pound the garlic with the saffron, parsley and a little salt. Add to the *cazuela* along with the rice, monkfish and prawns. Check for seasoning. Simmer uncovered for about 15 minutes or until the rice is practically done and the sauce thick but still liquid. Stir in the reserved clams, garnish with lemon quarters and serve.

# Cazuela de arroz con pollo

This simple *arroz caldoso* with chicken is a popular everyday rice dish.

4 tablespoons oil
salt and pepper
900g/2lb chicken, cut in small pieces and skinned
4 cloves garlic
2 medium-sized potatoes, peeled and cubed
1 green pepper, sliced
1 tomato, peeled and chopped
340g/12oz rice

juice of 1 lemon

about 1 litre/2 pints chicken stock

2 tablespoons chopped parsley

1 good pinch saffron

Heat the oil and fry the seasoned chicken until browned all over. Remove and reserve. Fry half the peeled garlic in the oil until browned and transfer to the mortar. In the remaining oil fry the potatoes until they start to brown, add the green pepper and let it brown slightly also before adding the tomato and letting it soften. Return the chicken to the *cazuela*, add the rice, lemon juice, some seasoning and the boiling stock. Pound the fried garlic with the two raw cloves, the parsley and the saffron. Stir the paste into the rice and cook for about 15 minutes, when the rice should be nearly tender. Remove from the heat and take to the table. By the time it is served it should be just right.

# Caldero murciano

Along with the very similar *caldero valenciano*, this is a famous fisherman's dish from the Murcian and south Valencian coasts. Whatever fish can be spared from the day's catch is boiled in a broth flavoured with *ñoras* and garlic. Once the fish is cooked it is removed and rice added to the broth. It is eaten as two courses, with an allioli to accompany the fish. There is some dispute as to which should be eaten first, the fish or the rice. I prefer to start with the rice, keeping the fish warm while doing so. Either way, it is all very delicious.

As to which fish to use, just buy whatever happens to be freshest and most appealing in the fish-monger's that day, with the proviso that it should be firm-fleshed. In Spain they tend to use rather bony rockfish which are otherwise difficult to sell.

1kg/2¼lb fish, with heads

salt

white wine

1 onion

6 peppercorns

1 bay leaf

4 parsley stalks

1 piece carrot

oil

2 tomatoes, peeled and chopped
4 *ñoras*, soaked as explained on pages 32-33
8 cloves garlic
400g/14oz rice
225g/8oz large, raw prawns, if available
allioli (see page 188) or garlic mayonnaise

Scale, clean and remove the heads from the fish. Either fillet it or cut it into thick slices. Sprinkle with salt and set aside.

Now make a broth with the fish heads: cover them with plenty of cold water (you will need to finish with about 2 litres/3½ pints). Add a little white wine, bring to the boil and skim. Add a sliced onion, peppercorns, bay leaf, parsley stalks, a piece of carrot and salt. Cover and simmer for 30 minutes. Strain.

Clean the pan and heat enough oil in it to cover its base. Soften the tomato in it and then add the 2 litres/3½ pints of broth. While it is coming to the boil, halve the *ñoras* and scrape the flesh from the skins into a mortar. Add the peeled garlic and pound to a pulp. Add this to the broth. When it boils put in the fish pieces and simmer for 10 minutes. Remove the fish to a plate, cover it with foil and keep it warm in a low oven.

Check the broth for seasoning. Add the rice and prawns and boil for 15 minutes. Taste the rice. If it seems nearly done, remove the pan from the heat. The rice should be fairly liquid and by the time you have served it it should be perfect. Follow it with the fish accompanied by a bowl of allioli or, perhaps better, garlic mayonnaise.

It should be stressed that 'wet' rice dishes such as this can't wait too long for people to come and eat them because they soon become soggy and unpleasant.

# Arroz a banda

*Banda* means here the side of a boat, hence the name of this rice dish which was originally cooked on the beach with the fishing boat acting as windbreak. The fishermen in and around Villajoyosa in Valencia probably invented it, but it is popular throughout much of the Mediterranean coast. It is often simply a 'dry' version of the *caldero* above, that is, the rice is cooked in less of the fish broth, the rest of which may go into a sauce called *salmorreta* of tomato, paprika, parsley, oil and sometimes vinegar which is eaten with the fish. Or it may be added to pounded garlic to form *allioli bord* and used to moisten the fish.

about 675g/1½lb fresh, firm fleshed fish cut into 8 slices

salt

1 onion, thinly sliced

4 tablespoons oil

2 cloves garlic, crushed

280g/10oz potatoes, thickly sliced (optional)

1 teaspoon paprika

about 1½ litres/2¾ pints broth made with the fish heads (locally they would also add

morralla, a selection of any available cheap rock fish, little crabs and so on)

1 bay leaf

*FOR THE RICE:*

1 good pinch saffron

3 tablespoons oil

4 cloves garlic, sliced

1 teaspoon paprika

400g/14oz rice

allioli (see page 188) or garlic mayonnaise

Season the fish with salt. Soften the onion in the oil, then add the potatoes and garlic and cook for 5 more minutes. Stir in the paprika and the water or broth, add the bay leaf and bring to the boil. Cover and simmer for 10 minutes. Add the slices of fish and cook gently, still covered, for 5 more minutes. Remove from the heat and set aside.

Now prepare the rice: soak the saffron in a little of the hot broth. Heat the oil in a paella or large shallow frying pan and gently fry the garlic until it starts to brown. Add the paprika, let it sizzle for a few seconds, then pour in the rice. Stir it into the flavoured oil for a few minutes. In the meantime transfer the fish, potatoes and onions to a plate, cover it with foil and put it in the oven to keep warm. Measure the broth – you need about 1.25 litres/2¼ pints, depending on the type of rice. Pour most of it into the rice, add the saffron and continue cooking the paella in the normal way (see page 172), adding more broth if necessary.

Serve the rice first, followed by the fish and potatoes, if using, or vice versa. Accompany both with the allioli or garlic mayonnaise.

# Salsas
## SAUCES

This is the shortest chapter in the book, for the idea of making a separate sauce to pour over a piece of meat or fish does not occur naturally to the Spanish consciousness. Their sauces usually act as condiments, that is they are strongly flavoured or very rich and are for eating as an accompaniment. One frequently comes across meat or fish bluntly and unhelpfully described as being in sauce, but these have been cooked in the sauce in question, not apart from it.

## Mayonesa

The best, most evocative word I ever saw used to describe mayonnaise was 'ointment' (in Elizabeth David's *French Provincial Cooking*) which seems to me to be exactly right, suggesting something smooth, glistening and elegant. Mayonnaise has a sensuous touch on the palate and makes one glad of summer days and salads. In Spain they eat it with a passion and, indeed, claim it as their own invention (from Mahón in Mallorca). They use it wherever they can – for enriching soups, dipping asparagus, eating with grilled fish, fried squid, fritters, instead of cheese for gratins, and so on.

Many people are reluctant to make it themselves, despite the efforts of hordes of cookery writers to persuade them that it can be made in next to no time. The received wisdom has always been to use egg yolks, oil and mixing bowl at room temperature. I was aghast therefore when my friend José, ignorant of culinary law, set about making mayonnaise with whole eggs straight from the fridge. In vain did I assure him that you can't make mayonnaise like that, it will curdle. Well, you can and it doesn't. He produced a two-egg mayonnaise in little more than a minute using a hand-held electric beater, and very good it was too: so much for received wisdom. José's recipe is the one I include here.

2 whole eggs from the fridge
300ml/½ pint light olive oil
¼ teaspoon salt
lemon juice *or* vinegar to taste

Break the eggs into a liquidiser goblet or food processor bowl. Add the salt and liquidise or beat with an electric beater until creamy. Start adding the oil: with this method there is no need to start drop by drop. Add it in a thin trickle at first, then, as it starts to thicken you can be more daring and add the oil in largish slugs until it's all thick and emulsified. Season with more salt if necessary and sharpen with lemon juice or vinegar.

# Allioli

Also known as *ajiaceite, ajolio, ajoaceite* and as *aïoli* in France. This is a very ancient sauce of which the Catalans especially are very fond, daubing it on anything they can lay their hands on. The name means garlic and oil in Catalan and that is all the true Catalan allioli (also spelt all-i-oli and alioli) consists of. Mayonnaise with garlic added is not the same thing at all, although delicious, but is often erroneously called allioli nonetheless. Such a mayonnaise can be used with abandon: allioli cannot, even, I suspect, by the most ardent garlic lover. It is better employed as a relish, as you would other powerful condiments such as horseradish sauce or mustard. The pure flavours of garlic and good oil, aided solely by a little salt, can have startlingly good effects on the plainest of foods.

As with any emulsion, the problems lie in the early stages, and allioli, without the benefit of egg yolk, is particularly delicate. However, once the garlic has 'taken' to the oil you should be all right.

Failure is inevitable from time to time; on such occasions use an egg yolk to rescue it and continue as for mayonnaise.

5-6 cloves of garlic, depending on size
½ teaspoon salt
about 90ml/3fl oz best olive oil

Peel and slice the garlic into the mortar. Add the salt and pound to a smooth paste. Now start adding the oil with extreme care, literally drop by drop at first, stirring vigorously with the pestle all the time *and always in the same direction.* I've no idea why this is vital but it does seem to be so. As the allioli starts to thicken you can be a little more adventurous with the oil, but only to the extent of increasing it to a small dribble. It takes time, and your wrist will ache, but the effort is worth it. You will end up with a beautiful golden sauce the colour of butter, and very solid. There won't appear to be much but a little goes a long way.

I particularly like allioli with fine-tasting vegetables – new potatoes or broccoli, for instance. With fish I have to admit a preference for garlic mayonnaise.

# Salsa romesco

One of the few certainties about this almost legendary Catalan sauce is that there is no one correct version. It originated in Tarragona, where it is particularly popular, but it is used throughout Cataluña to accompany plain fish or meat dishes or salad leaves. The only constants appear to be *ñoras*, garlic, nuts and bread pounded together. Tomatoes, chillies, oil and vinegar often find their way in, while some claim that the secret of a good *romesco* lies in a final touch of alcohol, for example, *vino rancio* or absinthe. All versions are better after being left for a few hours before use.

Here is one version. The quantities given produce about 600ml /1 pint of sauce.

2 *ñoras* (see pages 32-33)
450g/1lb tomatoes
4 cloves garlic
4 slices stale French bread
30g/1oz hazelnuts *or* almonds *or* a mixture of both
1 tablespoon vinegar
5 tablespoons oil

Remove the stalks from the *ñoras*, shake out as many seeds as possible and leave to soak in cold water for about an hour.

Heat the grill to medium-hot and place under it the unpeeled tomatoes, unpeeled garlic and bread. Slice the tomatoes in half if they are very big – the idea is to cook them just enough for them to lose their raw taste. Turn them over as they brown and remove them once they are browned all over. Slip off the skins of the garlic and tomatoes and remove the seeds from the latter. Place the garlic, tomatoes, bread, nuts and *ñoras* in a liquidiser with some salt, and process until very smooth. Add the vinegar, then the oil spoonful by spoonful, blending well between additions.

Leave the sauce to stand for 3-4 hours before you use it. It is particularly good with bitter salad leaves. When using the sauce as a dressing, thin it down with a little more oil.

## La picada

This is used to thicken and flavour stews in Cataluña, usually being stirred in at the end. There is no fixed recipe, but it will contain pounded garlic, parsley, toasted almonds, pine-nuts, hazelnuts, toasted or fried bread (or breadcrumbs) and sometimes the liver of the animal being used. The paste is thinned down to a cream with a little stock or liquor from the stew.

# Picadilla

An excellent sauce from Valencia for serving with poached fish – I particularly like it with trout, and it is also good with *arencas* (see sardines, page 218).

60g/2oz hazelnuts
60g/2oz almonds, blanched and peeled
3 cloves garlic
salt
120g/4oz oil
vinegar to taste

Toast the nuts in a hot oven until brown. Rub off the skins from the hazelnuts. Place the nuts and garlic in a mortar with a little salt, and pound to a paste; this is easier done in batches. Transfer the paste to a blender. With the motor running, gradually add the oil until you have a smooth, creamy-brown sauce. Season it very lightly with vinegar.

# Ajada, allada

A Galician sauce of oil, vinegar, garlic and paprika that acts as a hot dressing for fish. See recipes for *pulpo en ajada* (page 210), *bacalao con coliflor en ajada* (page 217) and *merluza a la gallega* (page 204).

# Pescado

## FISH

One is tempted to run amok in a Spanish fish market, like someone dying of thirst just arrived at an oasis. Then one discovers that even in Spain such things have a price. 'The turbot, señor? £30. That crawfish? £25. Perhaps some elvers at £2 an ounce? Or some fresh hake, a sea bream . . .' (These are prices from the early eighties!) The prices of the top fish have gone through the roof, for demand has now far outstripped supply, and one settles humbly for something a little more accessible.

It is impossible to say which part of Spain has the best seafood. Each coastal region is adamant that its fish is beyond compare, and it is true that certain fish are especially good in, or are the speciality of, particular places: hake in the Basque country, scallops and other shellfish in Galicia, eels in Valencia, anchovies in Andalucía, the *mero* and *corvallo* in Cataluña and so on. Popularity of species varies from region to region, and anything new on the slab will be eyed with suspicion. In my local market, for example, the occasional appearance of a John Dory will provoke curiosity and pointing fingers, but few people overcome their conservative instincts and actually buy one.

To an English visitor, the Spanish passion for fish is not only a delight and a surprise but cause for a little resentment. Coastal towns are full of bars and restaurants packed with people enjoying the fruits of the local sea. Madrid, in the dead centre of Spain and hundreds of miles from salt water, is the clinching proof that if the public wants something badly enough suppliers will respond. Walking through Madrid in high summer one sees window after window of the local bars stacked with the freshest and widest variety of fish imaginable. These have been rushed to the capital by plane.

But technology has not always kept up with demand. In the past, the long and hazardous journey from the coast, often taking four or five days, meant that much of the fish had to be dried or smoked en route. Salting and drying fish to preserve it goes back to Carthaginian times, when salt mines were opened in San Pedro de Pinatar in Murcia. Under the Romans, the invaders' passion for *garum*, that salty, fishy seasoning, led to the appearance of *garum* factories along the length of Spain's Mediterranean coast. In these areas the taste remains for fish cooked in salt (the whole fish, unscaled, is covered in coarse salt and baked); for *arencas* – salted and pressed sardines; for *ganyims*, a Catalan name for pieces of salted tuna preserved in barrels; and for *salazones*, these being fish or fish roe that are salted and wind-dried. The best quality can taste extraordinary but are extremely expensive, as is an Andalusian speciality of the salted, dried loin of the blue fin tuna. This is called *mojama* (from *musamma*, the Arabic for dried) and is a very ancient delicacy. Served in thin slices as a tapa with a drizzle of good oil it can be very good if not too salty or dry. I also like it marinated with a little chopped garlic, parsley, lemon juice and oil, though I wouldn't do this to the best quality *mojama*. A small piece left to dry out completely can be finely grated into fish dishes, in small quantities, for flavouring. Then, of course, there is salt-cod, but see more about that on page 212.

Recipes for fresh fish are best kept relatively simple, and I include very few recipes for shellfish precisely because these are usually enjoyed on their own. Some fish are better than others for richer, more aggressive treatment – I am thinking in particular of firm-fleshed creatures such as monkfish, squid and tuna. Others I feel should be enjoyed with little or no adornment so as to appreciate their fine flavour – red mullet and trout, for example –and fish such as these are usually best simply grilled or fried.

The Spanish, particularly the Andalusians, have a genius for frying fish, though this may not always be apparent in some restaurants. It sounds simple enough: the fish are seasoned with salt, dipped in flour and fried in hot oil; but the ease is deceptive. To fry fish the Spanish way you ideally need a deep, wide frying pan (I tend to use a saucepan – it's easier and feels safer) filled to half to two-thirds capacity with oil. Purists insist on olive oil but you get very good results with sunflower oil too, and it's much cheaper, something to consider when using such large quantities, which anyway soon become tainted and smell unpleasant. It should be heated until very hot – about 180°C/350°F. Experienced fryers hold the back of their hand close to the oil to see if it feels right. The pieces of fish should not be too thick or the coating will burn before the flesh is cooked, and they must be seasoned with salt *before* frying. The flour used should be a coarser one than normal (special flour for frying is sold in Spain). Do not cook too much fish at a time or the temperature of the oil will drop and the coating go soggy. Fried fish is often served garnished with lemon, but lemon juice is unnecessary, unwelcome even, if the fish is absolutely fresh. (We squeeze the lemons over our hands afterwards to mask the fishy smell.) Fried potatoes are *not* served with fried fish.

In Cádiz and elsewhere, freshly fried fish can be bought to take away. José Carlos Capel suggests, in *Comer en Andalucía* (1981), that it was from these *freidurías* that English sherry dealers and producers had the idea for fish-and-chip shops at home. I wonder.

Fresh fish is also excellent cooked on the *plancha* or iron hotplate common to Spanish bars and restaurants. You don't need special equipment at home, just a large heavy frying pan and a metal spatula or palette knife. Get it very hot, brush your fish with oil and put it into the pan. Do not be tempted to move it until a good crust has formed, then brush the upper side with more oil and flip the whole thing over (that makes it sounds easy; you get better with practice). When the fish feels firm to the touch it is done. I always try to remove the fish just before it seems ready because its residual heat continues to cook it.

## ANCHOVIES

### *(Boquerones)*

Known as *bocartes* in northern parts, as *anchoas* in the Basque country, as *aladrogues* in parts of the south-east and universally referred to as *anchoas* when canned. The best anchovies are said to be those fished in the stretch of sea between Estepona and Nerja on the Costa del Sol. In autumn look out for *victorianos*, especially small, thin anchovies netted around Rincón de la Victoria.

Anchovies are one of the best fish for frying. It is common to do this in *panojas*, or fan-shapes of five anchovies joined at the tail. This arrangement, I've been told, represents the fingers of the hand and symbolises hospitality to the traveller. The other very common way with them is to clean them (snap the head off, taking the entrails with it and opening the belly in one movement), remove the backbone and leave them in vinegar with a little salt for a few hours – just long enough to 'cook' them. Wash off the vinegar, drain them and cover with good oil, plenty of chopped garlic and parsley. This is a lovely, sharp tapa on a summer's day with a glass of cold Spanish lager – ask for *boquerones en vinagre*. (I should point out that it is now a legal requirement in Spain to freeze any fish that is to be eaten raw for a minimum of 24 hours as a precaution against the possible presence of the anisakis parasite.)

Spanish canned anchovies can be a real delicacy, especially those produced in Cantabria and the Basque country, and they have a price tag to match. If they are good they are never unpleasantly salty. Also worth looking out for are a speciality of the Costa Brava, *anchoas en salazón*, where the whole fish is preserved in coarse salt. Smoked anchovies in oil are now quite common and are excellent with a little hot bread.

## BARBEL

### (Barbo)

A freshwater fish that the people of Navarra marinate whole in white wine before frying, or they can be fried just as they are. Smaller ones are best.

## BONITO

This relative of the tuna and the mackerel is one of Spain's bargains – it has beautifully meaty and flavoursome flesh and is not very expensive. An ideal fish for soups and stews. The highly esteemed *bonito del norte* is, confusingly, the albacore or longfin tuna.

# Bonito a l'all cremat

Bonito with burnt garlic. The point about this excellent dish is that you don't actually burn the garlic. It is cooked gently in oil until dark brown, then pounded with nuts and added to the fish and potatoes, to which it gives a rich, powerful flavour. The recipe can also be used to advantage with mackerel or monkfish, the latter being seen to greater effect if fresh clams are added. From the province of Tarragona in Cataluña.

8-12 slices from a small bonito
6 medium-sized potatoes
salt
6 tablespoons oil
8-10 cloves garlic, peeled
12 almonds, blanched and peeled
12 hazelnuts, loose skins rubbed off

Season the fish with salt. Peel and chop the potatoes into largish cubes. Place them in a wide pan and just cover them with water. Add salt and cook uncovered until they are almost tender and the cooking water is slightly reduced.

Meanwhile, heat the oil in a small pan and fry the whole garlic cloves gently until very brown but nowhere near black. Transfer them to a mortar and pound to a paste with the almonds and hazelnuts. Thin this to a cream with some of the potato water.

When the potatoes are nearly tender, pour in the sauce and the garlicky oil, mix well and add the fish slices, pushing them down among the potatoes and sauce. Cover and leave to simmer gently for 10 minutes, by which time the sauce should be very thick.

Serve on its own, preceded by something simple and clean-tasting such as a green salad.

# BREAM

The best of the many sea bream to be found in Spain are the *dorada*, (the gilt-head), the *hurta* and the *besugo* (red bream).

The *dorada* is reputed to be a strict observer of Lent: during this time it will only eat a sort of seaweed called 'sea-lettuce'; the rest of the year it enjoys a diet of tasty crustaceans, particularly small crabs. It is the best fish for cooking whole in salt, a method that originated in Murcia. The fish, unscaled, is covered completely in coarse salt and baked for about 45 minutes, (allow 20 minutes per kilo, and 5 to 10 minutes rest after it comes out of the oven) by which time the salt has hardened to a shell which needs to be broken with a hammer. The salt is then removed, taking the scales and skin with it and exposing particularly moist flesh that isn't at all salty. Serve with allioli (page 188). Farmed dorada is now widely available in Spain. It's reasonable, but not a patch on the wild.

*Hurta* is famous *a la roteña*, in the style of Rota, the town that faces Cádiz on the other side of the bay. The fish is baked with a *sofrito* of onions, tomatoes and peppers, and is moistened with wine and brandy while it does so. Like the *dorada* it has strong teeth which it uses to devour large quantities of shellfish, and connoisseurs claim that this gives the *hurta* a special flavour.

The large *besugo* is popular baked, especially at Christmas when the prices for good-sized specimens soar. Smaller ones can be barbecued *al espeto* (see under sardines, page 218). To bake a *besugo* make four cuts along its side and insert halved slices of lemon into each one. Put the fish in an oven dish, season it, add a little white wine and sprinkle it with breadcrumbs mixed with chopped garlic and parsley. Finally pour over a little oil and bake. In the north you find *besugo a la espalda*, bream that has been spatchcocked and grilled.

## Besugo con piñones

Red bream in pine-nut sauce. In fact this can be made with any of the sea bream family, or indeed with any white fish.

1.25kg/2½lb red bream or similar, filleted
salt and pepper
2 lemons
6 tablespoons oil
3 tablespoons pine-nuts
2 cloves garlic
1 onion, finely chopped
2 tablespoons chopped parsley

125ml/4fl oz dry sherry
a little flour for coating

A couple of hours before you need them, season the fillets with salt and marinade them in the juice of one of the lemons and two tablespoons of the oil.

Heat the remaining oil and fry the pine-nuts and peeled garlic until brown. Remove them to a mortar. Soften the onion in the oil, then add that too to the mortar. Add the parsley and pound it all to a paste. Season with pepper and dilute to a cream with the sherry and the juice of the other lemon.

Pat the fish fillets dry and flour them lightly. Fry them quickly on both sides in the remaining oil. Add the sauce from the mortar and a little water if it's very thick. Simmer gently for 5-6 minutes and serve.

## CHANQUETES

The transparent goby (see Alan Davidson's *Mediterranean Seafood* ). Spaniards have a special regard for these tiny scraps. One writer reckoned, for example, that mermaids must eat them for pudding, and described them affectionately as 'little pins of silver, spume of the Mediterranean'.

Found in the waters round Málaga and famed throughout Spain, they are now something of a forbidden fruit because to satisfy the huge demand fishermen became none too fussy about what they were selling as *chanquetes* and started to label fry from other fish – most notably the anchovy – as such. The fishing and sale of *chanquetes* have been banned, with heavy fines for offenders.

(A frozen Chinese species of something resembling *chanquetes* is now available in Spain, as is a 'surimi' version. They are not like the real thing.)

## CONGER EEL
### (Congrio)

These can grow to a frightening size, when they make a spectacular if sinister sight in the fish market. Their drawback, like skate, is their smell – the first time I went to buy some I complained because I was convinced it had gone off. No, no, I was assured, all is well; the *congrio* is like that. And it is, but it makes it rather disagreeable to prepare. The flesh is good as long as you buy a thick piece: ignore the tail end where all the bones congregate. Skin the piece if possible, as this helps rid it of any unpleasantness.

Do not confuse the conger with ordinary eels, which they resemble only in their snake-like appearance. The common eel is infinitely superior in every way, as well as being considerably more expensive. Both of them can be dried and were once popular in this way among the poor of the north-east.

# Congrio con guisantes

Fish with peas is quite a common combination in Spain, particularly using cheap white fish such as conger or skate.

1kg/2¼lb conger, skinned and cut into 8 slices

salt

500g/18oz fresh peas, unshelled weight, *or* 175g/6oz frozen peas

3 tablespoons oil

1 onion, finely chopped

1 tablespoon flour

300ml/½ pint fish stock

2 cloves garlic

2 tablespoons chopped parsley

Season the conger slices with salt and shell the peas. Heat the oil in a *cazuela* or similar and gently soften the onion. Stir in the flour, cook for 2 minutes, then gradually stir in the stock. Pound the peeled garlic to a pulp with the parsley and a little salt. Stir it into the sauce, along with the peas. Lay the pieces of fish in among them and bring to the boil. Simmer for 20 minutes, turning the fish over halfway through cooking time and checking the seasoning.

**Note:** You have to be pretty sure of your fresh peas to cook them like this – you can sometimes finish with conger and cannonballs. If in doubt, cook the shelled peas in the fish stock for 10 minutes or so first, to soften them up.

## CUTTLEFISH

*(Jibia, Sepia)*

'A monstrous, flabby creature, as stupid as the squid or more so', according to Josep Plá, the Catalan writer. Cuttlefish are between squid and octopus in tenderness but are perhaps not as good as either in flavour, though this is not to say that you can't make some very good things with them, and like squid they will impart something of the essence of the sea to their sauce. (They also have inside them an extraordinary hard oval bone which occupies most of the body cavity and which is much esteemed by caged parrots.) Its ink was the original sepia colouring.

A very small breed of cuttlefish called *chopito* is delicious fried but is difficult to clean because of all its little bones and the ink that leaks out. Cleaning larger specimens (some of them are enormous)

is easier: cut off the tentacles from the head and reserve. Cut open the body cavity, take everything out, remove as much skin as possible and wash the flesh under the tap before cutting it into even-sized pieces. It can be cooked whole as for octopus, the Jane Grigson way (see page 209).

# Sepia guisada

A Galician recipe for stewed cuttlefish.

2 onions, finely chopped

1 red pepper, chopped

4 cloves garlic, crushed

2 tomatoes, peeled and chopped

2 tablespoons chopped parsley

4 tablespoons oil

salt

1 bay leaf

1 kg/2¼lb cuttlefish, about 600g/1lb 6oz after cleaning, cut up

chicken broth

4 potatoes, cut into small chunks

Make a *sofrito* by softening the onion, red pepper, garlic, tomato and parsley in the oil. Add the cuttlefish, season with salt and add the bay leaf. Stir over a good heat until the cuttlefish loses its waxy colour. Cover with chicken broth and simmer, covered, for an hour. Add the potatoes and more broth or water if necessary, and simmer uncovered until the fish and potatoes are tender and the sauce very thick.

## EELS

### *(Anguilas)*

These, rich, gorgeous creatures are not pleasant to deal with. Not only are they very slimy but they survive a long time out of water and can bite (in fact they should be bought live – their flesh deteriorates rapidly once they are dead). Elvers or baby eels (*angulas*) are considered a great treat in Spain, but they are now fantastically expensive (about a thousand euros a kilo for fresh ones at Christmas) partly as a result of pollution reducing stocks but also because of demand from Asia. Particularly prized are the ones from the town of Aguinaga near San Sebastián, which are distinguished by a grey-black line running down their backs. They are now very rare and there is said to be a cottage industry devoted to dyeing ordinary elvers to turn them into the kind from Aguinaga. Elvers last so long out of water that they are killed by being submerged in a bucket of water containing a cigar or two, or black tobacco. The nicotine in the water suffocates them.

The most popular treatment is to fry them briefly in olive oil with plenty of garlic and some pieces of chilli pepper. They are served sizzling hot (described by Jan Morris as 'like dishes of some fine-spun pasta') and traditionally eaten with a wooden fork. They taste of, well, garlic and chilli really. The texture is the thing. While worth trying, they strike me as a little dull, but then I've never had the wherewithal to be able to eat them often enough to form a reliable opinion. To make them go further you can make a tortilla of them as they do in Asturias, or dress them with oil, lemon, garlic and pepper in the Valencian way and eat them as a salad. An ersatz 'surimi' version is all most people can afford.

# All i pebre

This is the traditional way of cooking eels caught in the Albufera. The name is Valencian Catalan for garlic and pepper (i.e. red pepper), and the original dish consists solely of eel, oil, garlic, paprika, chilli and water. There are many slightly more complicated versions which add potatoes, peas, ground nuts, parsley, wine, and so on. However prepared, it is rich, and is usually eaten as a first course.

about 1.25kg/2½lb eels, cleaned and cut into 5cm/2in pieces
6 tablespoons oil
4 cloves garlic, crushed
1 tablespoon paprika
1 small dried chilli pepper, finely chopped
about 12 fried almonds (optional)

Season the pieces of eel with salt. Heat the oil and add the crushed garlic and chilli. Simmer them gently for a couple of minutes, but not enough to colour them. Add the paprika, cook very briefly and then put in the eels and about 600ml/1 pint of water. Bring to the boil and simmer uncovered for about 15 minutes, by which time the sauce should have reduced a little. To thicken it further you can pound some fried almonds and add them towards the end. (Turtle meat was also cooked in this way.)

*L'espardenya* or a*lpargatazo* (meaning 'large slipper') are both names for an *all i pebre* with the addition of chicken and sometimes beans – an echo of the meat and fish combinations popular in Cataluña. Use chicken breast and try it also with other meaty fish instead of eel – a successful combination is one with fillets of John Dory. *Espardenya* is also, incidentally, the Catalan name used for the sea cucumber, which is much sought after in the region for its meat.

<h1 style="text-align:center">GREY MULLET</h1>

(Mújol, Lisa)

Some of these can be good, though the flesh can be on the mushy side. They are popular in Valencia, where those caught in the Albufera and off Cullera find a ready market. They are sometimes sold, fraudulently, as *lubina* (sea bass) to the unknowing. Perhaps the best thing to come from this humble fish is its roe (*huevas de mújol*), which when salted and dried becomes a real delicacy.

# Lisa en amarillo

Grey mullet in a delicate and beautiful pale yellow sauce of saffron and lemon. The sauce goes well with any white fish.

2 slices stale French bread

3 tablespoons oil

1 onion, finely chopped

2 cloves garlic, crushed

1 good pinch saffron

1 large grey mullet, cleaned, scaled and sliced into cutlets

salt and pepper

juice of 1 lemon

Fry the bread briskly in the oil until brown. Transfer it to a mortar. In the remaining oil fry the onion and garlic until softened. Add them to the mortar along with the saffron and pound together until you get a fairly smooth paste. Thin the paste down with some water.

Place the pieces of mullet in a *cazuela* or similar, and season them. Sprinkle them with the lemon juice and pour over the contents of the mortar. Add more water if the sauce seems very thick, bearing in mind that the fish juices will thin it down to some extent. Simmer for 10-15 minutes and serve.

<h1 style="text-align:center">GROUPER</h1>

(Mero)

A hefty fish with a price to match. Very good *mero* is to be had in Cataluña, and excellent ones are caught around Almería. It should be sold in steaks; these have comparatively few bones, are firm-textured and of fine flavour. This is one of the best Spanish fishes, and is exceptionally good grilled.

# HAKE
## (Merluza)

Hake occupies much the same position on the Spanish table as cod used to on ours. Like cod, it is very good indeed when fresh, and pleasant but unremarkable when frozen. The latter is all many Spaniards can afford, fresh Spanish hake now being almost in the luxury price bracket as stocks become exhausted. When buying hake try to make sure it is the European version, *merluccius merluccius*, that you are getting, not a distant import. If you see *merluza de pincho* on sale and wonder why it's so pricey, it's because it was line caught by a system known as *palangre* rather than trawled, which better preserves both the fish and its environment. This system is still maintained by the hake fishermen of Celeiro in Galicia, and their catch is much sought-after. Some fishermen claim that hake shouldn't be eaten on the day it's caught, but gutted and hung head down overnight to rid it of mucus and excess water, and to compress the flesh.

A great delicacy is the hake's *kokotxas*, or chin, which are the v-shaped little pieces of slightly gelatinous meat from under the fish's lower jaw. These are prepared *a la donostiarra*: cooked very simply in oil with plenty of parsley and a little broth, the dish being shaken continuously so that the natural gelatine thickens the juices. As so often, I think, with fish, the tastiest and firmest meat is to be found in the head. Which is why I'm also a fan of the *cogote*, the head and neck of a large hake (eyes and nasty teeth removed), split, then grilled and dressed with garlic and chilli.

Small hake, *pescadillas*, are used for the soup on page 106, and if very small, *pijotillas*, they are good fried, their tails clamped in their mouths.

## Merluza a la vasca/merluza en salsa verde

Hake in garlic and parsley sauce from the Basque country. This is the simplest of many versions and the best one for really fresh steaks of hake or other white fish.

4 x 225g/8oz hake steaks

salt

4 tablespoons oil

4 cloves garlic, chopped

3 tablespoons chopped parsley

2 tablespoons flour

600ml/1 pint fish stock

2 teaspoons vinegar

Season the fish with salt. Heat the oil in a pan wide enough to hold the fish in a single layer. Add the chopped garlic and cook it gently for 2-3 minutes without browning. Add the parsley, let it sizzle briefly and stir in the flour. Gradually add fish stock until you have a fairly thick sauce – remember that the fish will thin it down with its juices – and stir in the vinegar. Place the fish in the sauce, cover and simmer for about 10 minutes or until the hake is just cooked. Check the seasoning and serve.

## Merluza a la koskera

A garlicky dish of hake in another 'green' sauce from the Basque country. Other white fish can be successfully substituted.

1kg/2¼lb hake, filleted

salt

2 dozen asparagus tips

225g/8oz peas

4 tablespoons oil

6 cloves garlic, chopped

flour for coating

2 tablespoons chopped parsley

Season the fish with salt. Boil the asparagus and peas until tender. Keep warm. Heat the oil in a *cazuela* and gently fry the chopped garlic for a couple of minutes without browning. Dip the fish in flour and add to the pan. Let the fillets colour on both sides, then gradually add water or the broth from the vegetables, shaking the pan the while, until you have a smooth, fairly thick sauce. Sprinkle over the peas and arrange the asparagus on top. Sprinkle with parsley and serve.

## Merluza a la gallega

Galician food can be so plain it borders on the dull. This dish of hake, peas and potatoes would be, were it not rescued by a good bath of *ajada*, the Galician dressing of oil, garlic and paprika.

4 x 225g/8oz hake steaks

salt

4 large potatoes

½ onion, sliced

8 cloves garlic

3-4 parsley stalks
225g/8oz shelled peas
8 tablespoons oil
1 tablespoon paprika

Season the fish with salt. Peel and thickly slice the potatoes. Cover them with water, add the onion, two of the garlic cloves, crushed, the parsley stalks and some salt. Cook for 10 minutes, then add the peas and the hake. Simmer for 10 more minutes. Strain (keep the liquor for soup, for example *pescado en blanco* on page 106) and discard the parsley stalks.

Slice the six remaining garlic cloves and heat the oil. Fry the garlic until it turns golden brown. Remove from the heat and sprinkle in the paprika. Quickly mix it in and then pour the dressing over the fish, peas and potatoes. Serve at once.

## Merluza al jerez
4 x 225g/8oz fillets or cutlets of hake

salt

juice of 1 lemon

175g/6oz fresh prawns, peeled (use the shells to make a little stock)

120ml/4fl oz dry sherry

4 tablespoons oil

225g/8oz mushrooms, wiped clean and sliced

3 tablespoons dried breadcrumbs

Sprinkle the fish with salt and the lemon juice. Set aside. Liquidise the prawns with the sherry, or pound them to a pulp in the mortar. Heat the oil and gently fry the mushrooms for a few minutes. Add the pieces of fish and pour in the sherry and prawn mixture. Add a little stock, enough to half-cover the fish. Cook very gently for a few minutes on either side. Add the breadcrumbs and cook a little longer until the sauce has thickened. Check the seasoning and serve.

## LAMPREY
### (Lamprea)

These ancient, ghoulish, parasitic creatures are particularly popular in Galicia, where as winter gets under way they start to appear in the rivers to spawn, clamping themselves onto wild salmon to feed on their blood as they travel upstream. They have a fiesta all their own in the town of Arbo the last weekend in April, where the fish is popular in a sauce of red wine and the creature's blood. Lampreys are also considered the best filling of all for a pie. Cipriano Torre Enciso offers the following guide to preparing this *empanada* in his *Cocina Gallega Enxebre* (1982):

> The lamprey must be well scraped and washed. Now remove its gall, which is a long, sharp-pointed piece of cartilage under the mouth. Without such preparation the lamprey would be bitter and tough. You must also remove the thick innards to be found in the middle of the animal. Bleed the fish, dry it with a cloth, reserve the blood and set aside the liver. Cut the lamprey into pieces, but without cutting all the way through. Turn them in flour, then briefly in a frying pan. In a casserole dish fry some chopped onion in oil with parsley, half a clove, salt, breadcrumbs moistened with vinegar, the blood and a tumbler of white wine. Once this is done incorporate the lamprey and let it cook about 10 minutes. Finally, put this stew in a pastry you have prepared for this purpose and put it in the oven until suitably cooked.

The idea of not cutting right through the lamprey is that it can then be formed into a circle to make a circular pie, rather than a rectangular one, the latter being more usual in Galicia.

## MACKEREL
### (Caballa)

One of my favourite recipes for one of my favourite fish: mackerel with garlic and lemon. The combination of the powerful flavour and aroma of garlic and lemon, the slightly resistant texture of the lemon slices and the soft richness of the fish produce a dish of real merit and delicacy.

# Caballa con ajo y limón

salt
3-4 mackerel, either in fillets or sliced across into little cutlets
10 tablespoons oil for frying
flour for coating
2 lemons
2 bay leaves
6-8 cloves garlic, lightly crushed with the flat of a knife
about 200ml/7fl oz water

Salt the pieces of mackerel, leave them for 10 minutes, then pat dry with kitchen paper. Heat the oil in a frying pan. Dip the mackerel pieces in flour, shaking off the excess. Fry in batches until brown on both sides. Drain on kitchen paper.

Remove all but about 5 tablespoons of the oil. Add the garlic cloves and let them sizzle until they start to colour. Add half a lemon cut into thin slices (halved if they're enormous) and the bay leaves. Fry for a couple of minutes, then add the juice of the remaining lemons and the water. Stir and return the fish to the pan. At this stage it all looks disgusting, but a few minutes' fast cooking amalgamates it all into a rich brown savouriness. Serve as soon as possible.

## MONKFISH
### *(Rape)*

It seems to have become part of cookery mythology that the flesh of the monkfish, or angler fish, is reminiscent of lobster. In my view it would difficult to confuse the two as far as taste is concerned, and anyway monkfish is now much too expensive in its own right to merit using it as a substitute for something else.

## Rap al conyac

A deceptively simple dish from Cataluña: monkfish cooked with oil, tomato, brandy and a considerable amount of parsley. Wateriness is the enemy of many fish dishes, especially those containing tomato, and the sauce here must be ruthlessly reduced. If done well this is an excellent, unfussy way of cooking monkfish, with a lovely fresh taste of parsley complementing the dark richness of tomato, brandy and fish juices, and the sturdy texture of the fish itself.

900g/2lb sliced monkfish, the bigger the better

salt

3 tablespoons oil

4 tomatoes, peeled, seeded and chopped

tomato concentrate (optional), to taste

6 tablespoons chopped parsley

black pepper

120ml/4fl oz Spanish brandy

Season the fish with salt. Leave the bone in as it contributes flavour to the sauce. Heat the oil and fry the tomato until it is reduced to a purée. Taste it: if it lacks flavour add a little tomato concentrate. Lay the slices of fish in the sauce and sprinkle with the parsley. Season with black pepper and let the dish simmer. When the fish starts to throw off its juices, add the brandy and turn the fish over if necessary. Cook for 10 minutes. Remove the fish and cook the sauce hard until it is thick. Return the fish to it and heat through.

A good accompaniment is some sliced new potatoes spread thinly with allioli.

# Rape a la malagueña

4 tablespoons oil
a dozen almonds, blanched and skinned
3 cloves garlic
2 slices stale French bread
1 onion, chopped
2 tomatoes, peeled and chopped
2 teaspoons paprika
1 good pinch saffron
450g/1lb tiny new potatoes, scrubbed
2 tablespoons chopped parsley
salt and pepper
900g/2lb monkfish, thickly sliced

Heat the oil in a *cazuela* or similar. Add the almonds, garlic and bread and fry until they are well browned. Remove and reserve. Soften the onion in the same oil, then add the tomato and paprika and cook for about 5 minutes. Add to the fried mixture with the saffron and either pound to a pulp or liquidise it. Thin the resulting paste down with water until you have a creamy sauce. Return this to the pot and add the potatoes, parsley and some salt and pepper. Simmer for 10 minutes. Add the monkfish and cook for about 15 more minutes. Serve hot, but not boiling.

**Note:** Skate can be treated in the same way. If you haven't got much monkfish, try the soup (*sopa de rape*) on page 102.

# OCTOPUS
## (Pulpo)

One of my favourite foods, for despite its terrifying aspect it provides exquisite meat. It is chewy, certainly, but not rubbery unless badly prepared. It responds well to strong, assertive flavours and, like squid, is perhaps best eaten in smaller quantities than other fish – as a tapa, for example.

Octopus is an interesting creature, since it has a complex nervous system and a good brain. With a little stealth they are easy enough to catch, as the local boys swimming off Spanish beaches frequently demonstrate: the octopus must be grabbed by its head, which causes it to throw its tentacles up and around your hand, exposing its beak which must be removed with a finger of the other hand. The octopus is now harmless.

Octopus, especially larger ones, can be as tough as old leather, and it is traditional to beat them against a rock to soften them. There are other methods: freezing the octopus helps considerably. Many Spanish cooks plunge it into boiling water three times, holding it by the head as if they were ducking a witch, before cooking it. Others add pieces of cork or cane to the cooking water. However, the easiest way is that give by Jane Grigson in *Fish Cookery* (1973). After cutting off the head and removing the beak from the tentacles,

> *Put it into a glass oven dish with plenty of room to spare, and cover it. Do not add water or seasoning.\* Leave in a cool oven (300°F/150°C/Gas 2) for one to two hours. It will exude a dark red liquid in surprising quantity. When it can be pierced with a pointed knife, rinse the octopus under the cold tap and discard the liquid. Now the fine skin and knobbly bosses can be rubbed off easily.*

\*It is particularly important not to add salt, which stops the meat becoming tender.

The octopus is now ready to be cooked with a sauce. With large octopus I would recommend the extra precaution of freezing it for a day first. Ready-cooked octopus is often on sale in Spain which is less bother but also rather more expensive than if you do it yourself.

One last thing to remember is that octopus shrinks drastically when cooked, losing about two-thirds of its weight, though this is offset by the richness of the meat.

## PULPO A FEIRA, PULPO A LA GALLEGA

*Pulpeiras* are octopus sellers who travel around the fairs and festivals of Galicia and neighbouring areas of Zamora with their octopus and their blackened copper cauldrons or *caldeiras*. The women arrive in the area first thing in the morning, set up their pots, fill them with water and boil the octopus in the open air. Once cooked, the octopus are cut up with great scissors, dressed with oil and red pepper (either sweet or hot, or both) and distributed to the many hungry takers. They will have brought along a wooden plate for the purpose and will eat the octopus on the spot or at a nearby bar, accompanied by bread and plenty of wine. The *pulpeiras* then pack up in the evening and head for the next place.

This is a very good way of enjoying octopus.

## Pulpo frito

Octopus can be good fried. Once it is cooked and cooled, cut it into individual tentacles if the octopus are small, into 2.5-5cm/1-2in pieces if large. Flour and fry them in the usual way, or turn them in frying batter. Done like this they are very popular in Cantabria where they are known as *rabas de pulpo*. Best served with an allioli or garlic mayonnaise.

## Pulpo en ajada

Dress hot, cooked octopus with a mixture of oil, pounded garlic, salt and pepper, and either hot or sweet red pepper.

## Ensalada de pulpo

Mix little nuggets of cooked octopus with a *pipirrana* salad (page 81).

## Pulpitos con chocolate

A rich Catalan dish of baby octopus and tiny new potatoes cooked in a thick sauce of wine, tomatoes, garlic, almonds and chocolate. Should baby octopus not be available, add pieces of cooked octopus to the sauce towards the end of cooking.

1kg/2¼lb baby octopus
2 dozen small new potatoes
6 tablespoons oil
4 cloves garlic
45g/1½oz almonds, blanched and peeled

2 onions, finely chopped
1 bay leaf
1 good pinch dried thyme
4 tomatoes, peeled and chopped
300ml/½ pint white wine
125ml/4fl oz aguardiente, dry anis *or* grappa
1 good pinch saffron
45g/1½oz bitter chocolate, grated

Cut off the tentacles and body sacs from the octopus. Cut open the sacs and scrape out all the guts. Wash the tentacles and sacs very thoroughly under the tap. Thinly peel the potatoes (or leave them as they are if you prefer).

Cover the octopus with cold water and bring to the boil. Drain, discarding the water, and rinse. Heat the oil in a small frying pan and fry the garlic and almonds until brown. Transfer them to a mortar. Strain the oil into a *cazuela* or sauté pan and soften the onion in it. Add the octopus, bay leaf and thyme. Cook briefly, then add the tomatoes and potatoes and cook until the tomatoes start to soften. Pour in the wine and aguardiente, season with salt and pepper, cover and leave to simmer until the octopus and potatoes are tender.

Pound the almonds and garlic with the saffron, then thin to a cream with a little water. Stir into the octopus, add the chocolate and let it heat through and thicken before serving.

## RED MULLET
### *(Salmonete)*

A fish of the highest class. There are two types, *salmonete de fango* (mud) and *salmonete de roca* (rock). They look much the same, except that the latter tends to have a more blushing complexion and looks as though its nose has been broken. It also has a slightly better flavour. However, both of them have beautifully meaty flesh and a fine-tasting liver. When tiny, the length of a finger or less, they are perhaps the best fish there is for frying, with a lingering intensity of flavour. When large I prefer them *a la plancha* or grilled, having first salted them, sprinkled them with lemon juice and left them to stand for half an hour. When your grill is nice and hot pat the mullet dry, brush them with oil and cook, brushing them occasionally with more oil. Large ones of about 450g/1lb in weight will take about 10 minutes a side. Serve them with a garlic mayonnaise and bread.

# ROSADA

The name means 'rosy' and is applied to cheap fillets of a rather ugly dogfish. It is reliably good with a pleasant texture, and popular because of its price.

# SALMON
## (Salmón)

To be had in northern areas where they are caught in the rivers that flow into the Atlantic and in the *rías*, the many fjord-like inlets that characterise parts of the coast. Superb salmon trout (*reo asalmonado*) are one of Spain's few fish bargains (but take care not to be palmed off with a large trout from a fish farm under the name *trucha asalmonada*).

# SALT-COD
## (Bacalao)

Portugal is said to have a salt-cod recipe for every day of the year. Add those of Spain and you'd have enough for another year, though not many people, unless forced by circumstance, would choose to eat salt-cod with such regularity. Its strong, unmistakable taste can produce some great treats, but in unknowing hands it can be dreadful. Whoever prepares it, the smell will be the same – 'like the lion house in the zoo,' said Gerald Brenan – and as penetrating as sardines or kippers.

This puts off many children:

> I won't go any further into the stench of those old food shops, where every spring the guillotine would cut up hundreds of these marine fossils, but I will recall with horror when our mothers, as a mark of mortification and Lenten penance, would force us to eat that abominable and reeking salted fish... salt-cod is a food for the adult gastronome. (Pepe Iglesias: *Enciclopedia de Gastronomía*)

Such a wealth of recipes demonstrates the importance of dried and salted cod in the everyday cooking of Spain and Portugal. It has been so for centuries, ever since those fearless Basque fishermen of the late Middle Ages went in search of whales and found cod in abundance around Newfoundland, cod which they soon found themselves sharing with the Portuguese, French and English. The fish was salted and dried to preserve it for its long journey home, and became a staple of the Iberian diet, which it continues to be, although, like fish generally, it is becoming too expensive for many people.

The type one often buys in Spain has not been completely dried after salting. This sort should be kept in the fridge, either in an airtight container or well wrapped to stop the smell escaping. It must be soaked in plenty of cold water prior to use in most recipes, the length of time varying according to the thickness of the fish. The usual recommendation is about 48 hours, changing the water every 8 hours or so for thinner pieces, every 6 hours for thicker ones. Keep it in the fridge while doing so. Do not remove the skin, as it provides an important gelatinous quality both to the fish and its sauce.

# Bacalao a la vizcaína

Salt-cod, from the Basque province of Vizcaya, which gives its name to the Bay of Biscay. Basque men are inveterate discussers of food, meeting in their traditionally all-male clubs called *txokos* to cook, eat and talk passionately about food. A great deal of such discussion surrounds this simple old dish of salt-cod. Should it have tomatoes or not? Peppers? What sort of peppers, fresh or dried? Should we thicken it with hard-boiled egg yolk or hazelnuts or chocolate? Or breadcrumbs? Should we toast the breadcrumbs? Add ham? This is one Basque dish that is not only hugely popular in its homeland but throughout the rest of Spain as well. There is no definitive version and the recipe I give is my personal favourite, for it comes closest, I like to think, to the original spirit of the dish through the simplicity of its ingredients – fish, onions and dried red peppers.

60g/2oz clean lard
3 onions, finely chopped
8 dried red peppers, *pimientos choriceros*, soaked
8 pieces of salt-cod, about 8cm/3in x 6cm/2½in, soaked

Melt the lard over a very low heat in a thick-based saucepan. Add the onions, mix in well and cover with a lid. Leave the onions to cook over the lowest possible heat for 3 hours. This long, slow cooking is crucial to the flavour of the sauce and under no circumstances should the onions be allowed to burn. If they seem to be cooking too fast place a heat diffuser under the pan or place the pan on top of a griddle over the heat. Stir the onions occasionally. After 3 hours they will have turned a rich brown.

Pass the onions through a sieve or liquidise them. Taste them and wonder at the transformation wrought on them by the slow cooking. Reserving the soaking water, halve the peppers and scrape out the thin layer of flesh. Add this pulp to the onion purée and put in a *cazuela* or sauté pan. Drain the pieces of salt-cod and place them, skin side up, on the purée. Pour in enough of the reserved water just to cover the cod. Bring slowly to simmering point and leave to cook for about 20 minutes. Add salt if necessary.

Serve with plain boiled potatoes, and precede the dish with a green vegetable such as green beans in oil and garlic (page 149).

The flavour of the sauce done this way is exceptionally fine and rounded.

# Bacalao de cuaresma

Lenten salt-cod. The name summons up dour, forbidding images but in fact this is a bright, colourful dish with a sauce of raisins and pine-nuts, and decorated with quartered hard-boiled eggs. Salt-cod was formerly cooked in many guises during Lent – with rice, for example (page 176). This particular version comes from Cataluña.

550g/1¼lb salt-cod, cut into 8 pieces and soaked
flour for coating
6 tablespoons oil
4 tomatoes, peeled and chopped
4 cloves garlic, crushed
2 tablespoons chopped parsley
100g/3½oz seedless raisins
60g/2oz pine-nuts
4 hard-boiled eggs, quartered

Drain the cod well and dip the pieces in flour. Heat the oil and fry the cod quickly until browned. Remove and set aside. In the remaining oil cook the tomatoes, garlic and parsley until set. Add the raisins, pine-nuts and cod, cover and cook gently for 20 minutes. Decorate with the hard-boiled eggs and serve.

# Bacalao a la calesera

'Coachman's cod', from Madrid. A splendidly fortifying dish.

400g/14oz salt-cod, soaked
2 onions, sliced
120g/4oz chickpeas, soaked
150g/5oz macaroni
60g/2oz raisins
4 tablespoons oil

Cut the cod into fairly small chunks and put it in a *cazuela* with the onions and chickpeas. Cover with water, bring to the boil and leave to simmer, uncovered, until the chickpeas are almost tender. Add the macaroni, raisins and oil and simmer until the pasta is cooked, adding more water if necessary. The stew should be quite thick.

The colour may be improved, according to taste, by a little saffron colouring.

# Albóndigas de bacalao con mayonesa

Fried salt-cod balls with mayonnaise. This is a little fiddly, and you have to plan ahead, but the result fully justifies the work involved. They are rather rich, and only need a few boiled potatoes as accompaniment.

450g/1lb salt-cod, soaked
2 tablespoons chopped parsley
4 cloves garlic, crushed
4 eggs
pepper
a little milk
dried breadcrumbs
300ml/½ pint oil
flour for coating
lemon juice
salt

Poach the cod for about 10 minutes. Drain, cool and remove all skin and bones. Break down the meat with a fork. Add the parsley, garlic, two of the eggs, pepper and a little milk to form a fairly smooth paste. Then add enough breadcrumbs to bind it all together so that the balls don't fall apart. Make the balls – there should be about two dozen.

Heat the oil. Roll the *albóndigas* in flour and fry until well browned all over. Drain on kitchen paper. Strain the oil and leave it to cool.

Separate the two remaining eggs. Make a mayonnaise with the yolks and oil. Flavour it well with lemon juice – it will only need a little salt. Gently reheat the *albóndigas* in a little water. When hot, whisk the water into the mayonnaise to thin it into a sauce, add the *albóndigas* and serve at once.

# Bacalao a la malagueña

One of the best salt-cod recipes, as well as one of the simplest, from Málaga. This is very delicious, but also very rich, so you may prefer to serve it as a tapa.

450g/1lb salt-cod, soaked
4 tablespoons oil
4 cloves garlic, crushed

3 tablespoons chopped parsley
200ml/7fl oz white wine
about 8 each, almonds and hazelnuts
1 good pinch saffron

Cover the cod with fresh water and bring it to a little below boiling point. Drain and remove all skin and bones. Crumble the cod into pieces.

Heat the oil and add the garlic. Let this simmer for a minute or so without browning, then add the cod and parsley and simmer for about 5 minutes, shaking the pan rather than stirring it. Pour in the wine.

Pound the almonds, hazelnuts and saffron in the mortar until more or less smooth. Thin it down with a little of the cooking liquor and add it to the cod; swill out the mortar with a little water if necessary. Cook for about 5 more minutes, until the sauce is of a good consistency and colour.

# Bacalao con dientes de ajos

Salt-cod with whole cloves of garlic. Though not quite as powerful as it sounds, this is nevertheless highly flavoured, and likely to be appreciated by garlic lovers.

550g/1¼lb salt-cod, soaked
3 tablespoons oil
1 onion, finely chopped
2 teaspoons paprika
peeled cloves of 1½-2 heads of garlic
2 tablespoons flour
6 peppercorns
4 cloves
2 tablespoons chopped parsley
2 tablespoons vinegar

Drain the cod and cover it with fresh water. Bring it to just below boiling point and drain it. Remove all the skin and bones. Place the fish in a *cazuela* or similar with the oil, onion, paprika, half the cloves of garlic and enough water to cover. Bring to the boil and leave to simmer gently.

In a small frying pan toast the flour until pale brown. Transfer it to a mortar. Add about 4-5 more peeled garlic cloves, a few peppercorns, the cloves and the parsley and pound to a paste. Moisten with the vinegar. Stir this into the salt-cod. Leave it to simmer for about 15 minutes more, adding a little extra water if it gets too thick. It should cook for about 30 minutes in all.

Serve it with boiled potatoes or plain rice to counteract its richness.

# Bacalao con coliflor en ajada

The blandness of cauliflower can be a good foil to the assertive flavour of salt-cod. Here the two are bathed in a barely cooked dressing of oil, vinegar, garlic and paprika, a version of Galicia's red sauce, *ajada*.

450g/1lb salt-cod, cut into 4 pieces and soaked

4 bay leaves

6 cloves garlic

8 tablespoons oil

2 tablespoons chopped parsley

1 cauliflower

4 teaspoons paprika

2 tablespoons vinegar

Cover the cod with fresh water, add two of the bay leaves, two of the garlic cloves, sliced, a tablespoon of oil and the parsley. Bring to the boil and simmer for about 15 minutes. Remove the cod to a plate and keep warm (remove the skin and bones now if you wish). Cook the cauliflower whole in the cod water until just tender. While doing so heat the oil and add 4 sliced garlic cloves and the other 2 bay leaves. When the garlic starts to brown add the paprika and vinegar and let it all boil together for a couple of minutes. Add 2-3 tablespoons of the cooking water and set aside.

Drain the cauliflower and cut into pieces. Set them around the cod and pour over the *ajada*.

## SAND-EELS
### *(Sonsos)*

Little eaten except in Cataluña, where they enjoy them fried. They are also used as live bait for tuna fishing.

## SAND-SMELTS
### (Pejerreyes, chirretes)

Resembling anchovies in appearance, these are popular eaten fried in the Mar Menor area of Murcia.

## SARDINES
### (Sardinas)

When I was a child, one of my favourite stories was *For the Leg of a Chicken* by Bettina Ehrlich. The story concerned poor Roberto, a little boy in Italy. He had nothing to eat but 'maize pudding' (polenta, presumably) and fried sardines every day, and so awful was this diet that he ran away from home to hunt the roast chicken of which he dreamed so fervently. I thus grew up with the idea that sardines and polenta were, like boiled celery and cauliflower, things to be endured rather than enjoyed. I think I was right about the polenta but I've revised my opinion about sardines since coming to Spain. Gerald Brenan thought them the 'cheapest and dullest of the Mediterranean fish' – perhaps he had to eat them every day like little Roberto – but though cheap and plentiful enough to be considered a poor man's fish, they are certainly not dull if very fresh and well grilled.

Before the age of tourism, sardine fishing was an important source of income for many coastal people, and Norman Lewis tells us how, in his Catalan village, '. . . the spring catch of sardines normally happened in March, immediately following which – if the catch proved satisfactory – a number of long-deferred marriages would take place.'

In many places sardines are covered, uncleaned, in coarse salt until used; this seasons and preserves them at the same time. On many a beach you can see them being cooked *al espeto*, on thin cane skewers in teepee formation over the fire, and indeed, sardines are usually best dry-cooked in this way, perhaps accompanied by baked potatoes and fried peppers.

The salting process can be taken a stage further by leaving the sardines in salt for anything from a week to a month or so while being pressed down by weights. These sardines are called *arencas* and are a good, if salty, breakfast when grilled and eaten with bread and oil (the saltiness can be reduced by soaking them in milk). For lunch I like them strewn with parsley and garlic, or accompanied by *picadilla* sauce (see page 191). Incidentally, a traditional way to skin *arencas* was to wrap them well in brown paper, then place them by a door hinge and slam the door on them. I feel I must try this one day.

Sardines are also good preserved *en escabeche*, first fried and then left in a bath of vinegar, garlic, thyme, oregano, paprika and the cooking oil. Or they can be smoked, as they are in Galicia.

# SCAD

## (Jurel)

When very fresh these are not only cheap but very good indeed cooked on the *plancha*; otherwise they can be rather uninteresting.

# SEA BASS

## (Lubina)

Another of the luxury fish and a beauty to look at, with good, quite firm flesh. Norman Lewis, in *Voices of the Old Sea* (1984). wrote:

> Mediterranean sea bass feed close to the rocks in heavy seas, favoured by the reduced visibility in their raids on small fish. Like incautious drivers in a fog they are subject to accident, and often stun or kill themselves by high-speed collision with the rock. In winter such casualties add to the gleanings of the sea provided by fish stranded in rock pools, helping the fishing community to eke out an existence at a time when the weather puts a stop to normal operations.

Another fish that is now efficiently farmed, though wild is preferable from the flavour point of view.

# SKATE

## (Raya)

This should pong a little bit before you eat it, or it will lack flavour. It starts to smell of ammonia, faintly at first, as the processes of decomposition get under way, and this is when it is at its best. The smell, which can be rather off-putting, disappears when the skate is cooked – or it will if the skate hasn't been matured too long, in which case it will be as repulsive as any other putrid fish. Unfortunately only the wings are sold in British fishmongers. In Spain the entire skate is displayed in all its glory, and Spanish cooks can enjoy the good flesh to be had from the tail.

Skate is the best fish of all for marinating and frying: see page 51.

# SOLE

## (Lenguado)

The name Dover sole conjures up wonderful images of flavour, texture and delicacy, but in Spain, though plentiful, many are frozen into anonymity to be served in yawn-provoking sauces in tourist restaurants. Fresh Spanish sole can be very good cooked on the *plancha* or baked in salt (see page 197).

Do look out though for *acedías* and *tapaculos* (literally, bum-covers) – small sole-like creatures which are very good fried.

## SQUID

### (Calamares, chipirones)

Squid is one of the most rewarding fish the sea can offer. When buying it, it is important to establish whether the squid comes from a frozen block or is fresh from the sea. It should be clearly labelled but if in doubt look at the price. In Spain, at least, fresh squid retails at about three times the price of frozen. Pluck up courage and pick one up in your hand. Frozen squid feels flabby and flexible, while the fresh product is firm and resistant to the touch.

There is a very considerable difference in taste. Fresh squid has an unmistakable sweetness which is completely lost when it is frozen for any length of time. For this reason only fresh squid should be used for frying. Fried squid has such a bad reputation (justifiably so) because it is so frequently made with frozen squid, and over-large ones at that. They have no more taste than the plastic draught-excluder they so resemble in texture, and are as bitter a betrayal to those who have tasted the genuine article as pub 'scampi' is to those who have eaten a fresh Dublin Bay prawn. This is not to say that frozen squid is not worth buying. If properly cooked it imparts a lovely, mysterious taste of the sea to it sauce.

Once you've decided to buy some squid, the most important thing is to pick out all the smallest specimens. It's more work when you get home but the rewards are in the tenderness of the meat. Larger squid taste all right – eventually. Once home, set to work to clean them, for short of giving him a very large sum of money it is unlikely that you will persuade your fishmonger to go through all the necessary palaver. It is particularly messy with fresh squid because the ink splashes. Wear an apron (and don't rinse them near a bowlful of white linen napkins in soak, as I once did).

### TO CLEAN SQUID

1 Sever the tentacles (or 'feet' as the Spanish call them) from the head and reserve them (for eating).
2 Holding the body sac in your left hand, take hold of the head and neck with your right hand and pull gently. With luck, out will slide all the squid's peculiar-looking innards, although there's often a thick, milky substance lurking at the very end of the beast. If the squid has recently eaten, you may find the evidence – I once came across an entire anchovy, almost the length of its captor, concealed in a squid I was cleaning.
3 Pull out the backbone: still holding the body in one hand, tug sharply on the tip of the backbone. Out slips a perfect transparent, plastic quill.
4 Though it is perfectly edible you may prefer to peel off the skin – it comes away very easily and then

sticks to your fingers, but persevere.

**5** Rinse the sac thoroughly inside and out, pulling out any remaining guts with a probing finger.

The following are some excellent recipes for squid, and there are more in the tapas section on pages 52-53. Frozen squid is acceptable for all of them, except where stated.

## Calamares fritos, calamares a la romana

Fried squid. As explained above, it is essential to use fresh squid for this. Allow about 4 small squid per person, or 2 largish ones. Clean them and cut them into rings. Use the tentacles too, but cut them close to the head so that you get them in a clump. Season with salt, flour them well and fry them in hot oil until they are a pale straw-gold in colour. Make sure you cover the pan while doing so, for they spit viciously as they cook.

Drain them well on kitchen paper and either serve them with salad or a garlicky mayonnaise and bread.

## Calamares a lo especiero

'Spice merchant's squid' – so called because of the ground saffron and black pepper used in the sauce, for the spice merchant had no more valuable wares than these. This recipe originates from Almería, that once great Mediterranean trading centre. I especially like the combination of textures of squid and fungi.

3 tablespoons oil
2 onions, finely chopped
400g/14oz sliced fungi (such as oyster mushrooms or big field mushrooms, although the latter will spoil the colour of the sauce)
900g/2lb squid, cleaned, sliced and seasoned with salt
300ml/½ pint white wine
1 good pinch saffron
about 20 peppercorns
4 egg yolks

Heat the oil in a *cazuela* or similar and fry the onion for about 5 minutes. Add the sliced mushrooms and let them wilt. Add the squid and fry until it changes colour. Pour in the wine. Pound the saffron and peppercorns to a powder. Add this to the pot and simmer for about 20 minutes.

Beat the egg yolks and stir in a few tablespoons of the hot sauce. Off the heat, stir this mixture into the squid. The sauce should now thicken of its own accord, but if it doesn't put the *cazuela* back on a low heat and stir until it does.

Serve at once, either simply with bread or with plain boiled rice.

# Calamares rellenos

Stuffed squid. Larger specimens are best for stuffing, as they are much sturdier and thus don't split or burst as smaller ones are liable to do. Use a piping bag to fill the squid – it's very much easier than fiddling with teaspoons. In this recipe the stuffed squid are served with a pine-nut sauce but you can serve them plain if you prefer.

4 large squid
salt and pepper
60g/2oz serrano ham, finely chopped
2 eggs, beaten
6 tablespoons dried breadcrumbs
juice of 1 lemon
4 cloves garlic, crushed
2 tablespoons chopped parsley
flour for coating
4 tablespoons oil
1 onion, finely chopped
60g/2oz pine-nuts
250ml/8fl oz white wine

Clean the squid, making sure the body sac is completely empty. Remove the wings from the sac and chop them finely, along with the tentacles. Mix these in a bowl with some salt, the ham, the beaten eggs, breadcrumbs, lemon juice, garlic and parsley. Fill the squid with the mixture, but not to bursting, and leave at least 1.25cm/½in free at the neck end. Fasten the necks together using 3-4 toothpicks or cocktail sticks per squid. You will find that a little of the stuffing may leak out while cooking, but this doesn't matter. Prick each squid in several places with a fork, then roll them lightly in flour.

Heat the oil in a large frying pan (large enough to hold the squid in a single layer) and add the squid. Cover, and leave to cook gently until browned on one side. Turn the squid over and repeat. Add the onion to the pan and let it soften. Pound the pine-nuts to a paste in a mortar. Thin the paste down to a cream with the wine and pour it over the squid and onions. Add a little water so that the squid are semi-immersed in liquid. Season. Cover and simmer for 30 minutes. Turn the squid over and repeat. The sauce should now be very thick and the squid tender.

Transfer them to a serving dish, remove the toothpicks and pour the sauce over them. This is good when eaten with buttery mashed potatoes.

# Calamares a la malagueña

The success of this simple little dish from Málaga lies in the quality and freshness of the principal ingredients: the squid should be fresh and the tomatoes and peppers should come from a reliable source (such as your garden) so that they actually taste of something other than water.

120g/4oz oil
2 onions, chopped
6 cloves garlic, crushed
2 green peppers, chopped
2 tomatoes, peeled and chopped
900g/2lb squid, cleaned and cut into rings, the feet chopped
120g/4oz red wine
2 tablespoons chopped parsley
2 teaspoons paprika

Heat the oil in a large, wide frying pan. Add the onion and garlic and let them soften. Add the peppers and 5 minutes later the tomatoes, and cook until they too have softened. Add the squid and stir until it changes colour. Pour in the wine and sprinkle in the parsley and paprika. Season and simmer for about 30 minutes – the whole thing should be thick, with no watery juices (the death of so many fish dishes).

Serve with fried bread cut into fingers or triangles. This is excellent reheated.

## CALAMARITOS

### (may also be called *puntillas* or *chipirones*)

Baby squid. These are tiny, shorter than the average thumb, and as tender and sweet as can be. One obstacle to overcome is that one eats everything bar the quill, which may be removed before cooking. There aren't any guts to speak of and the heads fry crisp. This may sound quite ghastly, and indeed I faltered when I first realised what was involved; but it's no worse than all those tiny eyes and brains and miniature innards one consumes without comment in a plate of fried whitebait. And in fact the easiest way to cook them is as for whitebait: having removed the little quills you wash them, salt them and leave them to drain (on an upturned plate wedged inside a pudding bowl – the fish stay up, the water goes down). Then toss them in flour and shake them in a sieve to get rid of the excess and keep them separate. Drop them in hot oil and cover as they tend to spit viciously. Leave them until they are a good colour, then drain.

Alternatively, turn them in frying batter for *gambas con gabardinas* (page 45) before frying them. Either way, this sort of cooking is far from ideal for large families or dinner parties: there is just too much to fry, and everything, including you, will smell like a chip shop. Keep it for intimate dos for two, when the other person can keep you company while you fry.

They can also be cooked on the *plancha* as they do at the Alhucemas restaurant in Sanlúcar la Mayor near Seville. Done this way they are one of the most delicious things it is possible to eat

**Note:** *Chipirones* in Spain may also refer to a type of tiny cuttlefish. They are a great deal of bother to prepare, but very good.

## SWORDFISH
### (Pez Espada, Pez Emperador, Aguja Palá)

The bully of the sea, amusing itself by persecuting shoals of mackerel or young tuna with mean-minded enthusiasm. It is a very imposing sight to see in the flesh: not the sort of creature one would wish to meet while out paddling – that sword means business. Like shark, it has flesh of convincing meatiness. In fact the similarity to shark is taken advantage of by some – it is not unknown for hammerhead shark to be sold as swordfish in Spain.

Its tendency to dryness is swordfish's drawback, for it lacks natural fat. This can be offset by cooking it in a sauce (the flesh responds well to strong flavourings) or, if cooking it *a la plancha*, it will stay juicy if you leave it slightly underdone.

# Pez espada con mariscos

Swordfish with prawn and clam sauce. To be successful this dish really needs fresh raw prawns and clams. It would be possible to make it with cooked prawns and tinned clams but the result would be rather a waste of a good piece of swordfish.

225g/8oz fresh clams

340g/12oz fresh, unpeeled prawns
salt
900g/2lb swordfish (two slices about 2.5cm /1in thick)
6 tablespoons oil
flour for coating
½ onion, finely chopped
2 cloves garlic, peeled
1 pinch saffron
2 tablespoons dry sherry

Open the clams in 2.5cm/1in of boiling water. Remove them from their shells. Strain the broth and reserve it. Peel the prawns. Put all the debris in a small pan and just cover them with the clam broth and some water. Add a little salt. Cook for about 10 minutes, then strain, reserving the broth.

Skin the swordfish and season it with salt. Heat the oil in a wide frying pan. Flour the fish well and fry it briefly until lightly browned on both sides. Remove it and set it aside. Pour off most of the oil (keep it for another fish dish) and fry the onion gently until soft. Return the fish to the pan and just cover it with broth. Pound the garlic with the saffron and stir that in as well. Add the sherry. Simmer, uncovered, for about 15 minutes. Add the prawns and simmer for 5 more minutes. Just before serving, stir in the clams to heat through.

## Pez espada a la cordobesa

If you should ever be lucky enough to encounter fresh swordfish, fresh prawns and fresh, preferably wild, asparagus at the same time, this dish will be heavenly. However, most of us will have to make do with frozen swordfish, cultivated asparagus and ready-cooked prawns. Notwithstanding, it should still be fit for a king.

A light hand with the sherry is essential; too much will be overpowering.

A much simpler version of this dish from Córdoba sees the fish served with a simple tomato sauce, garlic and parsley, as in *atún con tomate* (page 229).

675g/1½lb swordfish
340g/12oz thin asparagus (wild, if possible)
90ml/3fl oz oil
flour for coating

2 tomatoes, peeled and chopped
280g/10oz whole prawns, raw
450ml/¾ pint home-made beef stock
60g/2oz butter
2 tablespoons Montilla *or* fino sherry
salt and pepper

Skin the swordfish and cut it roughly into cubes. Slice the asparagus into 2.5cm/1in lengths, discarding the woody ends of the stalks. If using wild asparagus, blanch the pieces in boiling water for a minute in case it's very bitter.

Heat the oil in an earthenware *cazuela* or sauté pan. Dip the swordfish pieces in flour and fry them quickly until lightly browned. Remove and set aside. Add the chopped tomatoes to the oil and cook them rapidly until they start to form a sauce. Return the swordfish to the pot, along with the asparagus and prawns, then add the stock, the butter and the Montilla or sherry. Season lightly and simmer until the sauce is reduced to a good consistency.

## TROUT

### *(Trucha)*

The rivers of Spain are famous for their trout, but the ones in Spanish markets are increasingly from hatcheries, *criaderos*. There is one of these in the countryside to the north of Málaga called Río Frío (cold river) where the trout swim in a stream rushing by the path from which you watch. It's wooded, shady and cool, and seems perfectly natural except for the quantity of fish – the water is absolutely packed with trout. People throw them fragments of bread and the water seems to boil as the fish hurl themselves furiously in pursuit. It's like a permanent rush hour.

Most likely these same people have just eaten or are just about to eat trout in one of the basic restaurants that have sprung up next to the farm. They serve a few other things but not many, and most people go simply to eat good trout, spanking fresh.

## Trucha a la asturiana

Asturian-style trout. This beautiful dish is also one of the simplest and best fish dishes in Spain: the crisp, brown-skinned trout adorns the plate, with no garnish except the tiny nuggets of golden fat in which it was fried. The fat must be from a cured but unsmoked ham – ask in a delicatessen where they have Spanish or Italian hams and persuade them to set aside any excess fat they might discard, or else the rind, for there is often enough adhering to it for several trout.

Clean the trout carefully and sprinkle it with enough coarse salt to give it a good coating. Leave it like this for an hour, then brush off the salt. Take as much ham fat as you like, free of rind, and cut it into small dice. Fry these gently in a little lard until they are transparent and starting to brown. Flour the trout and add them to the frying pan over a medium heat. Fry, turning once, until the trout are brown and crisp on both sides. Garnish with the nuggets of fat, which should also have browned, and some of the cooking juices.

# Trucha con jamón y almendras

Trout with ham and almonds. For each trout allow:

1-2 tablespoons oil
flour for coating
60g/2oz serrano ham, diced small
3 almonds, blanched, peeled and chopped quite small
1 clove garlic, chopped
½ tablespoon chopped parsley
½ tablespoon lemon juice
½ tablespoon dry sherry

Heat a little oil in a frying pan. Season the trout and dip it in flour. Place in the hot oil and add the ham, almonds, garlic and parsley. Fry, turning the trout once. By the time the trout is well browned on both sides the rest will be cooked and coloured. Splash over the lemon juice and sherry, just enough to moisten it and form a little sauce. Let it all bubble, and serve piping hot.

# Trucha a la navarra

A contentious dish of trout from Navarra. Trout with ham is mistakenly served in many places under this name, at least according to various respectable authorities. I give both versions, for both are delicious, although there is no resemblance between them.

## VERSION 1

4 trout, cleaned but left whole

300ml/½ pint red wine

1 onion, finely chopped

1 bay leaf

pepper

small sprigs of mint, thyme, rosemary

3 tablespoons oil

salt

2 egg yolks

In a *cazuela* or similar, marinate the trout for 2 hours or so in the red wine mixed with the chopped onion, a bay leaf torn into pieces, a grinding of pepper, and small sprigs of mint, thyme and rosemary.

Add the oil, season with salt and place the *cazuela* over a good heat. Turn the trout over after about 5 minutes. After 10 minutes the fish should be done and the sauce well reduced. Remove the trout to warm plates. Beat the egg yolks and strain into the cooking liquor, stirring all the time. Put the sauce back on a low flame and heat, stirring, until it thickens enough to coat the back of the spoon. Pour it over the trout.

Accompany or garnish the fish with slices of boiled or steamed potatoes.

## VERSION 2

I find this combination of trout and serrano ham a magical one. Here the fish are fried in oil flavoured with smoked bacon – and that's it. If possible, get your fishmonger to gut the trout without slitting it all the way down the belly, so that the latter acts as a natural pocket for the ham.

4 trout, cleaned as on page 227

4 thin slices serrano ham

4 tablespoons oil

120g/4oz streaky smoked bacon, sliced

flour for coating

Dry the trout thoroughly with paper towels. Do not season them. Roll up the slices of ham into sausage shapes and insert them into the cavities of the trout. Heat the oil and gently fry the bacon until it is crisp. Remove it and set aside. Turn the trout in the flour, tapping them gently to get rid of the excess. Add them to the hot oil and fry over a medium heat, turning them once, until both sides are a good brown (about 15 minutes in all). Place them on a heated serving dish, garnish with the pieces of bacon and pour the hot pan juices over them. Serve at once.

Try serving this with a fine green vegetable such as broccoli, accompanied by a dish of allioli.

## TUNA/BLUEFIN TUNA
### (Atún rojo, cimarrón)

These massive creatures, one of the fastest in the sea, trek around the Mediterranean in huge shoals, or at least they used to. They have been fished since antiquity, when the Phoenicians, Carthaginians and Romans observed their migration patterns, patterns which led to an ingenious way of fishing them that still survives, called the *almadraba*. The fish are in effect herded, like sheep, through a labyrinth of submarine passages formed by vertical nets which intercept the shoals and guide the tuna to the *copa* or *buche*, the 'square of death', which closes round the fish and is lifted from the water. A battle now commences as the giant fish threshes and the fishermen try to haul it aboard with their gaffs, the water turning red with the gore that also liberally spatters the men and the boat.

The cost of buying and maintaining these nets, combined with dwindling stocks and quotas, has meant the gradual disappearance of these old ways, and though the *almadraba* survives, tuna are now taken by easier methods.

Demand continues to outstrip supply as much of the catch is sent off to Japan where fresh tuna is so appreciated raw. In places like Barbate or Zahara de los Atunes, close to the fishing grounds, you can try some very unusual cuts, the heart, for example, or the *criadillas* (testicles), and should you come across *bull* or *bullets* on the eastern seaboard they are the stomach and tripe, salted and dried. Nothing is wasted of this great fish.

Canned tuna is good, of course, but should not be substituted for fresh in the following recipes. Keep it for salads or sauces for pasta.

# Atún con tomate

The whole point in deceptively simple dishes like this is that the ingredients should be the best. Try to get the tuna cut from the belly of the fish called *ventresca* – because of its natural marbling with fat it's wonderfully tender – and use the best tomatoes you can find, boosting the flavour with tomato concentrate and a little vinegar if necessary. Swordfish can be prepared the same way.

900g/2lb fresh tuna, skinned
salt and pepper

juice of 1 lemon
a little flour for coating
4 tablespoons oil
900g/2lb fresh tomatoes, peeled and chopped
1 bay leaf
3 tablespoons chopped parsley
3 cloves garlic, chopped

Cut the tuna into 8 or 10 large chunks. Season well with salt and the lemon juice, then flour them. Heat the oil and fry the pieces of tuna quickly until brown. Transfer them to a *cazuela* or similar. In the remaining oil fry the tomato with the bay leaf and some salt and pepper. When it starts to soften pour it over the fish, which should be more or less covered by the sauce. Cover the dish and simmer for about 30 minutes. Just before serving, sprinkle with the chopped parsley and garlic.

## Putaco tarragoní

A thick tuna and snail stew from the province of Tarragona. It is built round a *samfaina* and finished, like so many Catalan dishes, with a *picada* of nuts and garlic.

2 onions, thinly sliced
1½ red peppers, peeled and chopped
4 tablespoons oil
3 tomatoes, peeled and chopped
340g/12oz potatoes, cubed
675g/1½lb small tinned snails
3 courgettes, sliced
salt and pepper
450g/1lb fresh tuna, cut into chunks
3 cloves garlic
1 good pinch saffron
2 tablespoons chopped parsley
24 toasted almonds
4 tablespoons *vino rancio* (or dry vermouth)

Soften the onion and red pepper in the oil in a large *cazuela* or similar. Add the tomatoes, let them soften and add the potatoes, snails and courgettes. Season, just cover with water and leave to simmer, uncovered, for 10 minutes. Add the pieces of tuna and continue cooking.

Pound the garlic, saffron, parsley and almonds to a paste. Thin to a cream with the wine. When the tuna is cooked through and the sauce reduced, stir in the *picada*, let it heat through briefly, enough to thicken the stew slightly, and serve.

# Pescado en ajillo

Fish with fried garlic and chilli. This is the sort of thing I make when I'm both short of time and without a clue as to what to do with the fish I've bought. It's perhaps best with whole fish rather than fillets or steaks.

*FOR 4 FISH OF ABOUT 225G/8OZ EACH, SCALED AND GUTTED:*
fish broth or water mixed with 1-2 tablespoons white wine
salt and pepper
6-8 (or more) cloves of garlic, sliced
2 dried red chillies, seeds removed (optional) and thinly sliced
4-6 tablespoons oil

Place the fish snugly in an oven dish and half cover with broth, or simply water and white wine. Season them and cook in a hot oven for about 15 minutes, turning them over at half-time. Drain off the liquid (keep it for soups or other fish dishes) and put the fish on to warm plates. Keep them warm while you fry the garlic and chilli in the oil until the garlic is a golden, aromatic brown. Distribute the garlic, chilli and oil between the four fish and serve at once.

**Note:** If you have a helper, get them to fillet the cooked fish for you while you are preparing the garlic.

# Mariscos
## SHELLFISH

The following are the commonest Spanish shellfish.

### CLAMS
#### (Almejas)

These are clams in general, and more exact names denote the many varieties, one of the best being the beautiful little *coquina*. I find the smaller varieties best, not only for flavour but for tenderness – some of the larger clams, such as *concha fina*, which is eaten raw, can be very chewy.

When buying fresh clams, they may be sandy. Put them in a big bowl of salty or seawater and let them sit in it for a few hours if possible. This will help to purge them of grit. Several recipes in this book call for the addition of fresh clams. If they are unavailable use fresh cockles (*berberechos*), or tinned clams at a pinch.

A good basic way to cook clams, hardly a recipe really, is the following: get a large heavy sauté pan as hot as you dare. Add a splash of olive oil, followed immediately by your well-drained clams. They will open in a very short time. Transfer to a dish, add a splash of raw oil, and eat while they are still spanking hot.

# Almejas salteadas

Sautéed clams. This is perhaps the commonest way of cooking the various sorts of excellent little clams available in Spain. Serve them as a first course or as part of a seafood dinner.

1kg/2¼lb fresh clams in the shell
8 tablespoons oil
4 cloves garlic, roughly chopped
salt
3 tablespoons chopped parsley
juice of 2 lemons

Put the clams in a colander and run them under the tap, removing any damaged ones. Place them in a large frying pan or *cazuela* with the oil and garlic. Put over a high heat and stir occasionally as the clams open. Sprinkle with a little salt and the parsley, and pour in the lemon juice. Add 2-3 tablespoons of water and let it boil together very briefly. Serve immediately.

# Almejas a la pescadora

A rich and garlicky dish of clams from Cádiz.

1kg/2¼lb fresh clams in the shell
6 tablespoons oil
4 cloves garlic, chopped
1 teaspoon paprika
100ml/3½fl oz dry sherry
2 tablespoons allioli (see page 188)

Wash and pick over the clams. Heat the oil in a large frying pan and fry the chopped garlic until it starts to brown. Add the paprika, let it sizzle very briefly and add the clams. Stir them round and add the sherry. Boil rapidly until the majority of the clams are open. Using a slotted spoon, transfer the clams to a serving dish. Beat the allioli into the pan juices, pour the sauce over the clams and serve.

# Almejas con setas

A recipe from Galicia that I include more in hope than in expectation, for it requires both fresh clams, preferably large ones, and fresh fungi. If you are fortunate enough to find both available one lucky day, try this lovely dish as a starter.

450g/1lb fungi (whatever is available)
1kg/2¼lb fresh clams in the shell
4 tablespoons oil
½ onion
1 clove garlic
½ green pepper
1 pinch saffron
1 tablespoon chopped parsley
½ dried red chilli
2-3 tablespoons white wine
salt

Clean and slice the fungi. Wash and pick over the clams. Heat the oil in a *cazuela* or similar and add the onion, garlic, green pepper and saffron, all finely chopped, and the parsley. Let them soften and add the fungi. When these start to throw off their juices add the sliced chilli and the white wine. Season with a little salt. Let this cook together for 10 minutes or so before adding the clams. As soon as they have opened serve the dish immediately.

## CRAB

### (Buey de Mar)

The large crab familiar in British fishmongers. The Spanish name means 'sea ox', so called because the large pincers or claws are thought to resemble cattle horns. When dried out these claws are used as kindling in some places, giving rise to another name for the crab – *esqueiro* or fire-lighter. Formerly these claws were not considered fit for human consumption and were discarded, but taste have changed and *bocas* are now a popular tapa in crab-catching areas.

# CRAWFISH AND LOBSTER

## (Langosta and bogavante, lubrigante)

Lobster can be easily distinguished from crawfish, the former being dark blue and with vicious-looking claws, and the latter clawless and brownish in colour. They both make superb, if expensive, eating. Crawfish are more common in Spain, but numbers have decreased owing to overfishing and being taken out of season. Particularly well-known are the crawfish of the Gallician port of A Guarda, where they have a fiesta in its honour in July.

# Langosta con pollo, langosta a la catalana

Catalan-style crawfish with chicken. The price of crawfish or spiny lobster in Spain is such that this old Catalan dish is really only suitable for special occasions. I have only tried it once but this dish made the occasion unforgettable. Its list of ingredients may read like something out of a medieval nightmare – chocolate, garlic, dry biscuits, nuts, saffron, paprika and so on – and some may even baulk at the idea of combining such a noble shellfish with a humble chicken. But rest assured, it all blends together into one of the supreme dishes of the Spanish repertoire.

This is the recipe I was given by the man who cooked our *langosta a la catalana*.

Take a live crawfish, remove its legs and cut it into regular-sized pieces. Cut the head through the middle. Reserve the blood that is released, the liver and the coral. Season the pieces of crawfish, and a quarter of a chicken per person, with salt and pepper. Place the pieces in a *cazuela* with some oil. Turn them over and add some chopped onion and a small bunch of aromatic herbs. When the onion appears to be a golden colour, add the paste you have previously prepared as follows:

Pound saffron, then garlic and paprika, almonds, hazelnuts, parsley, the biscuits,* the liver, the blood of the crawfish, the coral and some chocolate. Then dilute the mixture with some broth.

Once you've added the paste to the pan continue cooking: taste for salt and pepper and put it in the oven for 10 minutes.

It was served with small triangles of fried bread. In fairness to the crawfish one should perhaps cut the head through the middle to kill it first, before dismembering it. The recipe is similar to that of Ignacio Doménech in *La nueva cocina elegante española* (1915) which pins down some of the quantities: 40g/1½oz chocolate, 20 nuts, two or three biscuits, a ladleful of broth. You should not, in my opinion, be tempted to leave out the chocolate, and chicken breasts are preferable to chicken quarters.

*The biscuits referred to are small, dried slices of sponge and almonds called *carquinyolis*, similar to Italy's *cantuccini*, with a hint of vanilla.

## DATE-SHELLS

### (Dátiles de Mar)

These look rather like slimmed-down versions of mussels and are extremely expensive in Spain, chiefly because they live embedded in rock which makes it very difficult to get them out. This job is commonly done by the youngsters of places like Peñiscola in Valencia, who dive down to the rocks to chip the date-shells out. They formerly got by on lung-power, but scuba equipment is now more often used. This has increased yield but has accelerated the damage to the shells' natural habitat, and fishing them is now regulated. They are either eaten raw or steamed open and eaten with a few drops of lemon juice.

*Note: since this was written the date-shell has been declared a protected species and it is illegal to sell them. They are still poached and offered for sale by the unscrupulous. However, do not be tempted as they will not have been subjected to the normal quality controls for shellfish.

## DUBLIN BAY PRAWNS, SCAMPI

### (Cigalas)

Jane Grigson, describing her first taste of them, said: 'I thought I had discovered the secret of an earthly paradise.' (*Fish Cookery* 1973). I know what she means. Actually, it happened to me the second time, the *cigalas* having been too chilled the first. We only had four between the two of us but the taste was of dreams, especially the creamy part inside the head which must on no account be discarded out of squeamishness. The claws, too, are worth cracking, chewing and sucking. If you should encounter fresh, uncooked, rosy-pink *cigalas*, cook them for just a few minutes in well-salted (20-30g per litre) water. Let them cool before you eat them, but don't refrigerate them. If they are good and fresh nothing should be added to distract from their exquisite taste – no mayonnaise, lemon, nothing.

## GOOSE BARNACLES

### (Percebes)

These extraordinary creatures don't look remotely edible; in fact they don't even look like living things. When I first saw them in a Madrid bar my immediate impression was that they had been cut from the feet of some great bird. My mind jumped to Macbeth and the blasted heath – easy to imagine the witches tossing *percebes* with glee into the cauldron along with the bits of bat and toad.

*Percebes* grow like unhealthy protuberances from rocks – not just any rocks but the ones where the waves pound hardest and most dangerously. Plucking them from their habitat is an extremely perilous business – the picker must dash to the rocks in between waves or be lowered down to them swinging on a rope – and they fetch high prices as a result. Strange to think that they used to be food for the poor. *Percebes* that you can pick yourself from calmer waters are much less flavourful, as if the lack of excitement inhibited their development. In fact it's because rougher waters provide more oxygen to the barnacles, which explains in part why the *percebes* from Galicia's deadly Costa de la Muerte are so prized for their flavour.

To cook *percebes*, use sea water or salty water plus a bay leaf. Drop them in the boiling water, and when it returns to the boil remove from the heat and leave with the lid on for about 5 minutes. To eat them, snap off the nail-like pieces at the end and suck out the thin sliver of pink flesh from inside the leathery body. Have a large napkin draped over you for they can squirt. Or you can eat them raw, if you dare.

## MUREX
### *(Cañadillas)*

Murex provide delicious mouthfuls, though they are a little tough. When you see people eating them in Spanish bars you may wonder why, having eaten the meat, they start to shake the shells hard, like a thermometer. This is to dislodge the murex's *bonne bouche* hidden deep inside – a sliver of soft, dark meat, liver-like in texture and flavour.

## MUSSELS
### *(Mejillones)*

We should be grateful for mussels' cheapness and not condemn them as 'poor-man's seafood'. Thanks to mussel farms, they are the only commonly available shellfish many people can afford. In Galicia a common sight in the *rías* is the floating rafts on which they are grown. There they are picked when they are on the big side, but for flavour I prefer tiny wild mussels.

## PRAWNS
### *(Gambas)*

Like *almeja*, the word *gamba* is a general term for several similar creatures, and larger ones are called *langostinos*. This often leads to misunderstandings in restaurants, since foreigners tend to expect scampi (*langoustines* in France). Different regions lay claim to fishing the best ones. *Langostinos* can be a hefty size – the ones caught off Guardamar de Segura south of Alicante can reach nearly 30cm/1ft long, or so they say. They arouse fervent enthusiasm: in 1712 Louis-Joseph de Bourbon, duc de Vendôme, ate too many one day in Vinaròs as he was preparing to invade Cataluña, and died as a result. His body is buried in the Escorial, minus the intestines which failed him; these stayed behind, the remains of the *langostinos* still preserved inside them, to be displayed, in a local church.

Though very good, *langostinos* in my opinion generally cannot compare for fine flavour with smaller prawns and shrimps, the *gambas*, *camarones* and *quisquillas*, which are nibbled at endlessly in bars all over Spain.

# SCALLOPS

## *(Vieiras, peregrinas)*

Scallops are the pride, almost the emblem, of Galicia, and have a romantic background. Venus, so the legend goes, was born of a scallop (see Botticelli), which caused it to be associated with love and the ability to inspire it. Then it was adopted as the emblem for the pilgrims from all over Catholic Europe who trudged and sailed in their thousands to the shrine of the mythical St James – Santiago de Compostela – the association arising from the supposed imprint of the saint's cross on the shell. These shells were so common and cheap that they were used to face houses as a means of damp-proofing. Such plenty, as with oysters, seems inconceivable today when we have to pay a small fortune to enjoy just a few.

There are good smaller scallops also, the *zamburiña*, the variegated scallop, which is popular as a filling for *empanadas*, and the *volandeira*, the queen scallop.

# SEA ANENOMES

## *(Ortiguillas)*

If you saw these in their raw state you would think twice about preparing them, let alone eating them, but they are surprisingly good fried. A speciality in and around Cádiz.

# SEA SNAILS

## *(Cañabotas)*

These are easy enough to pick yourself from rocks while out swimming. Quite good, though chewy. They should be boiled, for a long time.

# SEA URCHINS

## *(Erizos, oricios, garotes)*

Another seafood that used to be thought of as poor people's fare, but now much of the catch is snapped up by Japanese buyers. They are popular on parts of the northern and eastern Spanish coasts; unpopular with unwary bathers who tread on them. In Cádiz they form the centrepiece, along with local oysters, of the fiesta at the start of their annual immensely popular carnival celebrations. Sea urchins are best in the winter months when the roes (which are what you eat) are fat and glossy.

## SHORE AND OTHER SMALL CRABS
### (Cangrejos, nécoras)

These are very cheap in Spain because they have so little meat – when I last bought a dozen or so for soup they cost me next to nothing. There's not a lot you can do with them apart from making soup, or putting them in the stockpot, but it will have a very good flavour.

# Sopa de cangrejos

Crab soup. Wash about a dozen small crabs (about 225g/8oz) then place them in a pot with some fried chopped onion, chopped red pepper, peeled and chopped tomato and parsley. Cover them with water, add salt and boil for 10 minutes. Put it all through the liquidizer in batches, then strain through a fine sieve. Melt 60g/2oz butter, add 2 tablespoons of flour and let the roux cook for a while. Gradually add the crab broth. Add a little tomato concentrate to bring up the colour, and pepper. Simmer for 10 minutes. Stir in a large knob of butter before serving.

## SPIDER-CRAB
### (Centollo, centolla)

The spiky-shelled, hairy-legged spider-crabs are particularly popular in the Basque country where they are known as *txangurros*. All crab recipes are suitable for *centollo*, and vice versa.

# La Carne,
## Las Aves y La Caza
### Meat, Poultry and Game

Game is included with meat and poultry here because for a long time virtually the only meat people got to eat was that of the wild animals and birds they could catch themselves, often illegally. Apart from Switzerland, Spain is Europe's most mountainous country, and the poor were lucky that these wooded hills and mountains contained an abundance of free protein – rabbit, hare, wild boar, venison and so on. Anything that moved was considered fair game, including thrushes and larks and other small birds which could be fried and eaten whole, bones and all. In hard times, fishermen would even eat sea-birds such as gannets, first removing all their fishy-tasting fat, then preserving them in brine. Hunger has driven the Spanish to eat even stranger things – donkey (disguised as beef), cat (disguised as rabbit), frogs, rats and, in Extremadura, Spain's poorest region, lizards. There you might still come across a lizard catcher, string of little dead bodies in one hand, small gaff in the other.

Apart from game, the meat eaten by the poor would be pork usually in the form of a little *tocino* eaten with bread. Pork is traditionally the most important source of meat in Spain, and many families used to keep a pig or two in the backyard until the *matanza*, the killing or slaughter, after which every scrap would be prepared so as to last as long as possible. The *matanza* came to be imbued with an air of ceremony, almost of a religious sacrifice, while at the same time being an occasion for joy: centred on the *matanza* was a family feast that brought together relatives and friends who all came to help – and to eat. Nowadays, many *matanzas* are simply an excuse for a celebration and a blow-out.

It is a grisly affair. The pig is dispatched by severing its jugular, and its blood flows into the *lebrillo*, an earthenware tub, where it needs to be stirred frequently to stop it congealing. Its skin is scalded with boiling water and scraped or scorched free of bristles, and the pig is then cut up. The hams and bacon are salted, the innards are washed and scrubbed (a revolting job) to make sausage casings, the sausages themselves – the chorizos, *butifarras*, and so on – are prepared, and the fat rendered down for lard. The bits left behind after rendering the fat are called *chicharrones* and are used to make pastries. The skin is cut into strips called *chiquillos* and cooked. The morcillas, the blood sausages, are boiled, the fat they give off being used as a spread for bread or toast. The head will be used for brawn, and the children present may appropriate the bladder to make a very serviceable football. This messy work takes all day and most of the night, the workers being sustained by pieces of the cooked pork and plenty of wine.

The *matanza* season depends on where you are, but will coincide with the first cold spells of winter. In Asturias the slaughter is known as San Martín because it traditionally starts at Martinmas, 11 November, and from this comes the phrase *a cada cerdo le llega su San Martín*, every pig has his Martinmas, often spoken as a reassurance when referring to the nefarious deeds of some unpleasant character. In the south the *matanzas* tend to begin somewhat later – in Murcia and Andalucía they often wait until mid-December or even Christmas.

Apart from pork, the most popular meat is lamb, which is reared in vast flocks, particularly on the plains of Castilla where it was formerly enjoyed almost exclusively by the feudal lords. Nowadays every other restaurant in Castilla y León seems to specialise in roast baby lamb (*lechazo*) or sucking pig (*cochinillo*), and they draw in people from miles around to enjoy them for a Sunday treat. A long-distance lorry driver told me how he always tried to get to this part of Spain for his lunch; even if it meant arriving very late in the afternoon, he said, the thought of the roast lamb always kept him going.

The lonely shepherds who keep these flocks have not only developed their own whistling language with which they communicate across valleys but also their own cooking tradition – dishes cooked *a lo pastoril*. These are especially associated with the regions affected by the *Mesta*, the cartel of Castilian sheep-raisers formed in the thirteenth century, whose members had the right to drive their flocks in the autumn to winter pastures over any land that happened to be in the way. The *Mesta* was to become the controller of wool, Spain's most important export. The shepherds who drove those flocks on their long treks went equipped with just a *caldero*, a knife and a wooden spoon and would prepare their simple dishes of lamb (they would use injured ones) or game or just *migas* on the way. Such dishes have gained a wider popularity, particularly at country fiestas or cattle fairs.

Spanish beef (*carne de vacuno*) has improved tremendously, especially in northern areas where the quality of native breeds is maintained and promoted by regional associations. Spanish butchers used to hinder things by selling beef too fresh and unhung. When I first moved to the south of Spain this was still considered to be a virtue, a throwback to the not-so-distant days when lack of refrigeration meant that meat had to be eaten as quickly as possible after slaughter. Luckily things are changing, and for the better.

Confusion may arise over the use in Spain of the word *ternera*, meat from a young beef animal. The word is always translated in English books on Spanish cookery or on tourist menus as veal. Though strictly speaking correct, it does lead one to expect the pale pink meat of the milk-fed animal which bears the name in Britain. In fact *ternera* usually looks and tastes much like normal beef and if you want the veal described above you should look for *ternera blanca, ternera lechal* or *ternera de Ávila*. It can be called *ternera* until the animal is about a year old. Then it becomes *añojo* for a year, then *novillo* until it's four, or *cebón,* if the animal has been castrated. More mature beef is simply *carne de vaca* or *carne de buey*, depending on whether it's from a cow or a bullock and is mainly used for processed meat. *Carne de toro* is what you get after bullfights.

Chicken has suffered much the same fate in Spain as in Britain. They were formerly (and still are in country areas) the family egg-layer and Sunday treat, and being home-grown were of especially good flavour and texture. Nowadays the majority are factory-farmed and almost taste-free, a production-line food within the reach of all but the very poor. I would recommend proper chickens for these recipes. The taste and texture more than make up for the expense.

# POULTRY AND GAME
## Pollo al ajillo

Headily flavoured with garlic, this dish is probably the most popular way of eating chicken in Spain. The method is also widely used for goat, rabbit, pork and lamb. (For a more complex version of the latter see the recipe for *cordero al ajillo* on page 279.)

900-1125g/ 2-2½lb chicken, divided into small pieces

9 cloves garlic

salt

6 tablespoons oil

200ml/7fl oz white wine or dry sherry

1 bay leaf

Skin the chicken pieces and trim away any fat. Place them in a dish. Peel 5 of the garlic cloves and crush them. Spread the paste over the chicken, mixing it in thoroughly with your hands. Leave for an hour or so, so that the flavour penetrates the meat.

When the hour is up rinse the pieces of chicken under the cold tap to rid them of all the crushed garlic. This is important, for otherwise the garlic will burn when you fry the chicken. Dry them thoroughly with paper towels and season with salt. Heat the oven to about 400°F/200°C/Gas 6.

Heat the oil in a frying pan and when very hot add the chicken. (This is best done in two batches.) Turn the pieces over as they brown, then remove them to an oven dish. Pour off all but 2-3 tablespoons of the oil (keep it for another chicken dish). Peel and thinly slice the remaining 4 garlic cloves and fry them in the hot oil until nicely browned. Pour in the wine and bring it to the boil, scraping up the chicken juices from the bottom of the pan as you do so. Pour the sauce over the chicken, add the bay leaf in 3-4 pieces and place the dish in the oven for 15-20 minutes, basting occasionally with the juices.

## Pechugas de pollo al ajo cabañil

Breast of chicken in a vinegar sauce, from Murcia. The vinegar combines deliciously with garlic, oregano and paprika to form the sauce, which is given body by adding breadcrumbs. This is a rich dish and calls for a simple accompaniment such as *papas a lo pobre* (page 152).

4 boned chicken breasts, skinned and divided into fillets
salt
150ml/¼ pint oil
10 cloves garlic, 4 of them sliced
1 tablespoon paprika
2 teaspoons dried oregano
6 tablespoons vinegar
about 300ml/½ pint water
2 tablespoons breadcrumbs

Season the chicken with salt and fry it in the oil until browned. While it is browning add the sliced garlic. Pound the rest of the garlic with a little salt, the paprika and oregano, then dilute the paste with the vinegar and water. Mix in the breadcrumbs. Tip this mixture over the chicken – the breasts should be just about covered. Cook fairly rapidly for about 20 minutes or until the sauce is quite thick. If there is any excess oil that hasn't amalgamated into the sauce and you object, skim it off.

This recipe can be adapted to other meats – lamb cutlets, for example, or liver.

# Pollo a la montañesa

Chicken, Santander style – *La Montaña* (the mountain) is the name given to the range running parallel to the Santander coast. The genius of this dish isn't revealed until the last minute: the chicken is strewn with chopped fresh mint. What was an ordinary chicken stew is thus transformed into something special.

2 tablespoons lard
900-1125g/ 2-2½lb chicken, quartered and skinned
2 onions, sliced
salt and pepper
120g/4oz green bacon, diced
2 red peppers, cut into large chunks
4 cloves garlic, crushed
4 tomatoes, peeled and chopped
900g/2lb potatoes, peeled and cut into small chunks
2 teaspoons paprika
300ml/½ pint white wine
chicken stock
1 bay leaf
3 tablespoons chopped fresh mint

Melt the lard in a large casserole dish and fry the chicken pieces over a medium heat until browned all over. Remove them and set aside. Add the onion and bacon and fry quite briskly until the onion softens. Add the red pepper and garlic and continue cooking fairly rapidly for another 5 minutes, stirring frequently. Add the tomatoes, potatoes and paprika and cook for 5 more minutes. Return the chicken to the pan, season the whole lot with salt and pepper, and pour in the wine and enough stock just to cover. Add the bay leaf, cover the pan and simmer for about 30 minutes. Remove the chicken pieces to a warmed serving dish and set aside (this allows the meat to 'settle'). Reduce the sauce over a high heat until it is very thick, stirring frequently. Check the seasoning. Pour the sauce over the chicken, strew generously with the chopped mint and serve.

# Pollo campurriano

Chicken stewed with *tocino* and white wine from Cantabria, and a dish which typifies simple Spanish home cooking, using limited ingredients but which is good and sustaining at the same time. It is eaten with rice, not a usual accompaniment in Spain.

900-1125g/2-2½lb chicken, cut into about 12 pieces
120g/4oz lard

150g/5oz piece of *tocino* or unsmoked streaky bacon, diced

2 onions, chopped

2 tablespoons flour

150ml/¼ pint white wine

water *or* chicken stock

1 bay leaf

1 red and 1 green pepper, chopped

225g/8oz rice

1 teaspoon paprika

salt and pepper

Season the chicken lightly with salt. Heat half the lard in a casserole dish and add the chicken and bacon. Let them colour before adding half the chopped onion. When this has softened mix in the flour. Gradually pour in the wine and enough water or stock to barely cover the meat. Pop in the bay leaf and leave it simmering uncovered for about an hour, the idea being that the sauce gradually reduces to a thick richness.

About 20 minutes before you want to eat, prepare the rice. Melt the remaining lard in a large frying pan or *cazuela* and soften the rest of the onion and the chopped peppers. Add the rice and paprika, cook briefly, stirring, then pour in roughly 1.75 litres/1¼ pints hot water or stock. Bring to the boil, and leave to cook, reducing the heat as the liquid is absorbed, for about 20 minutes, or until the rice is practically tender and still slightly moist. Remove from the heat and leave covered for 5 minutes or so, during which time you can take all the bones from the chicken if you wish.

## Pollo en pepitoria

Spanish chicken fricassee really, and one of the best recipes for chicken I know. Be sure to add the parsley mixture only a short time before the end of cooking, or its fresh taste will be lost.

2 tablespoons lard *or* bacon fat

4 cloves garlic

15-20 almonds *or* hazelnuts, blanched and peeled

2 cloves

3 tablespoons chopped parsley

salt

a little milk

200g/7oz slice green bacon, cut into small cubes

120g/4oz serrano ham, cut into strips
900-1125g/2-2½lb chicken, cut into small pieces and skinned
12 shallots or baby onions, blanched and peeled
150ml/¼ pint white wine
chicken stock
4 large egg yolks
lemon juice to taste

In a large, wide casserole, heat the fat and fry the whole cloves of garlic until brown. Remove them and place in the mortar with the almonds, cloves, parsley and a little salt. Pound well until more or less smooth. Thin to a cream with some milk.

Now fry the bacon and ham in the fat for a couple of minutes. Add the chicken and onions and let them brown all over. Pour in the wine and enough stock just to cover. Put a lid on the pan and let it all simmer for 35-40 minutes. Remove the lid and stir in the almond and parsley mixture. Leave to simmer for about 10 more minutes. Check for salt. Remove the chicken, onions, bacon and ham to a warmed serving dish.

Beat the egg yolks well. Gradually stir in a few tablespoons of the hot sauce. Pour this mixture back into the remaining sauce which will probably be hot enough to make the egg yolks thicken it straight away. If not, place the pan over a low heat, stirring all the time, until it starts to do so. Remove from the heat immediately. Taste, and sharpen the sauce slightly with a little lemon juice. Pour over the chicken and serve immediately.

This is a popular dish throughout Spain, probably originating in the north, for its name derives from *petite oie*, French for small goose. The bird's giblets were the original base for the dish. Hen and lamb are also commonly cooked in this manner.

## Pollo en pepitoria a la riojana

This version of *pepitoria* from La Rioja uses the local walnuts to thicken the sauce, but no egg.

900-1125g/2-2½lb chicken, cut into small pieces
salt and pepper
flour for coating
6 tablespoons oil
1 onion, finely chopped
12 shelled walnuts

1 clove garlic
125ml/4fl oz milk
125ml/4fl oz white wine
450ml/¾ pint chicken stock

Season the chicken pieces with salt and pepper and coat them with flour. Heat the oil in a wide pan and fry the chicken until browned. Drain off most of the oil and add the onion. While this is softening, pound the walnuts to a paste with the garlic. Thin the paste to a cream with the milk. Add the nut cream and the wine to the onion and chicken, pour in the stock and leave the chicken to simmer, covered, for 30 minutes. Remove the lid and continue cooking until the sauce is well thickened.

## Pollo con tomate

Chicken in tomato sauce. Basic cooking, but good.

4 tablespoons well-flavoured lard
salt and pepper
1 chicken (900-1125g/2-2½lb), cut into small joints
1 onion, finely chopped
4 cloves garlic, crushed
4 tomatoes, peeled and chopped
few drops vinegar

Heat the lard in a large frying pan or *cazuela*. Season the chicken and fry it until browned. Remove to a plate. Add the onion and garlic to the fat and fry until soft. Add the tomatoes and chicken, cover and simmer for 30 minutes. Again remove the chicken and purée the sauce. Taste and add a few drops of vinegar to bring out the flavour if necessary. Pour over the chicken and serve.

## Pollo con langostinos

Chicken with prawns. Another Catalan combination of meat and shellfish, and a more accessible one than the recipe for *langosta a la catalana*. Though perhaps less sophisticated, the flavour of this dish is remarkable, especially if you use a Spanish aguardiente which seems to have the effect of accentuating the taste of the seafood. Fresh, raw, large prawns are vital for this, otherwise it's a waste of time and effort.

Rabbit is sometimes used instead of chicken and scampi instead of prawns.

8-12 large prawns, depending on size
900-1125g/2-2½lb chicken, jointed
salt and pepper
flour for coating
4 tablespoons oil
2 onions, chopped
4 tomatoes, peeled and chopped
2 tablespoons chopped parsley
1 bay leaf
1-2 pinches thyme and oregano
40g/1½oz hazelnuts
3 cloves garlic
4 tablespoons *vino rancio* or dry vermouth
4 tablespoons dry *aguardiente* or grappa

Peel the prawns and slice them into 3-4 pieces. Set them aside and make a plain broth with the shells and heads, crushing the latter to squeeze out as much flavour as possible.

Season the chicken pieces, dip them in flour and fry them in the hot oil until brown. Remove them to a plate and soften the onion and tomato in the same oil. Return the chicken to the pan, add the parsley, bay leaf and a pinch or two of thyme and oregano. Just cover with the prawn broth and simmer, covered, for 45 minutes.

Rub the loose skins from the hazelnuts and pound them to a paste with the garlic. Thin the paste to a cream with the wine and aguardiente. Remove the chicken to a plate. If there is too much thin sauce, boil it hard to reduce it a little. Add the prawns and the cream from the mortar and cook for 5 minutes until quite thick. In the meantime, remove all the meat from the chicken pieces, stir it into the sauce, heat through and check the seasoning.

## Pollo a la andaluza

Chicken with sherry, saffron, almonds and garlic. Nothing could be more Andalusian – hence the title.

4 cloves garlic
15-20 almonds, blanched and peeled
4 tablespoons oil

the heads from 6 sprigs parsley

900-1125g/2-2½lb chicken, cut into small pieces

salt and pepper

4 tablespoons flour

1 onion, chopped

250ml/8fl oz dry sherry

1 bay leaf

750ml/1¼ pints chicken stock

2 hard-boiled eggs

1 good pinch saffron

Fry the garlic and almonds in the oil until brown. Just before you remove them throw in the parsley which will immediately crackle and go crisp. Remove all three to the mortar.

Season the chicken, dip in flour and fry in the oil until browned. Remove, and add the onion to the oil. Cook until softened. Return the chicken to the pan and pour over the sherry. Let this bubble away for a minute or two, then add the bay leaf and stock.

Add the yolks of the eggs to the contents of the mortar along with the saffron and pound it all down to a paste. Thin it with some of the stock from the chicken and stir it into the pot. Leave it all simmering about half an hour. Then sprinkle over the chopped egg whites and serve.

## Pollo asado con castañas

Roast chicken stuffed with chestnuts and apples. I like this fine dish from the Basque country for Sunday lunch in winter, accompanied by roast potatoes and *alcachofas estofadas* (see page 140). If you use dried chestnuts, start preparations the night before.

225g/8oz peeled chestnuts (half that quantity if using dried)

milk

salt and pepper

120g/4oz slice of unsmoked streaky bacon, diced

2 cooking apples, peeled and sliced

300ml/½ pint dry cider

1 chicken (about 1.35kg/3lb), liver reserved

1 large knob lard

flour

1-2 tablespoons white wine

If using dried chestnuts, cover them well with boiling water and leave overnight. Drain.

Cover the chestnuts with a mixture of half milk, half water and a little salt. Simmer them until just tender – about 45 minutes. Drain, reserving the cooking liquid. Meanwhile, blanch the pieces of bacon in boiling water for a couple of minutes and drain. Place the apple slices, cider and bacon in a pan and simmer until the apple goes pulpy and the cider evaporates. Stir in the chestnuts. Chop the chicken liver finely and add it to the stuffing. Season it all and place inside the chicken. Either sew up the opening or secure it with a couple of skewers.

Preheat the oven to about 400°F/200°C/Gas 6. Place the chicken in a roasting pan. Sprinkle it well with salt and place a large knob of lard on top. Roast for about 1½ hours, basting occasionally. Remove the chicken. Drain off the fat and juices from the pan. Skim off the fat with a spoon and return two tablespoons of the fat to the pan. Heat it and add a little flour. Let it brown. Gradually add the juices and the cooking liquor from the chestnuts, and a little salt and pepper. Add a splash of white wine. Let it cook for a few minutes, then strain.

Place the stuffing in the centre of a serving dish. Carve the chicken into large pieces and set them round the stuffing. Pour over a little of the sauce and serve the rest separately.

# Pollo con salsa de avellanas

Chicken with hazelnut sauce. The hazelnuts must be well roasted to give the right flavour to this rather unusual sauce.

900-1125g/2-2½lb chicken, cut into small pieces, skinned and seasoned with salt
3 tablespoons oil
1 onion, chopped
1 tomato, peeled and chopped
150ml/¼ pint white wine
4 cloves garlic, chopped
2 tablespoons chopped parsley
120g/4oz roasted hazelnuts, roughly ground in the mortar

Fry the chicken in the oil until well browned and cooked through. Remove. To the remaining oil add the onion, soften it and then add the tomato. Cook rapidly until a thick sauce results. Add the wine, garlic, parsley and nuts and simmer for a few more minutes. Liquidise the sauce until more or less smooth. Return it to the pan with the chicken and add a little water if the sauce seems very thick. Taste for salt and simmer for a few more minutes to let the flavours amalgamate.

# Pollo con salsa de ajos

Chicken with garlic sauce. If you like garlic as much as I do, you'll enjoy this.

6 tablespoons oil
4 slices stale French bread
8 cloves garlic
900-1125g/2-2½lb chicken, cut into small pieces, skinned and seasoned with salt
300ml/½ pint white wine
3 tablespoons chopped parsley
3 cloves
1 good pinch saffron
nutmeg
salt and black pepper

Heat the oil and fry the bread and 5 of the cloves of garlic until well browned. Remove these to the mortar. In the remaining oil fry the chicken and the 3 garlic cloves, crushed, until the chicken changes colour. Pour over the wine and enough water just to cover the chicken. Leave to simmer.

To the bread and garlic in the mortar add the parsley, cloves, saffron and a good grating of nutmeg. Pound it all to a paste. When the chicken is more or less tender (after about 25 minutes) and the sauce reduced somewhat, stir in the contents of the mortar. Leave to cook for another 10 minutes. Add salt if necessary and a little black pepper.

# Pato con judías a la catalana

Duck with beans from Cataluña. Duck is one of the most difficult meats to cook well. If you're not careful, you end up with greasy bits of bony meat enveloped in a wad of skin the texture of wet flannel. I find that the best way to start any duck recipe is gently to precook the duck under cover, drain off all the fat and then let it go brown and crisp in a very hot oven when you need it. It is a mistake to immerse the duck in a sauce – you lose that crispness.

Start preparations for this recipe the day before you need it.

1 large duck (about 1.8-2.25kg/4-5lb), cleaned
salt and pepper
oregano, thyme
120g/4oz rashers streaky bacon

1 onion, sliced
1 carrot, chopped
225g/8oz dried white beans
1 tomato, peeled and chopped
150ml/¼ pint red wine
1 bay leaf
60g/2oz hazelnuts
60g/2oz pine-nuts
1 clove garlic
1 good pinch saffron

The day before: sprinkle the duck with salt, pepper, oregano and thyme. Lay the rashers of bacon over it and place it in a roasting tin. Cover it tightly with foil and bake it in a moderate oven 330-350°F/170-180°C/Gas 3-4 for about 2½ hours. Drain off all the fat and juices into a bowl, not forgetting those that have accumulated inside the bird. Discard the bacon. When cold, put the duck and the bowl of juices in the fridge.

Cover the beans well with cold water.

The next day: remove the layer of fat from the bowl you left in the fridge. Melt a couple of tablespoons of it in a casserole dish and fry the onion and carrot until they start to soften. Add the drained beans and tomato and fry, stirring, for a couple of minutes. Add the jellied juices from the duck, a little salt, the red wine, a bay leaf and about 900ml/1½ pints water. Bring it to the boil, cover and simmer for about an hour.

Roast the hazelnuts in a hot oven for about 10 minutes, then skin them. (Bits of skin always stubbornly remain but these don't matter.) Pound the hazelnuts, pine-nuts, garlic and saffron in a mortar until very smooth. You'll find this easier if you do it in batches. After the beans have been cooking for an hour remove the lid and stir in the nut paste. Leave it to simmer, uncovered, until the sauce is very thick. Add salt if necessary.

Meanwhile, prepare the duck. Using strong kitchen scissors snip off the parson's nose and the flap of skin at the neck end. Cut the duck in half lengthways. Remove as many bones as possible and all excess fat. Cut the halves in two. Place on a baking tray and put in a very hot oven 450°F/230°C/Gas 8 until the duck's skin is brown and crisp. Transfer the duck pieces to a serving dish, surround them with the bean sauce and serve. Don't pour the sauce over the duck or the skin will go soggy again. All the fat that the duck throws off makes an excellent medium for roasting potatoes.

# Pato/Oca con peras

A rather extraordinary dish of young goose cooked with a bizarre hotchpotch of pears, pine-nuts, raisins, anis, and cinnamon, the whole thing coloured with caramel. The Catalans are very proud of it and it is much favoured by them for celebratory meals or fiestas. It is also made with duck, which is perhaps more suitable for British cooks as young goose is not generally available. Well worth trying.

1 large duck, about 1.8-2.25kg/4-5lb

1 onion, finely chopped

1 clove garlic, crushed

1 tomato, peeled and finely chopped

4 small cooking pears, peeled, quartered and cored

1 bay leaf

1 pinch ground cinnamon

60g/2oz pine-nuts

60g/2oz raisins

1 tablespoon parsley

3 tablespoons anis

2 tablespoons sugar

Cook the duck the day before you need it, as explained in the previous recipe, omitting the bacon and oregano. Drain off the fat and juices and chill them overnight.

The next day divide the duck into four, removing as many bones as possible. Use these and the giblets to make a stock.

Remove the fat from the juices and melt 2-3 tablespoons of it in a wide casserole. Soften the onion, garlic and tomato then add the pear quarters and let them cook gently for 10 minutes. Now add the bay leaf, a pinch of cinnamon, the pine-nuts, raisins, parsley, anis and the duck juices. Add enough stock nearly to cover the pears. Simmer uncovered until the pears are tender, turning them over occasionally; the sauce should reduce somewhat.

Meanwhile, place the duck pieces on a rack in a very hot oven to heat through and to crisp the skin. They can also be placed under a hot grill at the last minute if necessary.

Dissolve the sugar in a little water and cook until caramelised. Add the caramel to the sauce. To serve, place the duck pieces on 4 individual plates, each piece surrounded by 4 pieces of pear and some of the sauce.

# Pavo a la catalana

Catalan stuffed turkey. Christmas food in Spain isn't nearly so clear-cut as in Britain: Spanish families eat different food that is special to them. Among the most common Christmas dinners are *besugo* – baked red bream – and turkey, the latter especially so in Cataluña where the recipe below, with variations, has been popular for centuries and reflects the old Catalan habit of mixing fruit and meat (and seasoning everything with cinnamon).

Christmas dinner in Spain is eaten on the evening of 24 December – *la Nochebuena* – and the meal will be finished with a vast assortment of *turrones* and other sweetmeats. Then lots of people go off to midnight Mass – *la misa del gallo* – after which there is much cordial salutation of friends and consumption of alcohol into the small hours. The 25th is spent visiting family and friends, and eating leftovers from the night before. Presents, at least traditionally, aren't given until Epiphany – *Los Reyes*. The Three Kings will fill the shoe you've left out with presents if you've been good, with lumps of coal if not.

Start preparations the night before. Serves approximately 8 people.

1 turkey, preferably a hen (3.5-4.5kg/8-10lb)
120g/4oz lard *or* butter
225g/8oz fat streaky bacon

*FOR THE STUFFING:*
225g/8oz prunes
225g/8oz dried apricots *or* peaches
90g/3oz dried chestnuts
60g/2oz lard
225g/8oz boned loin of pork, diced small
90g/3oz pine-nuts
12 good sausages, thinly sliced (*or* 550g/1¼lb sausagemeat)*
1 cooking apple, peeled and diced
90ml/3fl oz *vino rancio* or dry vermouth
½ teaspoon ground cinnamon
salt and pepper

*Strictly speaking the sausages should be in slices, but I prefer to bind the whole thing together with sausagemeat. A small quantity of raisins is also often added, but with an eye to the Christmas pudding you may prefer to omit them.

The night before: cover the prunes and apricots with water, and, in a separate bowl, the chestnuts.

The next day: drain the chestnuts, cover with fresh water and boil for 30 minutes. Stone the prunes and apricots and chop them quite small. Melt the lard and mix it with the pork, sausages, prunes, apricots, chestnuts, apple, pine-nuts and wine. Season with the cinnamon and plenty of salt and pepper. Place some of the stuffing in the main cavity of the turkey and the rest in a pâté tin for baking separately. Sew up the opening of the cavity, or secure it with a couple of skewers.

Preheat the oven to 425°F/220°C/Gas 7. Place the turkey in a roasting tin and smear it all over with the lard or butter. Season well and lay the bacon over the breast (this is not authentic but helps keep the breast moist). Cover loosely with foil and put in the oven. After 30 minutes reduce the heat to 325°F/160°C/Gas 3 and continue cooking for 2½-3 hours, depending on the weight of the bird. Remove the foil and bacon and increase the heat again to 400°F/200°C/Gas 6. Leave the turkey 30 minutes more, basting it frequently, until its breast is a rich brown colour. Bake the extra stuffing while you are browning the turkey.

Leave the turkey for about 30 minutes in a warm place before carving it. While it's resting, skim off the fat from the juices and make the gravy in the normal way.

# Perdiz con judías

Partridge with beans. Partridge is one of the most plentiful forms of game all over Spain, and a common way of dealing with it is to cook it with the local form of dried beans. A good, simple dish.

1 head garlic
400g/14oz dried white beans, soaked overnight
salt
2 partridges, cleaned and quartered (preferably older birds)
1 bay leaf
1 sprig fresh rosemary

Roast the head of garlic over a flame until well charred. Drain the beans and cover with fresh water in a *cazuela* or similar. Add the partridge pieces and garlic and bring to the boil, skimming off the scum. Add salt, the bay leaf and the rosemary. Remove the latter after a few minutes. Leave to simmer for about 1½ hours, or until the beans are tender, topping up the water level as necessary. Leave the dish to settle for about 10 minutes before serving.

# Perdiz con chocolate

Partridge in chocolate sauce. There are several versions of this as it is popular in many places. This one comes from Navarra. The sauce is luxurious in style and the dish could be made more so by using just the partridge breasts (two per person); the carcass could go towards making the broth.

16 baby onions
2 partridges, halved
salt and pepper
flour for coating
4 tablespoons oil
2 celery stalks, cut into 2.5cm/1in lengths
about 600ml/1 pint light chicken stock
2 tablespoons vinegar
1 bay leaf
4 slices stale French bread
60g/2oz bitter chocolate, grated

Pour boiling water over the onions, leave for 1 minute, drain and then peel, leaving them whole.

Season the partridges with salt and pepper and dip them in flour. Heat the oil in a *cazuela* or similar and add the partridges and onions. Fry until they are lightly browned, stirring the onions to colour them evenly. Add the celery, cook briefly, then pour in the stock and vinegar. Add the bay leaf. Cover and simmer gently for 45 minutes.

Meanwhile, fry the bread in very hot oil until brown. Drain on kitchen paper and place on a serving dish. Remove the partridge halves from the sauce and place one on each piece of fried bread. Arrange the celery and onions around them. Remove the bay leaf and bring the sauce to the boil. Check the seasoning and sprinkle in most of the grated chocolate. Taste the sauce and add more chocolate if necessary. The chocolate melts instantly and thickens the sauce. Pour it over the partridges and serve.

# Codornices con uvas

Quail braised with grapes. Eating wild quail is a thing of the past, but they must have had more flavour than the farm-cosseted replacements we have to eat today. Nevertheless these tiny birds can be good eating, especially in a well-flavoured sauce like this one, with muscat grapes, from Castilla.

If the quails aren't already trussed when you buy them, push a cocktail stick through the legs and bottom of each bird. This neatens their appearance and stops their legs splaying outwards while they're cooking. Remove the sticks before serving.

8 quails
8 slices green streaky bacon
175g/6oz spring onion, thickly sliced
175g/6oz mushrooms, thinly sliced
2 small carrots, cut into thin strips
1 onion, thinly sliced
90g/3oz butter
1 tablespoon bacon fat or lard
250g/8oz muscat grapes, skinned and de-pipped (fiddly but essential)
4-5 peppercorns
nutmeg
225ml/8fl oz white wine
125ml/4fl oz Spanish brandy
2 cloves garlic, crushed

In an oven dish large enough to hold them in a single layer, place the quails with a slice of bacon over the top of each bird. Surround them with the prepared vegetables. Melt the butter and bacon fat and drizzle it over the top of the birds and vegetables. Place in the oven at 350-375°F/180-190°C/Gas 4-5 for 10-15 minutes, so that the bacon starts to brown and everything starts to sizzle.

Meanwhile, pound half the grapes in the mortar with the peppercorns and a good grating of nutmeg. Dilute with the wine and brandy, and add to the quail along with the garlic. Cook about 30 minutes more, basting occasionally, then add the rest of the grapes and let them heat through.

There will be a lot of juice. Drain it into a saucepan and boil it hard to reduce and strengthen the flavour. If it still seems too thin, slake a little flour in some cold water, add it to the sauce and let it cook for a few more minutes.

Arrange the quail on a dish with the vegetables and sliced bacon. Pour over the sauce and serve. This is excellent with saffron rice.

# PORK, BEEF AND LAMB
## Albóndigas sometimes called almóndigas (1)

Simply meatballs, usually of pork, and a very common tapa. Very easy to make. The recipe below produces succulent, subtly spiced meatballs in a rich tomato sauce. They are excellent reheated.

450g/1lb minced pork
225g/8oz fat salt-pork, minced
2 cloves garlic, crushed
2 tablespoons finely chopped parsley
nutmeg, ground cumin
salt and pepper
juice of ½ lemon
1 egg, beaten
2 tablespoons dried breadcrumbs
flour for coating
oil for frying

*FOR THE SAUCE:*
1 onion, chopped
2 tomatoes, peeled and chopped
150ml/¼ pint white wine
1 tablespoon paprika
1 bay leaf

Mix the meats with the garlic, parsley, a good grating of nutmeg, a pinch or two of cumin and some salt and pepper. Make sure you mix it very thoroughly, using your hands: they're much more effective than spoons. Mix in the lemon, egg and breadcrumbs. If the mixture seems soggy add more breadcrumbs; it should hold together but not be too dry. Then form the mixture into balls the size of a golf ball, more or less, using your hands. Roll them lightly in flour. (If you're not sure whether you've seasoned them enough, quickly fry a little bit and taste it.)

Heat about 1.25cm/½in of oil in a frying pan. Fry the *albóndigas* in batches until browned on all sides. Remove them to a *cazuela* or similar. In the remaining fat fry the onion until it starts to brown, then add the tomato and wine. Cook until pulpy, then add the paprika. Liquidise it and pour it over the meatballs. It'll probably be pretty thick and not quite cover them; add water until it does, just about. Add the bay leaf and leave the *albóndigas* to simmer for about 30 minutes.

These are best served when less than boiling hot, with fried potatoes and salad.

# Albóndigas (2)

Another version, with a sauce that has an unusual, almost gamy, flavour that comes from a combination of brandy and sherry.

*FOR THE MEATBALLS:*
250g/9oz minced beef
250g/9oz minced pork
1 egg, beaten
1 clove garlic, crushed
1 tablespoon chopped parsley
¼ teaspoon ground cumin
1 teaspoon dried oregano
salt and pepper
60g/2oz lard

*FOR THE SAUCE:*
1 onion, finely chopped
1 clove garlic, crushed
1 tomato, peeled and roughly chopped
1 tablespoon flour
5 tablespoons Spanish brandy
3 tablespoons dry sherry
1 smallish, firm apple, peeled and roughly chopped
30g/1oz almonds, blanched and peeled
30g/1oz pine-nuts

Mix thoroughly all the ingredients for the meatballs, except the lard. To check that the seasoning is adequate fry a fragment of the mixture and taste. Form the mixture into small balls with your hands. Heat the lard in a large frying pan and brown the meatballs all over. Transfer them to a *cazuela* or casserole dish.

In the remaining fat fry the onion and garlic until softened. Add the tomato and cook for 5 more minutes. Stir in the flour and pour the mixture over the meatballs. Add the brandy, sherry and enough water or stock barely to cover. Bring to the boil and simmer uncovered for 40 minutes, stirring occasionally. Add the apple pieces and cook for a further 10 minutes. Pound the almonds and pine-nuts to a paste. Thin it to a cream with a little of the sauce and stir back into the sauce. Check the seasoning and simmer for 10 more minutes.

# Lacón con grelos

A classic Galician dish using typical products of the area: *lacón*, the local ham made from the front legs of a pig; *grelos*, the turnip greens so popular in the region; and local chorizo and potatoes. Other bits of pig – bacon, ear, head – may be added. This is a warming dish for cold, wet days, in which Galicia specialises.

Care must be taken in choosing the ingredients or this will be insipid. Especially important are the greens: turnip greens will probably be unavailable, so alternatives have to be found. Spinach lacks the body of turnip greens and its bitterness upsets the balance of flavours; chard is a disaster, becoming slimy and tasteless. The best choice is to buy the crispest, freshest spring greens you can find, preferably with a slightly spicy flavour, or else cabbage.

900g/2lb turnip tops *or* suitable greens
900g/2lb joint of unsmoked ham *or* gammon
4 medium-sized potatoes (or more, depending on appetites)
4 chorizos
If using Spanish *lacón* it will need 48 hours soaking, changing the water every 12 hours

Trim the greens of any thick fibrous stalks or stalk-ends. Wash them thoroughly.

Put the ham in a large pot, cover it with water and bring to the boil. Taste the water and if it's very salty throw it away and start again with fresh. Boil the ham for about 30 minutes. Add the peeled potatoes cut into large pieces. Boil for 10 more minutes before adding the chorizos and greens. Cook for 10 more minutes, or until the greens are tender.

Drain everything well in a colander, reserving the broth for soups, e.g. with noodles, or for *papas pegas* (page 134). Slice the ham and put it on one plate with the chorizo. Roughly slice the greens and put them on another plate with the potatoes. Serve steaming hot.

# Solomillo de cerdo encebollado

Fillet of pork in an onion sauce thickened with almonds.

790g/1¾lb pork fillet, preferably ibérico, in a piece
salt and pepper
4 tablespoons lard
2 onions, quite finely chopped
6 cloves garlic

¼ teaspoon dried thyme *or* a sprig or two of fresh
nutmeg to taste
2 tablespoons wine vinegar
oil
2 dozen almonds, blanched and peeled
1 good pinch saffron

Trim the pork fillet carefully of all fat or it will buckle while it cooks. Season with salt and pepper. Heat the lard in a large *cazuela* or similar, and brown the fillet all over. Reduce the heat and add the chopped onions and 4 crushed cloves of garlic. Let them soften around the meat. Sprinkle in the thyme and a good grating of fresh nutmeg. Stir in the vinegar and enough water (or white wine) to half-cover the meat. Cover and leave to simmer gently for 30 minutes. Check the seasoning.

While the meat is cooking, heat a little oil in a frying pan and fry the almonds and two whole cloves of garlic until brown. Drain them and pound them to a paste in a mortar with the saffron. Add the paste to the sauce and cook for 10 more minutes, when it should be quite thick.

# Lomo al jerez

Loin of pork, larded with ham, spiked with garlic and roasted with sherry. It makes a delicious Sunday lunch. Remove the crackling and cook it separately.

60g/2oz serrano ham, cut into thin strips
900g/2lb boned loin of pork, preferably ibérico, in a piece and tied to keep its shape
2 cloves garlic, cut into slivers
salt and pepper
thyme, cumin to taste
2 tablespoons lard
150ml/¼ pint dry sherry
flour

Using a larding needle, push the strips of ham into the pork all the way along. Make holes with the needle and insert the slivers of garlic into them. Rub the meat with salt, pepper, thyme and a little cumin, then smear it all over with the lard. Heat the oven to 375°F/190°C/Gas 5.

Place the meat in a baking dish just large enough to hold it. Pour in the sherry and an equal amount of water. Cook in the oven, basting occasionally, for about 1½ hours. Roast the crackling at the same time. Pour off the juices and skim off the fat. Heat 2 tablespoons of the fat in a small pan. Add a little flour to bind it and cook for 2 minutes until browned. Gradually add the cooking juices and a little vegetable water or stock – enough to make a small quantity of gravy. Slice the pork, pour the gravy over and serve. This is excellent with fried green peppers.

# Lomo con castañas

Pork with chestnuts. The sweetness of chestnuts is frequently used in Spain as a foil to meat and game, being especially good with pork and rabbit, or with richer foods such as duck and hare.

flour for coating
900g/2lb boned loin of pork, or shoulder, preferably *ibérico*, diced
3 tablespoons oil
4 cloves garlic, chopped
120g/4oz serrano ham, chopped
1 onion, roughly chopped
2 carrots, diced
salt and pepper
good pinch saffron, toasted and crumbled
125ml/4fl oz Spanish brandy
125ml/4fl oz dry sherry
675g/1½lb chestnuts

Flour the pieces of pork and fry them in the hot oil with the garlic until browned. Add the ham, onion and carrot and let them soften for about 5 minutes. Season with salt and pepper, add the saffron and pour in the brandy and sherry. If the meat isn't quite covered by liquid add a little water or light stock. Cover and simmer for 45 minutes.

Meanwhile, slit the chestnuts around the rounded part of their shells. Drop them in a pan of boiling water and let them cook for a few minutes. Extract 2-3 at a time and with a small knife remove the outer shell and the inner brown skin. Keep the chestnuts very hot while you do this or the inner skin will be difficult to remove. When they are all peeled add them to the pork and cook for 15 more minutes.

# Picadillo de cerdo

Pork and potatoes in a rich gravy.

4 tablespoons oil
790g/1¾lb pork shoulder, or similar, cut into 2.5cm/1in cubes
60g/2oz serrano ham, diced small
60g/2oz cooked ham, diced small
1 bay leaf
about 300ml/½ pint white wine
450g/1lb potatoes, peeled and cut into chunks
4 large cloves garlic
1 good pinch saffron
2 tablespoons chopped parsley
2 teaspoons peppercorns
6 hard-boiled eggs, sliced

Heat the oil and add the pork and both sorts of ham. Cook them over a high heat until the pork has changed colour completely and thrown off much of its juice. Add the potatoes and bay leaf and enough wine more or less to cover. Pound the garlic, saffron, parsley and peppercorns to a paste. Add this to the pot and cover. Don't add salt. Leave it to simmer for about an hour. Remove the lid and leave it simmering for another 30 minutes or so, until the meat is very tender and the sauce very thick. Now taste for salt – it may well not need any. Serve with the eggs in a separate bowl: each person sprinkles a few slices over his or her helping.

# Costillas

Pork ribs. They are cooked in white wine, but this recipe is so popular where I live that the name is not elaborated upon. The ribs are the meaty ones taken from the belly, not spare ribs. They have an excellent flavour if slowly cooked, and being on the bone and with plenty of natural fat they are particularly succulent. This recipe is simple but extremely good.

4 tablespoons oil
salt and pepper
a good 900g/2lb pork ribs (or 'belly slices'), each chopped into 5cm/2in lengths
2 onions, finely chopped
1 bay leaf

about 300ml/½ pint white wine
about 12 small or new potatoes, peeled

Heat the oil in a *cazuela* or similar. Season the meat and add it to the hot oil. Fry it over a high heat until it has completely changed colour. Add the onions and let them soften, stirring frequently. Add the bay leaf, wine and enough water just to cover the meat. Cover and let it simmer a good hour. Remove the lid and put in the potatoes; it doesn't matter if they're not covered with liquid. Cover again and leave to simmer another 30 minutes, until the potatoes and meat are very tender.

Let it cool a little before eating.

# Lomo de cerdo con chícharos

Loin of pork with peas and spices. Since the flavour of peas is one of the main points about this dish, try to use fresh ones if possible.

1 tablespoon lard *or* bacon fat
1 onion, sliced
550g/1¼lb boned loin of pork, *or* shoulder, preferably *ibérico*, cubed
1 tablespoon flour
450ml/¾ pint meat stock
225g/8oz shelled peas (about three times that weight in the pod)
4 cloves
12 peppercorns
about ½ teaspoon freshly grated nutmeg
2 teaspoons oregano *or* marjoram

Melt the fat and fry the onion gently until it softens. Add the pieces of pork and fry them until they've lost all trace of their raw colour. Sprinkle over the flour, stir it in well and cook for a minute or so before gradually adding the stock. If you're using fresh peas add these now as well.

Pound the cloves, peppercorns, nutmeg and oregano in the mortar until they're powdery. Add these to the pot with some salt and simmer, covered, for about 45 minutes. (Add the frozen peas now if you're using them.) Remove the lid and simmer for a further 15 minutes, or until the sauce is good and thick.

# Lomo con tomate

Loin of pork in tomato sauce, which is also extremely popular as a tapa. Gammon is treated in much the same way in Aragón.

4 tablespoons oil
675g/1½lb boned loin of pork, preferably *ibérico*, cut into small cubes (*or use shoulder and cook the dish longer*)
salt and pepper
1 onion, finely chopped
6 cloves garlic – 3 of them crushed, the others sliced
2 red peppers, chopped
3 tomatoes (or about 790g/1¾lb), peeled and chopped
½ teaspoon sugar
1 tablespoon chopped parsley

Heat the oil in a frying pan and fry the pork until it has changed colour all over. Remove the pork pieces to a casserole dish and season with salt and pepper. In the remaining oil fry the onion until it softens, then add the crushed garlic and red peppers and cook until they too have softened. Add the tomatoes and cook for 5 more minutes. Liquidise most of this sofrito to a smooth purée. Add this purée, the remaining sofrito, the sliced garlic, the sugar and the parsley to the pork. Thin it down with a little water so that the pork is just covered by sauce. Simmer, uncovered, for about 45 minutes, by which time the sauce should have reduced considerably and be very thick (stir frequently towards the end or it may catch). Check the seasoning, and let the dish cool a little before serving.

# Lomo en manteca colorá

To British eyes, a weird sight in Spanish bars is that of a large earthenware dish filled with an arctic landscape of lard. On further investigation you learn that buried in it are pieces of pork, and very tender and succulent they turn out to be – if you can pluck up the courage to eat it, that is, for such a quantity of lard is a forbidding prospect, especially as it is drummed into us these days that we will practically drop dead on the spot if we partake of such things. However, most of the lard is scraped off before you are served and it has such a superb flavour that you will discover you don't object to it anyway. The original idea, of course, was to use the lard as a preservative in the days before refrigeration. I have been assured it lasts for ages and, as proof, my friend José told me how, during his military service, his mother, worried (with good reason) about the diet he would have to live on, used to pack for him a tin of *lomo en manteca*, into which he would delve in times of need during the weeks ahead. In England we had the same idea, using butter, to preserve our shrimp, and in France they make *rillettes* and *confit* along the same lines.

One may also come across bowls of orangey-red lard. This is the flavoured fat thrown off during the making of morcilla sausage and is spread on toast for breakfast. Or it may contain pieces of pork and have been prepared with chorizo; this is my favourite way, and the recipe below will, I hope, show why – the meat will be particularly flavourful and moist, the fat temptingly savoury and a treat on good hot toast. Avoid refrigerating it, for the fat will go solid and waxy and lose the buttery creaminess which is half its appeal. Or else make sure to bring it back to room temperature in plenty of time.

675g/1½lb boned loin of pork, preferably ibérico
salt and pepper
2 chorizo sausages
a little white wine
4 cloves garlic, crushed
2-3 teaspoons dried oregano
2 bay leaves
2 teaspoons paprika
450g/1lb clean lard (especially to be recommended is the lard you can render down yourself from chunks of *ibérico* pork fat)

Cut the pork into about 6 large chunks and season them well with salt and pepper. Skin the sausages and crumble the meat. Place the pieces of pork in a frying pan with just enough water to cover its base, a dash of wine, the crushed garlic, oregano and bay leaves. Place over a medium heat and cover the pan, lifting the lid only to turn the pieces of pork over as they change colour. After about 15 minutes they should have changed colour all over. Now add the crumbled chorizo, the paprika and the lard. Let the latter melt, then leave the pan covered to cook very slowly (the meat shouldn't even come close to frying) for about 45 minutes. Transfer to a dish which should be fairly deep – the cooling lard must more or less cover the meat – and set aside to cool at room temperature. Serve the sliced meat in small quantities with some of its fat and bread as a tapa, or else in sandwiches. The quantities given will feed quite a few if eaten thus.

# LECHAZO

Castillian roast lamb, and one of the most delicious things it is possible to eat in Spain, more specifically various towns and cities scattered about Castilla y León. The lamb (the *churra* breed is considered best) is killed very young and unweaned, 5 weeks old maximum. The carcass is cut into four, put in a *cazuela* and roasted for a couple of hours in a wood-fired baker's-type oven. And that's it. Very little if anything is added. Some chefs put a little water under the lamb, others smear the meat with lard. The meat is served well-done with little to accompany it bar a lettuce salad and bread.

Nobody travelling through this part of the world should pass up the opportunity of trying this roast lamb, for example in Sepúlveda at Figón Zute el Mayor – Tinín. Be aware, however, that restaurants serving *lechazo* are enormously popular at weekends or *días festivos*, when hordes of hungry *madrileños* descend on these places. You should always book well ahead anyway and reserve your lamb; if you turn up on the off-chance you are liable to be given reheated meat.

# COCHINILLO/TOSTÓN

The Castilians are very proud of their *cochinillos*, sucking pigs, and wherever you go, in Segovia, for instance, no restaurant worth its salt is without roast piglet on the menu. The creatures are often displayed in the restaurants' windows: bald, poignant little things, for they are killed very young while still feeding on their mothers' milk. The most famous place to eat it is the Mesón de Cándido, a charming, very old restaurant by the Roman aqueduct. Despite all the razzmatazz with which Cándido and others surround the sucking pig (carving it with the edge of a plate, etc.) the meat itself, to me at least, is something of a disappointment, though it would be heresy to say so at the time. It seems to have none of the advantages of fully grown pork, while it retains the disadvantages. The flesh itself is almost preternaturally tender: it practically dissolves in the mouth without aid from the teeth, a quality I find vaguely unpleasant. The pork flavour has yet to develop – one knows it's pork, but only just – and the thin crackling is as nothing compared to the robust crunch you get from a fully grown pig (the Spanish unfortunately sell the latter *without* the crackling), yet the meat is as rich as pork, perhaps richer.

All this, however, is just a personal opinion. If you are ever in that part of Spain you should give it a try. For a Spaniard it is one of the most delectable things imaginable, and you may well find that you agree.

# Guiso de cordero a la ampurdanesa

A thick lamb stew rich with fungi from the region of Ampurdán in northern Cataluña. The Catalans are very fond of combining lamb or beef with fungi, especially their beloved *rovellons*.

120g/4oz lard
675g/1½lb shoulder *or* leg of lamb, diced

salt and pepper
1 onion, finely chopped
2 tomatoes, peeled and chopped
12 baby onions, peeled
280g/10oz fungi (whatever is available), wiped clean and sliced
4 tablespoons oil
4 slices stale French bread
4 cloves garlic
2 tablespoons chopped parsley

Heat half the lard in a *cazuela* or similar, season the lamb and fry it until it has changed colour. Add the onion and let it soften, then add the tomatoes. Cover and leave to simmer.

Heat the rest of the lard and fry the baby onions very slowly with a little salt until they are browned all over. Add to the lamb, along with the fungi.

Heat the oil and fry the bread until it is a good brown colour. Pound it to a paste with the peeled garlic and chopped parsley. Stir the paste into the stew, and let it finish cooking uncovered. The lamb should cook for about 45 minutes altogether, and the stew be very thick.

## Pebre de cordero murciano

A Murcian two-in-one dish – the cooking liquid from the lamb is used to make a soup, which is followed by the meat itself. A chicken can be used instead of the lamb, in which case it would be called *pebre de gallina*.

900g/2lb neck of lamb, in cutlets
1 tomato, peeled and sliced
1 green pepper, chopped
salt and black pepper
4 slices stale French bread, crusts removed
3 cloves garlic, peeled
30g/1oz pine-nuts
2 tablespoons oil
1 tablespoon chopped parsley
¼ teaspoon ground cumin
tomato sauce (page 131)

Put the lamb in a deep pot and just cover it with water. Bring to simmering point and skim off the scum. Add the tomato and green pepper, season with salt and simmer, covered, for an hour. Remove the meat and set aside. Add the bread to the broth so that it soaks while you fry the garlic and pine-nuts in the oil until brown.

Place the boiled tomato, green pepper, nuts, garlic, parsley and bread in the liquidiser goblet with some of the broth. Add the cumin and some black pepper and liquidise until smooth. Return the purée to the broth in the pan – there should be roughly 1.5 litres/2½ pints altogether. (If there's a great deal more set it aside for use in other lamb dishes.) Reheat the soup and serve it with croutons of fried bread.

Remove all bone and gristle from the meat and dice it. Add it to the tomato sauce and serve after the soup. Alternatively, mix it with some lightly cooked tomato, onion, hard-boiled egg and oregano or thyme and use as a filling for little fried pies, *empanadillas* (page 73).

# Caldereta de cordero

Just as fishermen will call their daily meal after their cooking pot the *caldero*, so will shepherds call their stews (of lamb, venison, kid, chicken, small birds or snails) after theirs.

4 tablespoons oil
3 cloves garlic, peeled
2 dozen almonds, blanched and peeled
120g/4oz lamb's liver, skinned
790g/1¾lb boned shoulder of lamb, diced
salt and pepper
good pinch each thyme and oregano
2 tablespoons vinegar
150ml/¼ pint dry sherry *or* white wine

Heat the oil in a *cazuela* or similar and fry the garlic and almonds until brown all over. Remove them to a mortar and fry the liver in the same oil for 5 minutes. Add it to the mortar. Now fry the lamb, seasoned, until the pieces change colour. Add the thyme and oregano, the vinegar and wine, bring to the boil and simmer, covered, for an hour.

Pound the almonds, garlic and liver to a paste. Thin it to a thick cream with a little water and pour it into the lamb. Heat through, check the seasoning and serve.

# Cordero al Txilindron

## (Chilindrón)

A nationally popular dish that originated in Navarra (hence the Basque spelling). The *pisto* of tomatoes and red peppers was originally used for the lamb that is so common in much of northern Spain, but it is used also for poultry and rabbit.

4 large, meaty red peppers
60g/2oz lard
1kg/2¼lb boned shoulder of lamb, diced
salt and pepper
4 cloves garlic
1 onion, sliced
6 tomatoes, peeled and chopped
2 tablespoons chopped parsley

Roast the peppers in the usual way (see page 31) and leave covered in a bowl for 15 minutes before peeling and slicing them quite thinly.

Heat the lard in a large earthenware *cazuela* or similar. Season the lamb with salt and pepper and fry it in the fat until browned. Remove to a plate and mix with the crushed garlic. In the remaining fat fry the onion until it starts to soften. Add the tomatoes and peppers and cook for 5 more minutes. Return the lamb to the pan and mix well with the sauce. Cover and simmer gently for about an hour. Stir in the parsley and simmer uncovered for 10 more minutes to reduce the sauce.

In the same way as roasts, stews like this benefit from a few minutes' rest before eating.

For chicken, turkey or rabbit: add 120g/4oz diced serrano ham with the onion and a glass of white wine with the tomatoes. This is best if made ahead of time so that, once cooked, you can take all the meat from the bones and reheat it in the sauce.

This is how most Spaniards know their *chilindrón*, but a book of Navarrese recipes, *Cocinar en Navarra* (1986) by Francisco Abad and Marfa Rosario Ruiz contains a sharpish rebuke:

*Let's be agreed; the experts say that chilindrón is pimiento, or a stew of it. For this reason a chilindrón does not contain tomato or water, just pimiento. There are excellent stews of lamb that bear the name of chilindrón and which are agreeable to the most demanding palates, but the real chilindrón of old is made like this:*

*First prepare some dried red peppers (about two per person), washing them, halving them lengthways and letting them soak in hot water for a good hour. Then take out the pieces of pimiento one by one and extract the pulp by scraping the insides with a sharp knife. With this you will make a smooth paste by carefully pounding it in the mortar. Now that the chilindrón is ready waste no time in frying in a cazuela the lamb, best cut in small pieces, along with a lot of finely chopped onion. The onion will provide the liquid for the stew. When the pieces of lamb are done on the outside add some diced potatoes, as many as you like, salt and the paste of the red peppers. Stir, lower the heat and let the whole thing cook gently until the potatoes and meat are tender.*

This is indeed excellent, and the best chilindrón I ever had, in the Shanti restaurant in Pamplona, bore no trace of tomato (nor potatoes for that matter).

# Cochifrito

A stew of lamb or kid, traditionally popular with shepherds and cattle dealers. From Navarra. Good with *patatas al montón* (see page 159)

790g/1¾lb boned shoulder of lamb, trimmed of fat and thickly diced
salt and pepper
4 tablespoons oil
1 onion, roughly chopped
6 cloves garlic, crushed
4 tablespoons chopped parsley
2 teaspoons paprika
juice of 2 lemons

Season the lamb well with salt and pepper. Heat the oil in a *cazuela* or similar and fry the pieces of lamb until coloured all over. Add the onion and garlic and continue cooking fairly rapidly until they soften. Sprinkle in the parsley and paprika, mix well and pour in the lemon juice. Cover and simmer for a good 45 minutes. If during this time the sauce becomes too dry and starts to catch, add a little water, but bear in mind that the sauce at the end should be thick and concentrated.

# Cordero a la campesina

Marinated lamb in a tomato sauce. A rich and beautifully flavoured dish.

900g/2lb leg of lamb, cubed
salt

2-3 teaspoons dried oregano

3 cloves garlic, crushed

2 tablespoons paprika

6 cloves

3 tablespoons vinegar

3 tablespoons oil

2 tablespoons flour

thick tomato sauce (see page 131)

nutmeg

Place the lamb in a non-metallic container. Sprinkle with salt, the oregano, garlic, paprika, cloves, vinegar and a little water. Mix all very thoroughly, and leave it for several hours (out of the fridge) so that the lamb absorbs all the flavours.

Drain the lamb well. Remove the cloves. Heat the oil and add the pieces of lamb. Brown them well, then sprinkle in the flour. Let this cook a minute or two before adding the tomato sauce and a good grating of nutmeg. Simmer for about 15 minutes.

Serve with bread or fried potatoes.

# Chuletas de cordero a la Navarra

A wonderful way of cooking lamb chops from Navarra, where the local chorizo, more like a thick, fine-textured salami than a sausage, gives a special piquancy to the sauce. Ordinary chorizo works well too. As the chops have to cook in a single layer in a frying pan you may find this a bit tricky for more than two or three people. Serves 2-3.

550g/1¼lb small lamb chops from the loin, *or* meaty cutlets

salt and pepper

30g/1oz lard

30g/1oz oil

½ onion, finely chopped

60g/2oz slice of serrano ham, roughly chopped

2 tomatoes, peeled and chopped

60g/2oz *chorizo de Pamplona*, thinly sliced then cut into strips

Season the chops with salt and pepper. Heat the fats in a wide frying pan. Add the chops, onion and ham and cook briskly for a couple of minutes. Turn the chops over. After another couple of minutes' fast cooking add the tomatoes. Leave to simmer for 10 minutes, then stir in the strips of chorizo. Heat through, and serve. The sauce should be thick and concentrated.

# Cordero a la antigua española

Lamb in the style of old Spain. The more restrained, almost English style of this stew does indeed remind one of the Spain of old, the Spain of empire. This stew comes from Burgos in the north, a city that stands roughly at the border between the green and mountainous lands of Cantabria to its north and the high moorland to its south that marks the beginning of the *alta meseta*, Spain's high central plain.

120g/4oz lard
1 onion, chopped
1.25kg/2½lb leg of lamb, in slices with the bone
450g/1lb peeled potatoes, cut into chunks
2 tablespoons flour
450g/1lb turnips, peeled and cut into chunks
stock
3 cloves
2 bay leaves
4 parsley stalks
salt and pepper

Melt the lard in a large casserole and fry the onion and lamb until the meat changes colour. Add the potatoes and turnips and fry for 2 more minutes. Sprinkle in the flour and mix well. Gradually add enough stock just to cover the cloves, bay leaves, parsley stalks and some salt and pepper. Cover and simmer for about an hour. If the sauce seems thin reduce it by rapid boiling, or remove a few pieces of potato, mash them and stir them back in. Try to remove the parsley stalks and cloves before serving.

# Cordero a la murciana

Murcia is perhaps the most fertile region in Spain and is justifiably thought of as *la huerta de España*, much as Kent is known as the garden of England. For this reason *a la murciana* usually signifies a dish containing vegetables, in this case lamb with a medley of peas, asparagus, red peppers and tomatoes.

4 tablespoons oil

2 cloves garlic, crushed

120g/4oz serrano ham, diced

1.25kg/2½lb boned shoulder of lamb, cubed

salt and pepper

flour for coating

1 onion, roughly chopped

2 teaspoons paprika

1 teaspoon oregano

1 tomato, peeled and chopped

120g/4oz peas, fresh or frozen

3 tablespoons white wine

2 red peppers

280g/10oz fresh asparagus, trimmed

1 tablespoon chopped parsley

Heat the oil in a large casserole and fry the garlic and ham until the garlic starts to brown. Season and flour the pieces of lamb and add them to the pot, frying them till they've changed colour. Now add the onion and let it soften. Add the paprika and oregano, the tomato and the fresh peas if you are using them. Add the white wine and enough water just to cover. Simmer, covered, for about 45 minutes.

Meanwhile, roast the peppers on a griddle or under the grill until they are charred all over. Place them in a bowl and leave them covered with a plate for about 10 minutes. Peel the peppers and cut them into strips.

Remove the lid from the casserole and stir in the frozen peas if you are using them, the strips of pepper and the asparagus (cut the spears into pieces if they are very long). Leave to simmer for another 15 minutes until the sauce is thick and the asparagus tender. Sprinkle with the chopped parsley and serve.

## Paletilla de cordero a la bejarana

This recipe for boned shoulder of lamb stuffed with sausages comes from the town of Béjar, south of Salamanca in the beautiful sierra that divides Castilla from Extremadura.

1 shoulder of lamb, boned

salt

150g/5oz sausages
3 tablespoons oil
1 clove garlic
450g/1lb potatoes, peeled (small new ones are best)
12 button onions, peeled
225ml/8fl oz white wine
2 tablespoons tomato purée

Season the lamb lightly with salt, both inside and out. Slit open the sausages (which should be of good, meaty quality), take out the meat and spread it over the cavity of the lamb. Fold the lamb round it and tie the meat up in a neat parcel with string.

Heat the oil in a *cazuela*, brown the clove of garlic and discard it. Add the potatoes and onions and let them colour slightly in the hot oil. Make a space for the meat and brown it on both sides. Pour in the wine and place the dish in the oven, 400-425°F/200-220°C/Gas 6-7, for about 1¼ hours. There is no need to baste the meat; the action of the sausagemeat inside and the wine outside keep it very moist.

Remove the meat from the oven and set it aside to rest. Add the tomato purée to the sauce in the pan, plus a little water if it's very thick. Check for seasoning and simmer for a few minutes. Return the meat to the pan and serve.

# Guisado de cordero

Lamb stew. The original recipe, an old one from Córdoba, called for breast of mutton. As mutton never seems to be available I make it with shoulder of lamb, and the result is exceptionally good.

790g/1¾lb boned shoulder of lamb, in largish chunks
salt and pepper
60g/2oz lard *or* bacon fat
120g/4oz *tocino or* unsmoked streaky bacon, sliced
10 cloves garlic
4 tablespoons chopped parsley, plus a few sprigs
4 tablespoons oil
90g/3oz pine-nuts

Season the lamb with salt and pepper. Heat the lard in a *cazuela* or large shallow casserole dish and fry the lamb and bacon until the lamb has completely changed colour. Add 6 of the garlic cloves, sliced, and cook for 2-3 more minutes – enough for the garlic to take a little colour. Add the chopped parsley and enough water to half-cover the meat. Cover and leave to simmer.

While the meat is cooking, heat the oil in a small frying pan. Add the remaining garlic cloves, peeled but left whole, and the pine-nuts, and fry them to a golden-brown. Remove them to a mortar, and in the remaining oil fry the well-dried parsley sprigs for a few seconds. Add these to the mortar (the oil can be used on another occasion). Pound the garlic, nuts and parsley to a smooth paste.

When the meat has been cooking for about 45 minutes stir in the paste, plus a little water if the whole thing's getting too dry (though the stew should be thick). Leave to simmer for 10 more minutes, uncovered, and check the seasoning. Let the stew cool for at least 5 minutes before serving.

# Cordero al ajillo

Lamb in a rich sauce made with typical Andalusian ingredients – paprika, saffron, cumin, wine and, of course, garlic. Trim as much fat from the lamb as possible – the flavour of lamb fat can be obtrusive. Try this with *puré de patatas con setas* (page 154). See also the recipe on page 245 for a simpler version.

4 cloves garlic
1 pinch cumin
1 larger pinch saffron
salt and pepper
2 teaspoons flour
150ml/¼ pint red wine
3 tablespoons oil
900g/2lb boned leg of lamb, diced quite small
1 tablespoon paprika

Pound the garlic, cumin and saffron in a mortar with a little salt. Add the flour and mix it in well. Gradually stir in the wine.

Heat the oil in a *cazuela* and fry the lamb until it has changed colour and thrown off a good amount of juice. Add the paprika and some pepper. Stir in the mixture from the mortar and taste for salt. The lamb should now be enveloped in a small quantity of sauce. Add a little water if it seems on the thick side. Simmer uncovered for about 20 minutes, and it's ready.

# Guiso de ternera

A beef stew with fungi from Cataluña.

90g/3oz lard
salt and pepper
flour
900g/2lb braising beef, in 4 slices
2 onions, peeled and sliced
2 carrots, sliced
2 tomatoes, peeled and chopped
120ml/4fl oz *aguardiente* or grappa
1 bay leaf
4 cloves
340g/12oz fungi, wiped clean and sliced

Heat the lard in a large *cazuela*. Season and flour the meat and fry it until brown on both sides. Remove to a plate. Add the onions and carrots to the fat and let them soften before adding the tomatoes. Let this sofrito cook briefly, then replace the meat and add the aguardiente or grappa, the bay leaf and the cloves. Add enough water just to cover the meat, check the seasoning and simmer, covered, for 2 hours. Add the fungi and continue cooking, uncovered, for another hour, or until the stew is very thick and concentrated and the meat especially tender. Remove the cloves and bay leaf before serving. This is even better if reheated later.

# Fricandó con moixernons

A version of a Catalan beef stew which was originally an adaptation of an old French veal dish called *fricandeau*. Among the ingredients are *carquinyolis*, small biscuit-like slices of dried sponge with a pronounced vanilla flavour. These are used to thicken the sauce at the end. As an alternative, use plain biscuits and a very little vanilla extract – like a good committee member, the vanilla should make its presence felt without being too conspicuous.

30g/1oz dried fairy-ring mushrooms (*moixernons*)
2 onions, chopped
2 carrots, chopped
4 tablespoons oil
900g/2lb diced shin of beef

2 tomatoes, peeled and chopped
bay leaf
¼ teaspoon each thyme, oregano
150ml/¼ pint dry white wine
salt and pepper
4 cloves garlic
12 toasted almonds
3 *carquinyolis*

Pour boiling water over the mushrooms and leave them to soak. Soften the onions and carrots in the oil. Add the pieces of beef and continue cooking until they change colour. Add the tomatoes, mushrooms, herbs and white wine. Cook until the tomatoes have softened. Season with salt and pepper, filter in the water from the mushrooms and add enough water just to cover the meat. Cover tightly with a lid and place the casserole in a very slow oven (285°F/140°C/Gas 1), or leave over the merest thread of heat, for 3-4 hours. Pound the garlic, almonds and biscuits to a smooth paste. Remove the casserole from the oven and if necessary boil down the liquid to reduce it. Use a little of the liquid to thin the paste to a cream, then stir this back into the stew. Check the seasoning, and leave to stand for a few minutes before serving.

## Ternera a la sevillana

An unusual pot roast from Sevilla. The beef is larded with olives and toasted almonds and lightly flavoured with cinnamon.

900g/2lb top rump of beef, tied to keep its shape
2 dozen green olives, stoned and halved
2 dozen toasted almonds
ground cinnamon
salt and pepper
flour for coating
4 tablespoons oil
2 cloves garlic, chopped
1 onion, chopped
150ml/¼ pint dry sherry
300ml/½ pint beef stock
2 tomatoes, peeled and chopped

Using a sharp knife, make deep incisions all over the meat into which you push two olive halves and an almond. Keep back a few of each for the sauce. Sprinkle the joint sparingly with ground cinnamon and some pepper. Rub these into the meat and leave it to stand for an hour.

Season the meat with salt and roll it in flour. Heat the oil in a casserole dish and put in the meat. Let it brown all over. Add the chopped garlic and when it starts to brown add the onion. Let the onion soften. Add the sherry, stock and chopped tomatoes, bring to the boil, cover well and simmer for 1¼-1½ hours. Pour off the juices and vegetables and liquidise them. Slice the meat quite thickly. Reheat the sauce gently with the reserved olives and almonds, then pour it over the meat.

**Note:** The meat will be better if you leave it to settle for about 15 minutes before carving.

# Ternera en su jugo

Beef in gravy, and a most delicious gravy it is too.

60g/2oz lard *or* bacon fat
900g/2lb braising beef, e.g. topside *or* silverside (in Spain, ask for *tapa de ternera*)
60g/2oz fat salt-pork, diced
1 carrot, sliced
900g/2lb marrow bones, sawn into pieces by your butcher
salt and pepper
150ml/¼ pint white wine
flour (optional)

In a large casserole melt the fat over a low heat. Add the beef, salt-pork, carrot and bones, and cover with a lid. Leave over a low heat for 30 minutes, by which time the underside of the beef should be nicely browned. Turn it over, along with the bones, cover and leave for another 30 minutes. Season with salt and pepper and add the wine. Leave to simmer, covered, for an hour or so.

The beef needs to rest for a few minutes before carving. You may wish to thicken the gravy slightly, as it tends to look a little thin and unappetising as it is. In this case beat a little flour into some cold water, stir it into the gravy, bring it to the boil and let it simmer for a few minutes.

# Cachopos de ternera

Fillet steaks stuffed with Manchego cheese and serrano ham. This is a good way of making a piece of precious fillet go further than it otherwise might. Other cuts can be used but won't be quite so tender. If these steaks are to be part of a large meal, the quantities below will serve four; if not, two.

8 thin slices of fillet steak, taken from the centre
Spanish brandy
about 90g/3oz serrano ham
about 90g/3oz strong Manchego cheese, sliced
flour
3 eggs, well beaten with a little salt
breadcrumbs
oil for frying

Place each slice of fillet between two pieces of waxed or greaseproof paper and gently flatten them out with a rolling pin or the heel of a heavy bottle. Sprinkle each slice with a little brandy. Place a slice of ham on four of the fillets – it should be smaller than the fillet it sits on. Do the same with the cheese. Now cover these with the remaining four fillets, brandied side inwards. Tuck the edges of the fillets in and around the filling to form a sort of parcel – the idea is completely to enclose the stuffing. Roll each parcel in flour, then beaten egg, then breadcrumbs. Roll them again in the egg and breadcrumbs – this double layer helps to fill in any cracks through which the filling might leak. Leave them to rest for a couple of hours in the fridge if possible – the coating will stiffen slightly. Heat about 6mm/¼in of oil in a frying pan and when hot add the meat parcels. Fry them, turning once, until they are well browned on both sides. Drain them on kitchen paper and serve with something saucy, like *papas en ajopollo* (page 153).

# Ternera con puré de castañas

Chunks of beef in a red wine sauce, served on a bed of creamed chestnuts.

675g/1½lb chuck steak, cubed
4 cloves garlic, crushed
½ teaspoon dried thyme
3 tablespoons oil
1 onion, sliced
1 carrot, sliced

1 tomato, peeled and sliced

flour

300ml/½ pint red wine

salt and pepper

450g/1lb peeled chestnuts (see *pilongas con chorizo*, page 126,

if you want to use dried chestnuts)

milk, butter

Mix the cubes of beef with the crushed garlic and thyme, and set aside. Heat the oil in a casserole and fry the onion and carrot until they start to soften. Add the tomato and cook for 5 more minutes. Add the beef and cook until it changes colour. Sprinkle over a little flour to bind it all together and gradually stir in the red wine. If necessary add some water so that the meat is just covered with liquid. Season with salt and pepper, cover and simmer for 1½ hours.

While the meat is cooking just cover the chestnuts with a mixture of milk and water, bring them to the boil and simmer, covered, until tender – the time depends rather on the chestnuts, but they will be ready in good time for the beef.

Remove the lid from the beef and reduce the sauce if it seems too thin. Mash the chestnuts with a little of their cooking liquid, a large knob of butter and some salt and pepper. The purée should be the consistency of mashed potato. Spread it over a serving dish and pour the beef over the top.

# Filetes con aceitunas

An old Madrid dish of steak with olives, cooked in the blink of an eye.

*FOR 4 STEAKS:*

salt and pepper

flour for coating

4 tablespoons oil

2 cloves garlic, thinly sliced

200ml/7fl oz white wine

2 dozen olives stuffed with anchovies

2 tablespoons chopped parsley

Flatten out the steaks a little with a meat mallet, season them and dip them lightly in flour. Heat the oil and fry the steaks and sliced garlic until the meat is brown on both sides. Add the wine and olives and cook rapidly until the wine has more or less evaporated. Sprinkle with the parsley and serve.

# RABO DE BUEY, RABO DE TORO

Oxtail – some of the best meat on the whole beef carcass is to be found in the humblest position: hanging off its bottom. If cooked properly oxtail should be so tender that it falls easily from the bone and be of a very special flavour. It doesn't require much work if you plan ahead, for its one drawback, its fattiness, can be overcome by cooking the meat the day before you need it. You chill the dish overnight and then skim off the solidified fat the next day. This fat should not be thrown away, but used for roasting potatoes or making beef stews.

Both the recipes below start the same way: the oxtails are cooked gently in water with various flavourings and the resulting broth is strained, chilled and de-fatted for use in the making of the sauce.

*FOR BOTH RECIPES:*
1 oxtail, sliced
1 carrot, washed and sliced
1 onion, sliced (use the skin to colour the stock if you wish)
½ stick of celery
salt
2 bay leaves
4 cloves
4 parsley stalks
¼ teaspoon each thyme and oregano
6 peppercorns

In a deep saucepan or casserole place the oxtail, carrot, onion and celery. Add a little salt and cover well with cold water. Put a lid on it, and bring to the boil. Skim very thoroughly (oxtail throws off a lot of evil-looking scum). Add all the herbs and spices, cover and leave to simmer gently for 2 hours. Strain the broth into a bowl and add the pieces of oxtail (the vegetables and herbs should be discarded). Let it get cold and then leave in the fridge overnight. The stock will set to a jelly and the fat solidify on top. Scrape the fat off the next day. If you love your fellow eaters (and yourself) very much, it makes life infinitely easier if you now also detach all the meat from the bones and cartilage before continuing.

## Rabo de toro guisado con vino tinto
Oxtail stewed with red wine.
3 tablespoons oil *or* fat from the stock
1 onion, sliced

1 carrot, peeled and sliced
120g/4oz serrano ham, diced
4 cloves garlic, crushed
2 tablespoons flour
2 teaspoons paprika
¼ teaspoon cayenne
175ml/6fl oz red wine
about 600ml/1 pint of the broth*
1 oxtail, prepared as above

Heat the oil or fat in a casserole and fry the onion and carrot until they start to soften. Add the ham and garlic and cook for 2 more minutes. Stir in the flour, paprika and cayenne, cook for a minute, then gradually add the red wine and broth. Add the pieces of oxtail, bring to the boil, check the seasoning and leave to simmer, uncovered, for an hour.

*If any is left over, use it to make soup, or poach some dumplings in it to serve with the oxtail (unauthentic but good). Alternatively boil some vegetables in it (chunks of artichoke and carrot, for example) without a lid, and no added salt. Let the liquid boil down to a delicious glaze, adding a little olive oil right at the end to give the veg a gloss.

# Rabo de toro al jerez

Oxtail in sherry sauce.

4 tablespoons oil *or* fat from the broth
4 cloves garlic
2 slices stale French bread
1 onion, chopped
1 green pepper, chopped
2 tomatoes, peeled and chopped
1 teaspoon paprika
1 oxtail, prepared as above
600ml/1 pint oxtail broth
125ml/4fl oz dry sherry
1 good pinch saffron

Heat the oil or fat and fry the garlic and bread until brown. Transfer them to a mortar. In the remaining oil soften the onion and green pepper. Add the tomatoes and paprika and cook for 5 more minutes. Add the oxtail, broth and sherry. Pound the garlic, saffron and bread to a paste and add it to the pot. Bring to the boil, check the seasoning and simmer, uncovered, for an hour.

# Ropavieja

Old clothes. This is one of any number of recipes bearing the name and is useful for using up the remnants of a Sunday joint. I suppose the slices of aubergine do vaguely remind one of the odd sock or bit of jersey as you fish them out of the stew.

1 large aubergine

salt

oil

450g/1lb cooked beef

1 onion, sliced

4 cloves garlic, crushed

2 red peppers, sliced

2 tomatoes, peeled and sliced

150ml/¼ pint stock

2 cloves pounded in a mortar with 6 peppercorns and a pinch of saffron

Slice the aubergine thinly, sprinkle with salt and leave to drain in a colander for a couple of hours. Pat them dry and fry in very hot oil until brown. Drain and reserve.

Tear the beef into thick shreds. In a couple of tablespoons of the oil from the aubergines fry the onion, garlic and peppers until softened. Add the tomatoes and cook until pulpy. Add the beef to the sauce and moisten with a little stock. Add the pounded spice and some salt. Simmer for about 15 minutes. Reduce it further if necessary until you have a very thick stew. Stir in the aubergine slices and heat through before serving.

# RABBIT

Rabbit, like chicken, is a very accommodating meat, and lends itself well to many different treatments. You could probably use all the chicken recipes in this book for it.

# Conejo a la montañesa

A rich rabbit stew from Cantabria, thickened with nuts and flavoured with herbs and a touch of cinnamon. This is a good way of pepping up the rather bland flavour of domestic rabbit. It is best made a day ahead of time and gently reheated.

120g/4oz lard *or* bacon fat
1 rabbit, jointed, rinsed and dried with paper towels
flour for coating
450g/1lb button onions, peeled (much easier if they're left in boiling water for a minute or two)
280g/10oz mushrooms, sliced (preferably the big field ones)
300ml/½ pint white wine
bay leaf, 2 sprigs thyme, 2-3 parsley stalks, and ½ stick
cinnamon, all tied up in a piece of muslin or old tea-towel
salt and pepper
1 tablespoon pine-nuts
12 toasted almonds
4 cloves garlic

Heat the fat, dip the pieces of rabbit in the flour and fry them until they're brown all over. Add the onions and let them brown a little. Now add the mushrooms, wine, herbs and salt and pepper. Cover and simmer for about 45 minutes.

Pound the nuts with the garlic until you have a smooth paste. Stir this into the pot and let it simmer, covered, for another 45 minutes. Remove the herb packet before serving.

# Conejo con castañas

Rabbit with chestnuts. The tenderness of rabbit is rather offset by its bland flavour, so it needs stout, aggressive treatment to make it interesting, which is exactly what it gets in this Galician recipe. As in the recipe for meatballs on page 262, a combination of Spanish brandy and sherry imparts a gamy flavour to the sauce, while the chestnuts provide a slight sweetness.

225g/8oz dried chestnuts, soaked overnight
1 rabbit, cut into small pieces
salt and pepper
6 tablespoons oil
4 cloves garlic, chopped

1 onion, finely chopped
120g/4oz serrano ham, diced
2 carrots, sliced
4 tablespoons Spanish brandy
4 tablespoons dry sherry
1 good pinch saffron, toasted

Drain the chestnuts, cover them with fresh water or chicken broth and boil them for 45 minutes. Set aside, reserving the cooking water. Season the rabbit pieces and fry them in the oil in a *cazuela* or similar, along with the garlic, until they start to brown. Add the onion, ham and carrot and let them soften a little. Pour in the brandy and sherry and let it bubble for a couple of minutes. Add the chestnuts, their cooking water and the crumbled saffron. The rabbit should be just covered with liquid – add more if not. Partly cover the *cazuela* and simmer for 45 minutes. Remove the lid and reduce the sauce further if it's still thin – there shouldn't be a great deal. Check the seasoning and let the meat rest for a few minutes before serving.

# Conejo con chocolate

Rabbit with chocolate sauce. Dark chocolate is used quite frequently in Spain to flavour sauces for game, and the taste is not as outlandish as one might suppose, for only a comparatively small amount is used and it lends a flavour that is very difficult to identify if you aren't in the know.

This recipe is an adaptation of the one to be found in Josep Lladonosa Giro's *Cocina de ayer, delicias de hoy*, a treasury of old Catalan recipes. Here the rabbit is given a good marinade to strengthen its flavour, then cooked in the marinade, the sauce being thickened with nuts and chocolate.

Start the recipe a day ahead of time.

1 rabbit, cut into small pieces
4 cloves garlic, crushed
600ml/1 pint red wine
1 small glass dry sherry
1 onion, sliced
4 tablespoons oil
4 cloves garlic, peeled
flour for coating
1 carrot, sliced
60g/2oz almonds, blanched and peeled

salt and pepper
thyme
1 bay leaf
small piece of cinnamon stick
60g/2oz pine-nuts
40g/1¼oz dark chocolate
120ml/4fl oz Spanish brandy

Mix the rabbit with the crushed garlic and pour over it the red wine and sherry. Mix in the onion and carrot, season with salt and pepper and some dried thyme. Tuck in the bay leaf and piece of cinnamon stick. Leave in the marinade for a minimum of 12 hours, turning the meat occasionally if it isn't covered.

Next day, drain the rabbit, reserving the marinade. Heat the oil in a *cazuela* and fry the whole, peeled garlic until browned. Transfer it to a mortar. Toss the rabbit pieces in flour and fry in the oil until browned. Add the pieces of onion and carrot from the marinade and let them soften. Pour in the strained liquid, bring to the boil and simmer for 40 minutes, covered.

Pound the garlic with almonds, pine-nuts and chocolate until you have a smooth paste. Dilute this with the brandy and add to the rabbit. Cook for a few more minutes, checking the seasoning. (You may need to add a little sugar, for the sauce can be somewhat bitter from the wine and chocolate.)

# Conejo con peras y nabos

Rabbit with pears and turnips. The Catalans combine richer meats with pears – duck and goose for example – and produce combinations about which I sometimes have reservations. This recipe works well, though, especially with the addition of young fried turnips. I also give the meat a more robust flavour by marinating it in the wine and brandy that go to make the sauce. Otherwise, it is more or less the same as the recipe of Lola Pijoán given in *Damas guisan y ganan* by Carmen Casas.

1 rabbit, jointed
½ glassful brandy and 1 glassful white wine (*or* dry sherry)
flour for coating
6 tablespoons oil
chicken stock *or* water
1 onion, chopped
2 cloves garlic, crushed
2 leeks, sliced

1 tomato, chopped
1 bay leaf
¼ teaspoon each thyme, oregano
8 small turnips, peeled
2 large firm pears (or 3-4 small ones)

About 2-3 hours before you want to start (or overnight if you prefer), prick the rabbit all over with a fork and pour over it a good glassful of white wine and about half that of brandy. The idea is more or less to cover the meat, though you will need to turn it over at least once to give it a thorough soaking.

When you are ready, drain the pieces of rabbit (reserving the marinade) and dip them in flour. Fry them in hot oil until browned, then pour over the marinade and set the whole thing alight, shaking the pan while it burns. Let the alcohol reduce, then cover the rabbit with light chicken stock or water. Leave to simmer with the lid on.

Fry the vegetables (except the turnips) and herbs until tender and soft. Liquidise this sofrito with some of the liquid from the rabbit. Pass the purée through a sieve over the rabbit, season and leave simmering.

Now blanch first the peeled turnips, then the peeled and quartered pears, for about 5 minutes in boiling water. Roll the turnips in flour and brown them quickly in hot oil. Add them to the rabbit. When the latter has been cooking about an hour altogether, add the pears to heat through, then serve.

# GOAT

*Choto*, *cabrito* and *chivo* are all words for young goat, which is quite a popular dish in spring. It is not to everyone's taste, for the meat tends to be hidden in large quantities of bone and fat. Some people enthuse about the meat in the head. The most popular way of cooking it, where I live, is *a lo pastoril*, shepherd's style. The meat is marinated in lemon juice and chopped onion (this is said to remove a slightly unpleasant 'milky' taste), while a sauce is made by frying almonds, garlic, tomato, stale bread and the kid's liver. These are then pounded to a paste. The pieces of kid are fried, the sauce and some white wine added and the whole left to simmer and thicken. Everyone seems to prefer the sauce, which is very delicious.

# OFFAL
## Hígado al ajillo

A deliciously savoury and quick little dish of liver with oil, garlic and chilli. The quantities of garlic and chilli are up to the cook, but one should bear in mind that the liver is supposed to be highly flavoured.

450g/1lb lamb's *or* veal liver, thinly sliced
8 cloves garlic
2 red chillies
6 tablespoons oil
salt and pepper

Cut the slices of liver into thin strips. Slice the garlic and chilli thinly. Some red chillies have many seeds and you may wish to discard some of them. Heat the oil in a wide frying pan and fry the garlic and chilli until the garlic browns. Add the strips of liver, season and fry, stirring, for just a very few minutes until the liver is tender – test a piece if you are unsure.

Serve immediately, perhaps with fried potatoes and a green salad.

# Hígado a la pastoril

Liver in a rich sauce of pounded almonds and garlic. You may prefer to serve this in half quantities as a tapa.

1 dozen almonds, blanched and peeled
4 cloves garlic, peeled
4 tablespoons oil
2 slices stale French bread
450g/1lb lamb's or veal liver, thinly sliced and cut into strips
1 teaspoon paprika
1 teaspoon dried oregano

In a small frying pan, fry the almonds and garlic in the oil until well browned. Remove them to a mortar. Fry the bread in the same oil until brown, then pound it to a paste with the almonds and garlic. Put any remaining oil into a larger pan, heat it and add the liver, paprika and oregano. Fry, stirring, over a high heat until it just loses its raw colour. Add the paste from the mortar and enough water to form a little sauce. Bring to the boil and simmer the liver very briefly in the sauce.

# Hígado a la molinera

Liver in a white wine sauce with hazelnuts and pine-nuts.

4 tablespoons oil
1 handful each hazelnuts and pine-nuts
90ml/3fl oz white wine
1 onion, sliced
450g/1lb lamb's *or* veal liver, thinly sliced and cut into strips
3 tablespoons chopped parsley

Heat the oil in a small frying pan and fry the nuts until brown (rub off the loose skins from the hazelnuts first). Put the nuts in a mortar and pound to a paste. Thin the paste down with the wine. Transfer the oil to a larger pan and cook the onion slowly until tender and starting to brown in places. Pour in the mixture from the mortar and cook until the wine has evaporated. Add the liver and enough water to form a little sauce. Simmer for a few minutes until the liver is just cooked and coated by the sauce, then stir in the parsley.

# Riñones a lo señorito

Kidneys with ham, garlic, mushrooms and sherry. Good fungi or dried mushrooms (especially the very aromatic *Boletus edulis*) are preferable, but plain ones can be used. *Señorito* is the term of rather grovelling respect used to address rich landowners and the like by their workers. The name of this dish from Córdoba is said to reflect that only a *señorito* could have afforded the ingredients.

900g/2lb lamb's kidneys
30g/1oz dried mushrooms *or*
225g/8oz fungi, sliced
4 tablespoons oil
175g/6oz serrano ham, diced
4 cloves garlic, chopped
salt
6 tablespoons dry sherry

Cut each kidney into several pieces, cutting away all the tough core. Blanch the pieces in boiling water until the kidneys throw off their scum, then drain and rinse them under the cold tap. Soak the dried mushrooms until tender in hot water, then rinse them to get rid of any hidden grit. Chop them roughly. (The soaking water isn't required, but can be strained through a fine sieve lined with muslin or gauze and used for another mushroom dish.) Heat the oil in a wide frying pan and add the mushrooms, ham and garlic. Fry over a good heat until the garlic starts to brown. Add the kidneys and a pinch of salt, stir and fry for a couple more minutes, then add the sherry. Cook until it evaporates, then serve immediately.

# Postres y Dulces
## PUDDINGS AND DESSERTS

Puddings, desserts, sweets, call them what you will, they don't enjoy the same prominence at Spanish mealtimes as they traditionally do in Britain. Sensibly, in view of the quantities eaten at other courses, Spaniards neither expect nor ask for much at the end of their meal. They will peel an orange, or chew a few grapes or any other fruit in season. There are some delicious exotica to choose from: the creamy-fleshed chirimoya; the persimmon (*caqui*), eaten when it's as soft as an overripe tomato; loquats, pomegranates, figs, dates and prickly pears. These are traditional fare, and many growers in the south now also produce mangoes, papayas, Cape gooseberries, passion fruit and others. At times one can feel almost overwhelmed by the choice.

For a little clean sweetness the Spanish might have a *flan*, a crème caramel in a little pot, or some other milk-based pudding such as *natillas* (egg custard), *crema catalana* (a version of burnt cream), *arroz con leche* (rice pudding) or *cuajada con miel* (junket with honey).

All such sweets have their origins in the northern milk-producing areas. The south caters for the Spanish sweet tooth with a bewildering variety of sweetmeats and pastries. Every region in Spain has its local specialities, but in these southern areas, which were under Moorish dominion the longest, the Islamic taste for sticky, spicy things, for honey and almonds, for cinnamon, aniseed and sesame, has manifested itself most noticeably. Entire towns are given over to producing the sweetmeats that the Spanish devour at Christmas: Estepa in Andalucía devotes itself especially to rich things like *mantecados*, a soft, meltingly textured mixture of lard, flour and spices; while Jijona in Valencia produces a rich array of *turrones*, best translated as nougats, some nutty and crunchy, others soft and smooth. At first try, some of these things might seem alien to British tastes, but one soon begins to like them. (Unlike some of the ghastly concoctions of the poorer-quality *pastelerías*.)

It is not just at Christmas that such sweets are enjoyed: the Spanish year is full of national and local feast days, of ferias and fiestas, which are often marked by making some traditional sweet considered appropriate for that particular day and frequently with religious names such as saint's bones, nun's sighs, bishops' tongues or friar's ears.

The connection between sweets and the Catholic Church is not only found in the names: Spain's greatest sweet-makers are nuns. Nobody knows quite why they started; possibly the sweets were made as presents for generous benefactors or the parish priest. It wasn't until 1836, when president Mendizábal appropriated and sold vast amounts of church-owned land, that the nuns had to fall back on their sweet-making skills to survive. The sweets are often rich with egg yolks; some are called simply that, *yemas*, are the size, shape and colour of egg yolks, and of ethereal flavour. The dozens and dozens of yolks required were an offshoot of wine and sherry making – wine was, and still is occasionally, clarified with egg whites, and many of the yolks would go to the convents for the sisters to work their magic.

Other things can be bought at these convents, delicate pastries, jellies, cordials, jams and even rabbits (at the Convent of the Incarnation in Baeza). It is always worth turning up at the convents to see what they have: some provide such a choice of sweetmeats that it is best to ask for a selection, a *surtido*.

Few Spanish cooks attempt such things at home; except for *flan*, rice pudding and one or two other things, sweet dishes are usually left to professionals. I include the more accessible recipes here, as well as a few of the immensely popular fried sweets and pastries.

# Flan

What we would call crème caramel, and Spain's national pudding – often the only one offered in cheap restaurants. It can be very refreshing after a big Spanish meal, when all one wants is a little sweetness to finish off with, but it can also be on the bland side; I prefer to follow Delia Smith's example and use brown sugar in the custard which gives the *flan* a boost. An important point is that the *flan* should be cooked in a very low oven – if it's too hot the custard becomes coarse and grainy.

120g/4oz granulated sugar
4 eggs
40g/1½oz dark brown sugar
vanilla essence
450ml/¾ pint creamy milk

First make the caramel: put the sugar in a small heavy saucepan over a lowish heat. It will soon start to blister and brown round the edge. Reduce the heat to a minimum and shake the pan occasionally to caramelise the sugar evenly. Once it is all a good brown colour, add about a tablespoon of hot water – be careful, for it splutters and spits. Return the pan to the heat and let the caramel dissolve in the water. Pour it into small moulds – soufflé dishes, for example.

Beat the eggs with the brown sugar and a little vanilla essence. (Alternatively, infuse the milk beforehand with a vanilla pod.) Heat the milk until it is very hot and pour it on to the eggs, stirring. Pour the custard into the prepared moulds. Now place the moulds in a roasting tin and carefully pour enough hot water into the tin to come halfway up them. Place the whole thing in a very slow oven and cook for about an hour until just set, that is, when an inserted knife blade comes out clean.

Either serve straight away, or chill for later.

# Natillas

A popular Spanish pudding that is really no more than English custard (the sort made with eggs, not the kind that comes out of a tin). Its name is the affectionate diminutive of *nata* cream, so it could be translated as 'little creams' or 'creamies'.

500ml/18fl oz creamy milk
2 strips lemon peel
120g/4oz sugar
1 vanilla pod (*or use vanilla sugar*)
6 eggs
2 tablespoons cornflour
ground cinnamon

Bring the milk to the boil with the lemon peel, sugar and vanilla. Leave it to simmer very, very gently for about 15 minutes so that the milk becomes thoroughly infused with the flavourings.

Beat the eggs well with the cornflour. Strain the hot milk over them, stir well and return the mixture to the pan. Over a low heat, stir the custard until thickened and hot. If the eggs start to set (the tell-tale signs will be bits of scrambled egg on the wooden spoon), don't panic. Remove the pan from the heat and whisk frantically to break it all up. Leave the custard to get cold, then put it in the fridge, covered, and leave it until thoroughly chilled.

Serve in individual bowls sprinkled with a little cinnamon, and with a plate of sponge fingers or similar to hand.

*Crema catalana*, the national sweet of Cataluña, is *natillas* topped with sugar and caramelised with a salamander.

# Leche Frita

Fried milk. The name tells only part of the story – this popular pudding originating in the Basque country, is really fried pieces of pastry cream flavoured with cinnamon and lemon (it is also sometimes known as *crema frita*). The cream is made extra thick so that it is just solid enough to cut into pieces when cold. The pieces are then given a coating – flour, breadcrumbs or beaten egg – and fried. All this sounds sinful enough by today's puritanical standards, but to cap it all the *leche frita* is then rolled in cinnamon sugar. The result is a delicious contrast between the crunchy, sugary coating and the gooey filling.

Start several hours ahead of time. Serves 6.

2 whole eggs
2 egg yolks
120g/4oz sugar
75g/2½oz flour
500ml/18fl oz milk
grated rind of ½ lemon
small piece cinnamon stick

*FOR COATING:*
2 beaten eggs
breadcrumbs for coating
oil for frying
about 200g/7oz icing sugar mixed with ground cinnamon to taste

Whisk the eggs, yolks, sugar and flour to a cream. Gradually bring the milk to the boil with the lemon rind and cinnamon stick. Strain it over the egg mixture and mix well. Rinse out the saucepan and pour in the custard. Whisking all the time, bring the custard to the boil and simmer for 2-3 minutes, by which time it will be very thick. Pour it into a buttered square dish about 2.5cm/1in deep, and leave to cool before refrigerating it for several hours.

Unmould the custard and cut into small fingers or squares. Dip them into beaten egg and coat with breadcrumbs. Heat a good 2.5cm/1in of oil and fry the custard until browned all over. Drain with a slotted spoon and roll in the cinnamon sugar – it helps to have someone else doing this while you continue frying. Place the *leche frita* on some kitchen paper on a plate and either eat straight away or keep them warm in the oven while you have your meal first.

**Note:** As mentioned above, you can fry the custard in alternative coatings. Plain flour is very good but tends to break away from the custard. Flour and beaten egg are also commonly used, but they soak up the cooking oil.

# Flan de naranja

A relative of *natillas* from Valencia. It is made simply with orange juice, egg yolks and sugar and baked. If you want to serve it hot, reduce the stated amount of sugar by 30g/1oz or so and don't expect it to set solid, although it will thicken considerably once chilled. Either way, it is deliciously creamy, rich yet light, with an intense, arresting taste of orange. Quantities serve 4 to 6 people.

6 egg yolks
150g/5oz sugar
juice of 3 large oranges, *or about* 360ml/12 fl oz

Preheat the oven to 300°F/150°C/Gas 2. Whisk the egg yolks with the sugar until thick and creamy. Gradually beat in the orange juice. Don't strain the juice – the little pieces of flesh help form a most delicious crust on the custard. Pour it into a shallow mould (or into individual ramekins) and place in a baking or roasting tin. Pour in enough cold water to come halfway up the sides of the mould. Place in the centre of the oven and cook for about 1½ hours.

**Note:** It is always galling to be told that a recipe doesn't work, but people have had problems with the quantities as originally published, which called for double the amount of orange juice. I have re-tested the recipe and found that the new quantities as described above work fine, so apologies to Lesley Butcher and any others who were frustrated by my mistake.

# Tortada de naranja

Orange and almond sponge flan. This comes from Valencia, the land of sweet oranges and lemons. It has a superb flavour, the taste of orange really lingering on the palate. Try to find time to pound the almonds yourself in the mortar; it's laborious, but it means you get lovely little pieces of almond studding the flan, instead of a uniformly smooth texture.

4 eggs, separated
170g/6oz sugar
rind and juice of 3 large oranges
120g/4oz ground almonds
a round, shallow cake tin about 29cm/11in wide, buttered and floured

Heat the oven to about 425°F/220°C/Gas 7. Beat the egg yolks with 120g/4oz of the sugar and the orange rind until thick, creamy and pale yellow in colour. Gradually beat in the ground almonds. Whisk the egg whites stiffly. Fold them gently into the almond mixture. Pour this into the prepared tin and put it in the centre of the oven. Cook for about 15 minutes, then turn the oven down to about 330°F/170°C/Gas 3 and leave for another 15 minutes (the flan should cook for about 30 minutes). It will have risen and collapsed, but don't worry – it's supposed to. Remove it from the tin.

Strain the orange juice and stir the remaining sugar into it until it dissolves. Gradually pour it over the flan until it's all absorbed. Eat the flan hot or cold; it does not need cream.

# Soplillos

'Little puffs of wind'. In fact, these are meringues with toasted almonds embedded in them. They come from the province of Granada.

3 large egg whites
175g/6oz sugar
finely grated rind of ½ lemon
120g/4oz split almonds, toasted in a hot oven or fried and well drained

Preheat the oven to 300°F/150°C/Gas 2. Whisk the egg whites until fairly stiff, then whisk in the sugar a tablespoonful at a time. Stir in the almonds and lemon rind and mix well. Oil a large baking sheet and line it with greaseproof or baking parchment. Lightly oil the paper as well. Distribute large spoonfuls of the mixture around the baking sheet – there should be about twelve in all. Bake for about 1½ hours, by which time the meringues should have coloured slightly. Switch off the oven and leave the meringues alone until the oven has cooled completely. Don't open the oven door in the meantime because the residual heat helps to dry the meringues out.

# Arroz con leche

Simply rice pudding, and one of the very few puddings eaten with any regularity in Spain. It is not usually baked but simmered slowly on top of the stove.

150g/5oz pudding rice
600ml/1 pint milk
150ml/¼ pint single cream
3-4 tablespoons sugar
1 vanilla pod
2-3 strips lemon rind
3 egg yolks
ground cinnamon

Place the rice, milk, cream, sugar, vanilla pod and lemon rind in a heavy-bottomed saucepan. Heat it slowly to the point where the milk just starts to bubble. Turn the heat down to an absolute minimum and leave the pan like that, uncovered, for about 45 minutes, shaking the pan occasionally to stop the rice sticking, or until the rice is just tender. Beat the egg yolks to a cream and stir a few tablespoons of the hot milk into them. Stir this mixture back into the rice, the heat of which should be enough to just cook the eggs and thus thicken the pudding. Remove the lemon rind and vanilla pod. Divide the rice between small bowls (I deviate from the Spanish way here – they often eat it in absolutely stomach-bursting quantities). Sprinkle lightly with cinnamon and chill well before serving.

# Pasteles de boniato

Sweet potato pies. Sweet potatoes are a legacy of Spain's discovery and conquest of the Americas, of her brief moment of glory in history before Drake and the ignominy of the shattered Armada. They quickly established themselves as part of the staple diet of the Spanish poor and continue to be grown in large quantities, though they seem to be declining in popularity as the bounty of other vegetables increases. Every Christmas, where I live, there is a competition for the best *boniato* recipe, but enthusiasm has sunk to the extent that this year only two people entered: myself and the lady who always wins (this year was no exception). It is a shame, for the sweet potato has a delicious flavour all its own, delicate (that much abused word, but applicable in this case) and interesting.

In this recipe from Valencia a sweetened and spiced purée of *boniato* is used as a filling for a pie of sweet, orange-scented pastry. The pies can be like pasties, or the size and shape of a mince pie – I use a Yorkshire pudding tin.

1 sweet potato of about 225g/8oz
90g/3oz sugar
grated rind of ½ lemon
ground cinnamon

*FOR THE PASTRY:*
340g/12oz plain flour
60g/2oz sugar
salt
90g/3oz lard, chopped
3 tablespoons oil
juice of 1 orange

Boil the sweet potato, washed but unpeeled, in plenty of water in a covered pan. While it is cooking make the pastry: mix the flour and sugar with a pinch of salt. Add the lard and rub it in. Stir in the oil and orange juice and mix well. The dough should be quite elastic (add a little water if not). Set it aside to rest.

The sweet potato should be done in about 40-45 minutes. Drain it and, when it is cool enough to handle, peel it. Mash it until smooth and then stir in the sugar, lemon rind and a touch of cinnamon. Leave it to cool.

Heat the oven to 425°F/220°C/Gas 7. Divide the dough into two parts, one larger than the other (the larger one for the pie bases, the smaller for the lids). Roll the larger piece out rather thinly. Cut out rounds to fit the base and sides of the Yorkshire pudding moulds – I find a large teacup is about the right size. Line the moulds and prick the bases with a fork. Place a spoonful of the purée in each, leaving a little space at the top. Roll out the smaller piece of pastry and cut out the lids of the pies (I use a smaller teacup). Moisten the edges with water and place them on top of the pies. Press the edges together to seal. Sprinkle each pie with a little sugar and bake until lightly browned – about 25 minutes. Remove the pies from the tin and leave to cool on a wire rack (or eat them while still warm if you can't bear to wait that long).
**Note:** The pastry will seem soft when you remove the pieces from the oven but will become crisp as it cools.

# Plátanos con brandy

Bananas with brandy. I came across this charming dish in the recipe section of a book on Spanish brandy by Néstor Luján, *Libro del Brandy y de los Destilados* (1985). The bananas are simply cooked in honey, sharpened with orange juice, and finally flamed with brandy – irresistible.

6 tablespoons honey
4 large bananas, peeled
juice of 2 oranges
3-4 tablespoons Spanish brandy

Choose a frying pan just big enough to hold the bananas in a layer. Heat the honey in it and add the peeled bananas. Let them cook gently, turning once, for about 10 minutes. Add the orange juice and cook for another 5 minutes. Divide the sauce between 4 plates. Pour a good slug of the brandy over the bananas and set them alight. Shake the pan until the flames go out.

Serve with a jug of cream.

# Orejuelas

These are crisp little diamond-shaped pieces of fried pastry flavoured with cinnamon and anis.

200g/7oz plain flour
½ teaspoon ground cinnamon
30g/1oz sugar
salt
60g/2oz lard, chopped
1 egg, beaten
3 tablespoons aniseed liqueur
oil for deep frying
honey

Mix the flour, cinnamon and sugar in a bowl with a pinch of salt. Rub in the lard as you would for pastry. Bind it together with the beaten egg and anis so that you have a soft-textured dough. Roll it out thinly on a floured surface and cut it into small diamond shapes. Heat the oil and fry the pastries in batches until brown, puffed and crisp. Drain them well on kitchen paper before placing them on a serving dish and drizzling a generous quantity of clear honey over them.

# Panecicos

Eggs and breadcrumbs are here transformed into little fritters resembling fried profiteroles. They are soaked in a strongly flavoured syrup and taste like rum babas without the rum, if you see what I mean.

300ml/½ pint water
120g/4oz sugar
4 cloves
1 small piece of cinnamon stick
peeled rind of ½ orange and ½ lemon
2 eggs
1 egg white
35g/1¼oz breadcrumbs
oil for frying
1 tablespoon brandy

Bring the water, sugar, spices and rinds slowly to the boil, and leave to boil steadily, uncovered. While the syrup is cooking, beat the eggs with the extra white very thoroughly. Gradually stir in the breadcrumbs – you may need more or less – until you have a very soft paste that just holds together. Heat about 12mm/½in of oil in a frying pan, and when hot add small teaspoonfuls of the mixture. These will quickly puff up. Fry them in batches until well browned all over. Drain on kitchen paper, then transfer them to a serving dish. When the syrup has been cooking for about 15 minutes add a dash of brandy and strain it over the *panecicos*, making sure that they are all bathed in it. Leave them to get cold, turning them occasionally, by which time they will have absorbed most of the syrup.

Serve as they are or with whipped cream.

Instead of the syrup you can use about 120g/4oz clear honey. Heat it with half its weight in water, then pour it over the *panecicos* and sprinkle them with a little ground cinnamon.

# Bartolillos

These famous specialities of Madrid are heavenly when the main course hasn't been too taxing, or for tea-time. They are another of Spain's fried sweets that some would label with a government health warning. *Bartolillos* consist of pastry cream wrapped inside a pastry shell and fried – in the same way as savoury *empanadillas*. For those without too many qualms, they are every bit as delicious as they sound.

*FOR THE PASTRY CREAM:*
275ml/9fl oz milk
rind of ½ lemon (*or* vanilla pod)
1 egg
38g/1¼oz sugar
30g/1oz flour
knob butter

*FOR THE PASTRY:*
120g/4oz plain flour
45g/1½oz lard
45g/1½oz sugar
1 egg
3 tablespoons milk
oil for frying
caster sugar and cinnamon

First make the cream, as it must be completely cool before filling the pastries. Put the milk to infuse over a low heat with the lemon rind or vanilla pod. Beat the egg with the sugar and then the flour. Bring the milk to the boil and strain it into the egg mixture, beating with a spoon. Rinse out the saucepan, return the custard to it and bring it back to the boil, *whisking all the time.* The custard will thicken very quickly. Simmer it for 5 minutes, stirring continuously so that it doesn't catch. Pour it into a dish, stir in a knob of butter and leave it to cool.

Now make the pastry. Sift the flour and rub in the lard. Stir in the sugar, make a well in the centre and pour in the beaten egg. Gradually incorporate the egg into the flour. If the pastry is still on the dry side, add a little milk until the pastry holds itself together without being sticky. Wrap the pastry in plastic film or metal foil and leave it in the fridge for an hour.

Flour your work surface and roll out the pastry thinly, aiming for a square or rectangle rather than a circle. Trim the edges straight. Now cut the pastry into triangles roughly 7.5cm x 7.5cm x 7.5cm/3in x 3in x 3in. Place a little pastry cream in the centre of one triangle, dampen its edges with water and place another triangle over the top. Seal the edges carefully (using the prongs of a fork, for example). Continue until all the triangles are stuffed.

Heat a good quantity of oil and when it is very hot slip in the triangles 3-4 at a time. Turn them over as they cook, and when brown on both sides drain them on kitchen paper. Keep them warm while you fry the rest.

Finally, sprinkle them all with some caster sugar mixed with a little ground cinnamon.

# Buñuelos

The same pastry cream can be used to fill buñuelos, another of Madrid's specialities. These light little puffs of choux paste are fried instead of baked as they would be for profiteroles.

120g/4oz butter
150ml/¼ pint water
2 tablespoons milk
4 eggs
150g/5oz flour, sifted with a pinch of salt
oil for frying

Melt the butter and pour in the water and milk. Bring to the boil and pour in the flour in one go. Mix it in quickly and thoroughly, then cook over a low heat, stirring continuously, for a couple of minutes. Remove the pan from the heat and beat in the eggs one by one, mixing very thoroughly between additions.

Heat a good quantity of tasteless oil until it is quite hot but not as hot as the temperature you would use to fry potatoes. Now drop in it small rounded teaspoonfuls of the mixture. If you have the heat too high they will brown too quickly without cooking in the centre. Remove them when they are puffed and light and well browned, and drain them on kitchen paper.

Either serve them still warm and sprinkled with cinnamon sugar, or leave them to cool, split them and sandwich them with pastry cream.

# Arrope

My version of an Andalusian fruit compote for autumn, when quinces all too briefly appear. It can be eaten hot, but I prefer to leave it to cool so the flavours can mature, and eat it with whipped cream. Serves 6.

1kg/2¼lb black *or* green grapes
1 quince
2 peaches
225g/8oz green plums
2 cooking apples
2 cooking pears

225g/8oz sugar

First press all the juice from the grapes. Ideal for this is a mouli-légumes, but putting the grapes in a large bowl and pressing them with the end of a rolling pin or some such instrument works well enough. You can use a liquidiser but go carefully or it will break up the pips and make the juice bitter.

Remove the peel and core from the quince and place them in a small pan. Cover with water and leave to cook while you peel and roughly chop the rest of the fruit, with the exception of the plums which should be left whole. Place all the chopped fruit in a large *cazuela* or casserole, add the sugar, grape juice and strained quince water. Add enough water just to cover the fruit. Bring to the boil and cook steadily until the cooking liquid is very thick and reduced. Try not to stir too much, and reduce the heat towards the end so the fruit doesn't catch. Remove from the heat and leave to cool.

# Further Reading

It is perhaps easier to list books about Spain itself than about its food and wine. Of the books available in English I can recommend the following:

Andrews, Colman. *Catalan Cuisine*, Grub Street, 1997

Casas, Penelope. *The Foods and Wines of Spain*, Penguin, 1985

Casas, Penelope. *Tapas*, Pavilion, 1991

Clark, Sam and Sam. *Moro, The Cookbook*, Ebury Press, 2001, and *Casa Moro*, Ebury Press, 2004

Luard, Elisabeth. *The Food of Spain and Portugal*, Kyle Cathie, 2004

MacMiadháchain, Anna. *Spanish Regional Cookery*, Penguin, 1976

Pohren, D. E. *Adventures in Taste: The Wines and Folk Food of Spain*, Society of Spanish Studies, Finca Espartero, Morón de la Frontera, Sevilla, 1972

Richardson, Paul. *A Late Dinner*, Bloomsbury, 2007. My favourite book of all. He even gets to eat *niu*.

Searl, Janet Mendel. *Cooking in Spain*, Lookout Publications, 1987

For Spanish speakers there is obviously an enormous variety. Here are some personal favourites:

Abad, Francisco, and Ruiz, María Rosario. *Cocinar en navarra*, Editorial Pamiela, 1986

Bazán, Condesa de Pardo. *La cocina española antigua*, Ediciones Poniente, 1981

Cunqueiro, Alvaro, and Iglesias, Araceli Filgueira. *Cocina gallega*, Editorial Everest, 1987

Doménech, Ignacio. *La nueva cocina elegante española*, various publishers depending on the edition, first published by Imprenta Helénica, 1915

Enciso, Cipriano Torre. *Cocina gallega 'Enxebre'*, Editorial Tres-Catorce-Diecisiete, 1982

Giró, Josep Lladonosa. *Cocina de ayer, delicias de hoy*, Editorial Laia, 1984

Isusi, José María Busca. *La cocina vasca de los pescados y mariscos*, Editorial Txertoa, 1985

Llopis, Manuel Martínez, and Ortega, Simone. *La cocina típica de Madrid*, Alianza Editorial, 1987

Luján, Néstor, and Perucho, Juan. *El libro de la cocina española*, Ediciones Danae, 1972

Mapelli, Enrique. *Papeles de gastronomía malagueña*, Ediciones La Farola, 1982

Montalbán, Manuel Vázquez. *La cocina catalana*, Ediciones Peninsula, 1979

Piera, Josep. *Los arroces de casa y otras maravillas*, Ediciones Península, 2000

Sordo, Enrique. *España entre trago y bocado*, Editorial Planeta, 1987

The series of books on regional food entitled *'Comer en . . . .'*, Dédalo Ediciones

# Index

frito, 210; *pulpo a la gallega*, 209
offal, 291-93
olive oil, 25-7
olives, 25-7; *filetes con aceitunas*, 284; *patatas a la malagueña*, 152; *preparing*, 26
*olla de trigo*, 125
*olla podrida*, 128
onions, 29; *calabacines en pisto*, 142; *calçotada*, 142-3; *solomillo de cerdo encebollado*, 263; *zarangollo*, 142
oranges: *caldo de perro*, 106; *flan de naranja*, 299; *remojón*, 83; *sopas cachorreñas*, 107; *tortada de naranja*, 300
oregano, 35
*orejuelas*, 303
*ortiguillas*, 240
oxtail, 285; *rabo de toro al jerez*, 286; *rabo de toro guisado con vino tinto*, 285

*paella*, 169-71; *croquetas de paella*, 173; *making*, 170; *paella nuestra*, 172; *paella valenciana*, 172
*paletilla de cordero a la bejarana*, 277
Pamplona, 14, 38, 87, 139, 274, 275
*pan*, 27; *pa amb tomàquet*, 5
*panadoms*, 73
*panecicos*, 304
*papas*, 134, 150; *espárragos y papas en adobillo*, 65; *papas en ajopollo*, 153; *papas a lo pobre*, 152
paprika, 32
parsley, 34
partridge: *perdiz con judías*, 258; *perdiz con chocolate*, 259
*pasas*: *espinacas con pasas y piñones*, 145
*pasteles*: *pasteles de carne*, 10; *pasteles de boniato*, 301
pastry, 302, 305
pastry cream, 304-5
*pata negra*, 36
*patatas*, 150; *buñuelos de patatas*, 154; *ensalada de patatas y gambas*, 66; *patatas aliñadas*, 82; *patatas a la malagueña*, 152; *patatas en salsa*

verde, 150; *patatas panaderas*, 153; *puré de patatas con setas*, 154
*pato*: *pato con judías a la catalana*, 254; *pato/oca con peras*, 256
*pavo a la catalana*, 257
pears: *conejo con peras y nabos*, 290; *pato/oca con peras*, 256
peas: *arroz con atún*, 175; *congrio con guisantes*, 199; *guisantes con jamón*, 147; *guisantes a la valenciana*, 146; *guisantes y alcachofas a la catalana*, 146; *lomo de cerdo con chícharos*, 267; *merluza a la gallega*, 204; *merluza a la koskera*, 204; *patatas en salsa verde*, 150
*pebre de cordero murciano*, 271
*pebre de gallina*, 271
*pechugas de pollo al ajo cabañil*, 246
*pejerreyes*, 218
*pelotas*, 130
pepper (spice), 32
peppers, 11, 15, 22, 31; *chilindrón*, 273; *cordero al txilindron*, 273; *ensalada de pimientos asados*, 81; *escalivada*, 80; *gazpacho*, 92; *paella nuestra*, 172; *pimientos fritos*, 64; *porra antequerana*, 93
*peras*: *conejo peras y nabos*, 290; *pato/oca con peras*, 256
*percebes*, 237
*perdices*: *perdiz con judías*, 258; *perdiz con chocolate*, 259
*perdices de capellán*, 66
*perejil*, 34
*pericana*, 11
*perol*, 168
*pescado*, 193-231; *pescado en adobo*, 51; *pescado en ajillo*, 231; *pescado en blanco*, 106; *romescada de pescado*, 110; *sopas de pescado y mariscos*, 99
*pez emperador*, 224; *pez espada*, 224; *pez espada con mariscos*, 224; *pez espada a la cordobesa*, 225
*picada*, 190
*picadilla*, 191
*picadillo*, 22
*picadillo de cerdo*, 266
pies: *empanadas*, 75-7; *empanadillas*,

73-5; *pasteles de boniato*, 301; *pasteles de carne*, 10
pig's trotters: *cocido madrileño*, 130-3
*pilongas con chorizo*, 126
*pimentón*, 32-33
*pimientos*, 31; *ensalada de pimientos asados*, 81; *pimientos fritos*, 64
*pimporrete*, 91
*pinchitos*, 69
pine-nuts (*piñones*), 31, 55, 60, 91, 111, 190, 214, 222, 255, 256, 257, 262, 271, 278, 288, 290, 292; *besugo con piñones*, 197; *cazuela de setas y piñones*, 60; *espinacas con pasas y piñones*, 145; *gazpacho de piñones*, 94
*pintxos*, 15, 41, 43
*piparrada*, 111
*pipirrana* (*piriñaca*), 81
*pirri*, 91
*pisto*, 111; *pisto manchego*, 112; *pisto riojano*, 112
*plátanos con brandy*, 303
*pollo*: *arroz con pollo y setas secas*, 178; *cazuela de arroz con pollo*, 182; *empanada de pollo*, 77; *langosta a la catalana*, 236; *langosta con pollo*, 236; *pechugas de pollo al ajo cabañil*, 246; *pollo al ajillo*, 245; *pollo a la andaluza*, 251; *pollo asado con castañas*, 252; *pollo campurriano*, 247; *pollo con langostinos*, 250; *pollo con salsa de ajos*, 254; *pollo con salsa de avellanas*, 253; *pollo con tomate*, 250; *pollo a la montañesa*, 247; *pollo en pepitoria*, 248; *pollo en pepitoria a la riojana*, 249
pork, 244; *albóndigas*, 261-62; *arroz con costillas*, 177; *costillas*, 266; *flamenquines*, 70; *lomo adobado*, 55; *lomo de cerdo con chícharos*, 267; *lomo con castañas*, 265; *lomo con tomate*, 268; *lomo al jerez*, 264; *lomo en manteca colorá*, 268; *paella nuestra*, 172; *picadillo de cerdo*, 266; *pinchitos*, 70; *pisto riojano*, 112; *pote asturiano*, 118; *solomillo de cerdo encebollado*, 263
*porra*, 91; *porra antequerana*, 93